HERMES BOOKS

John Herington, Founding Editor

Also in this series:

Aeschylus, by John Herington
Catullus, by Charles Martin
Herodotus, by James Romm
Hesiod, by Robert Lamberton
Homer, by Paolo Vivante
Horace, by David Armstrong
Ovid, by Sara Mack
Pindar, by D. S. Carne-Ross
Virgil, by David R. Slavitt

PLUTARCH

ROBERT LAMBERTON

FOREWORD BY JOHN HERINGTON

YALE UNIVERSITY PRESS
NEW HAVEN AND LONDON

Published with assistance from the Mary Cady Tew Memorial Fund.

Designed by Sally Harris.
Set in Palatino type by Keystone Typesetting, Inc.
Printed in the United States of America by Sheridan Books, Chelsea, Michigan.

Library of Congress Cataloging-in-Publication Data
Lamberton, Robert.
   Plutarch / Robert Lamberton ; foreword by John Herington.
       p. cm. — (Hermes books)
"The works of Plutarch": p.
Includes bibliographical references and index.
   ISBN 0-300-08810-8 — ISBN 0-300-08811-6 (pbk.)
   1. Plutarch. 2. Greece—Biography—History and criticism.
3. Rome—Biography—History and criticism. 4. Dialogues, Greek—History and criticism. 5. Philosophers—Greece—Biography. 6. Biographers—Greece—Biography. 7. Biography as a literary form. 8. Ethics, Ancient. I. Title.
PA4382 .L36 2002
938'.007'202—dc21   2001002862

A catalogue record for this book is available from the British Library.

JOHN HERINGTON

μνήμης χάριν

CONTENTS

FOREWORD *by John Herington*   ix
PREFACE   xiii
LIST OF ABBREVIATIONS   xix

I PLUTARCH'S PRESENT   1
    Plutarch in Context   1
    The Internal Autobiography   2
    The Reader, the Writer, and His Books   12
    Plutarch the Thinker   26
    Plutarch the Educator   44
    Plutarch the Priest at Delphi   52

II PLUTARCH'S PAST   60
    The Project of the *Parallel Lives*   60
    The *Lives* and the Function of Biography   69
    The Mythic Limits of History   74
    Conquerors   91
    Heroes and Villains   115
    The Project in Retrospect   143

III BETWEEN PAST AND PRESENT: THE DIALOGUES   146
    The Dialogue as a Genre   146
    The Delphic Dialogues   155
    The Face in the Moon   172
    Socrates' Sign   179

IV PLUTARCH'S READERS   188

APPENDIX 1: THE WORKS OF PLUTARCH   197
APPENDIX 2: TRANSLATIONS AND SELECT BIBLIOGRAPHY 211
INDEX   215

FOREWORD

"It would be a pity," said Nietzsche, "if the classics should speak to us less clearly because a million words stood in the way." His forebodings seem now to have been realized. A glance at the increasing girth of successive volumes of the standard journal of classical bibliography, *L'Année Philologique*, since World War II is enough to demonstrate the proliferation of writing on the subject in our time. Unfortunately, the vast majority of the studies listed will prove on inspection to be largely concerned with points of detail and composed by and for academic specialists in the field. Few are addressed to the literate but nonspecialist adult or to that equally important person, the intelligent but uninstructed beginning student; and of those few, very few indeed are the work of scholars of the first rank, equipped for their task not merely with raw classical erudition but also with style, taste, and literary judgment.

It is a strange situation. On one side stand the classical masters of Greece and Rome, those models of concision, elegance, and understanding of the human condition, who composed least of all for narrow technologists, most of all for the Common Reader (and, indeed, the Common Hearer). On the other side stands a sort of industrial complex, processing those masters into an annually growing output of technical articles and monographs. What is lacking, it seems, in our society as well as in our scholarship, is the kind of book that was supplied for earlier generations by such men as Richard Jebb and Gilbert

Murray in the intervals of their more technical researches—the kind of book that directed the general reader not to the pyramid of secondary literature piled over the burial places of the classical writers but to the living faces of the writers themselves, as perceived by a scholar-humanist with a deep knowledge of, and love for, his subject. Not only for the sake of the potential student of classics, but also for the sake of humanities as a whole, within and outside academe, it seems that this gap in classical studies ought to be filled. The Hermes series is a modest attempt to fill it.

We have sought men and women possessed of a rather rare combination of qualities: a love for literature in other languages, extending into modern times; a vision that extends beyond academe to contemporary life itself; and above all an ability to express themselves in clear, lively, and graceful English, without polysyllabic language or parochial jargon. For the aim of the series requires that they should communicate to non-specialist readers, authoritatively and vividly, their personal sense of why a given classical author's writings have excited people for centuries and why they can continue to do so. Some are classical scholars by profession, some are not; each has lived long with the classics, and especially with the author about whom he or she writes in this series.

The first, middle, and last goal of the Hermes series is to guide the general reader to a dialogue with the classical masters rather than to acquaint him or her with the present state of scholarly research. Thus our volumes contain few or no footnotes; even within the texts, references to secondary literature are kept to a minimum. At the end of each volume, however, is a short bibliography that includes recommended English translations, and selected literary criticism, as well as historical and (when appropriate) biographical studies. Throughout, all quotations from the Greek or Latin texts are given in English translation.

In these ways we hope to let the classics speak again, with a minimum of modern verbiage (as Nietzsche wished), to the widest possible audience of interested people.

John Herington

PREFACE

Janus-like, Plutarch looks both forward and backward. He is the lens through which the subsequent European tradition has most often and most consistently viewed the Greeks and the Romans. In his own time, his vision of that past was revisionist in interesting and idiosyncratic ways, but that vision was canonical within a generation of his death. It reflected, and, by reflecting, cemented into the tradition, Roman values with regard to Greek culture—and the opposite, Greek attitudes toward Rome—that can in many cases be documented elsewhere. But in retrospect and for lack of any comparable surviving corpus of historical and philosophical writing, Plutarch's vision of Greece and Rome from the perspective of the high empire is uniquely his own. If it has ever been supplanted as the most powerful and influential account of the Greco-Roman past, one would have to say that it was Gibbon in the eighteenth century—in so many ways himself dependent on Plutarch—who was the successor. Here a symmetry emerges that was no doubt deliberate: Plutarch had written the authoritative account of the rise of Greece and Rome; complementing it, Gibbon wrote the story of their decline.

As a biographer, Plutarch rewrote the history of Greece and Rome from their Bronze Age beginnings, obscured in myth, down to the wars of the successors of Alexander and those of the warlords of the late Republic. As an essayist and a writer of dialogues in the tradition of Plato, he is also the principal witness to the intellectual life of his time—roughly the half-century between the death of Nero in 68 and the accession of Hadrian in 117. Before him, there is a drought of preserved Greek literature extending over several centuries. By the time of his death, the imperial flowering of Greek literary productivity known as the Second Sophistic was under way. Viewed in this perspective, Plutarch emerges as a curiously creative and innovative figure, although much Plutarch scholarship has tended to obscure any trace of this originality. And it is true that it is only by the chance of preservation that he stands at the beginning of the history of Greek biography and that his dialogues are the first after Plato's to tell us of the evolution of that genre. But what is genuinely new and even bewildering in Plutarch is his experience of the world and his shaping of that experience into literature.

Perhaps most striking of all, Plutarch is a thinker—a writer—who interrogates the phenomena of his world in unprecedented ways. He interrogates books, symbols of cult, myths, and even natural phenomena and asks what they *mean*. What this indicates, first of all, is that the scope of his understanding of meaning itself is quite different from anything previously documented in Greek literature. He is committed to an ontology and a metaphysics by virtue of which phenomena are naturally viewed as symbols, as signs referring to other things, and therefore as inherently meaningful. The elucidation of such meanings is raised to the level of literature for the first time in the Greek tradition in the vast preserved corpus of his nonbiographical writing, misleadingly labeled the *Moralia*. It is perhaps this belief, this orientation toward the world, that constitutes his most characteristic and engaging trait. It sometimes makes him sound naive and sometimes—in the rich variety of interpretations or readings of a given phenomenon that he is willing to entertain simultaneously—even fatuous. But that very pluralism, rooted not (as many have maintained) in lack of

intellectual rigor, but rather in a deep sense of the abyss sepa-
rating us, in this sublunary realm of appearances, conceptions,
and misconceptions, from the truth, is the intellectual hallmark
of Plutarch (see, e.g., "Slowness" 549e–550b). He is the furthest
thing from a facile pluralist: he is a dogmatic pluralist.

Because he interrogates everything, he very often seems
about to offer us answers to semiotic and hermeneutic questions about the Greco-Roman world to which we would dearly
love to possess clear answers. If he seldom in fact provides
them, this is no more to be charged to his inadequacies than to
be attributed to our inability to formulate those questions any
better than he was able to do. And if he frequently infuriates us
by his failure to deliver the elucidation or interpretation we
seek, he nevertheless delivers a great deal.

Plutarch made literature of his experience of the world. The
invitation he offers to share in this interrogation of present phenomena, which include the vast accumulation of facts and anecdotes about the past, is an invitation to enter into an ancient
consciousness that is exceptionally accessible, in part because it
is so well documented. But there are hazards in accepting, and
one should be aware of them from the start. In Plutarch's world,
nothing is lost; at worst, it passes from the light of being known
into the obscurity of being forgotten, but what has been known
can be known again. As phenomena emerge and recede, their
relations are in constant flux, and their meaning is a function of
those relations. This is in part the effect of the pervasive role of
rhetoric in the corpus: Plutarch all too often turns his eloquence
to the task of demonstrating a point while leaving in us the sus-
picion that he would be equally capable of arguing the contrary
position. Viewed in another perspective, however, these doubts
have a philosophical dimension, related to Plutarch's pervasive
sense of alienation, of remoteness from any fixed truth. What we
do know, what we can know, is by its very nature a tentative

configuration of meanings, often conflicting and even contradictory. There is a built-in regress in his epistemology, a commitment to the idea that every phenomenon a is a metaphenome-
non, subsequent to and a function of some previous phenomenon b, by virtue of which it is what it is and means what it means.
But the previous phenomenon itself stands in the same relationship to some c, and so on, in a vertiginous series seemingly
doomed to perpetuity. Plutarch's own belief—grounded in the
Platonism he was heir to—that this regress in fact has a terminus,
in some remote sphere accessible to intellect (but seldom if ever
to our own fragmented consciousness), is not the issue. Rather,
what he gives us as his experience of the world turned into literature is the exploration of those ambiguities that are the immediate facts of our lives.

The effect of all this is—vertigo aside—a corpus that is re-
petitive and open-ended in the extreme. It is also vast. Since any
conclusion remains a remote goal, the exploration becomes an
end in itself. This quality of Plutarch's writing is summed up
most vividly (and devastatingly) in the quintessentially *velléi-
taire* and episodic *Table Talk*. The wit and elegant ingenuity of
the discussion are savored for their own sake. To reach a conclusion, with the inevitable consequence that one account
would prevail over others, would be a breach of intellectual
etiquette. One does well to approach this corpus armed with
clearly formulated questions with which to confront it, for it has
a capacity and a predisposition to absorb and digest those not
so prepared.

It is the primary goal of this book to provide a map of the
corpus in the form of a series of possible modes of interrogation—to formulate a range of questions that Plutarch, at our
moment in history, might be called upon to answer. To do that,
we will have to look at the historical context in which he lived
and then remove him from that context to assess his role in

shaping subsequent perceptions of his culture and its antecedents. Everything about Plutarch, for whom history itself was
an endless recycling of human possibilities, encourages us in
this endeavor.

This book's greatest debts are to the students at Washington
University in St. Louis, at the American School of Classical
Studies in Athens, and at Princeton University with whom I
have had the privilege of reading Plutarch over the past decade.
The opening section of Chapter 2 incorporates material from
my "Plutarch and the Romanizations of Athens," pages 151–60
in Michael C. Hoff and Susan I. Rotroff, eds., *The Romanization of
Athens*, Oxford: Oxbow Books, 1997. It would be impossible to
list all the individuals who have contributed ideas that will be
found here. Indeed, as the project nears completion, my greatest worry is that I can no longer be sure where a given notion or
interpretation originated: with me, with a student or colleague,
or in some commentary read years ago. The following people,
however, are particularly likely to recognize some idea or insight of theirs that I have appropriated or built on: David Blank,
Tad Brennan, David Furley, Tony Grafton, John Keaney, John
Kroll, Stephen Menn, Christopher Pelling, Tony Woodman. I
hope neither they nor others unnamed will feel ill used. Susan
Rotroff read and reread the manuscript and offered a wealth of
corrections and improvements. At the Press, Mary Pasti slashed
many a superfluous word and strengthened more than one
tangled sentence. Like all students of Plutarch today, I am constantly indebted to the prosopographic and historical work of
C. P. Jones. This and some other debts will be evident from the
brief annotated bibliography in Appendix 2.

The book has a further, now unrepayable debt to the founder of the Hermes Books series, John Herington, who invited
me to write it more than a decade ago. John's combination of

scholarship with a feisty and demanding literary imagination breathed life and energy into the field of Classics for decades. He wanted a *Plutarch* for his series that would communicate both the qualities of the Greek writer and the centrality of the oeuvre. I cannot hope that this book will please every reader, but I do hope it would have pleased him.

ABBREVIATIONS

IN THE FOLLOWING CHAPTERS, THE READER IS OFTEN REFERRED to specific passages in the corpus of Plutarch's works. Appendix 1 shows the complexity of the matter. References to the forty-eight surviving *Parallel Lives* are to title and section—for example, *Numa* 10. Any abbreviation that is not immediately clear may be sought in Appendix 1, part I.

The traditional sections (or chapters) of the *Lives* are respected and uniformly numbered in all editions of the Greek text and in most translations, providing a convenient system of reference that is not dependent on the pagination of a specific edition or translation. The *Moralia* in their diversity present even greater difficulties, solved here by the use of a title (in italics) or short title (in quotation marks) followed by page and section of the Frankfurt edition of 1599 (see Appendix 1, part II). All editions of the Greek text (as well as the Loeb translation, facing the Greek) mark these divisions, and Appendix 1, supplemented by the index, will serve as a guide.

Not all translations will provide the reader with the necessary information for locating a given reference by this system. Parenthetical numbers after *Moralia* titles that do not include both number and letter (as in "Oracles" 408c) designate sections of the composite pieces (e.g., *Table Talk* 4.6 refers to book 4, question 6). These references should be self-explanatory when the work in question is consulted.

The small number of other works, both ancient and modern, to which reference is made in the text are identified briefly in parentheses. The following standard abbreviations are used.

CIG   A. Boeckh. *Corpus Inscriptionum Graecarum.* Berlin, 1828–38.
DK   H. Diels and W. Kranz. *Die Fragmente der Vorsokratiker.* 6th ed. Berlin, 1961.
FGrHist   F. Jacoby. *Die Fragmente der griechischen Historiker.* Berlin (later Leiden), 1923–.
Il.   *Iliad*
Od.   *Odyssey*

PLUTARCH

I PLUTARCH'S PRESENT

Plutarch in Context

THE MAN LATER KNOWN AS L. MESTRIUS PLUTARCHUS WAS
born, probably at his family's home in Chaeronea, sometime in
the fifth decade of the Common Era. The society into which he
was born was explicitly and self-consciously Greek and pervasively and inevitably Roman. He was born within a few
years of the addition of Britain, Thrace, and Mauretania to the
empire of the Romans, which under its princeps Claudius was
well on its way to fulfilling what it constantly reminded itself
was its destiny—to rule the world. That expansion continued
through the seventy-some years of Plutarch's life, although at
the time of his death, early in the reign of Hadrian, the con-
centric waves of conquest and domination had reached the At-
lantic, the Danube, and the Euphrates and ceased to advance.
The extraordinary century of affluence and security for the elite
of that empire—the period Gibbon singled out, with characteristic Eurocentric eloquence, as "the period of the history of
the world during which the condition of the human race was
most happy and prosperous"—had begun.

Whatever the manifest shortcomings of Gibbon's formulation, it is clearly relevant to Plutarch's situation. The violence of
the consolidation of Roman power in Greece was two centuries
in the past. In the previous century, the challenge to that power
in the East by Mithridates of Pontus had again brought Roman
armies and repressive force, and later in that century Octavian's

1

own consolidation of power had once more exported Roman violence to Greece. But all of that was finished some seventy-five years before Plutarch's birth. Families like his own, who had learned to live well within the system the Romans oversaw, prospered. In Chaeronea and in Athens, in Rome and in Delphi—in the places where Plutarch spent his life—the Pax Romana was the single pervasive social fact. If, for Plutarch, a shadow lay across all of this, it was a sense that somehow, in his moment in history, little was at stake. As he tells us, the Delphic oracle that in its days of greatness had been consulted on affairs of state and military conquest was in the time of his own priesthood asked such questions as "Should I get married?" or "Should I take a trip?" and the civic consultations that occurred were about public health or the next harvest ("Oracles" 408c). But the speaker in Plutarch's dialogue in whose mouth this nostalgic observation is placed makes it explicit that this state of affairs is quite acceptable to him—as it doubtless was to Plutarch himself.

This brings us immediately in touch with one of the fundamental contradictions that lurk beneath the rather serene surface that Plutarch presents to his reader. Plutarch consistently praised and recommended the active, engaged life. He admired leaders and statesmen and spent much of his life thinking and writing about the great generals of the past, in whose lives a great deal was at stake. But he lived in a place and an age without politics, where there was no foreign policy, no scope for military excellence—except at the limits of the empire, a part of the world that on the whole does not seem to have interested him much.

The Internal Autobiography

The technique of moving continuously from the subject at hand to the writer's personal experiences and opinions and

back again is one that we associate, in modern European literature, primarily with Montaigne. By no means fortuitously, in
antiquity it was associated in particular with Plutarch:

> Oracular Plutarch . . . sowed bits of the biography of his
> teacher [Ammonios] and his own autobiography through
> all of his works, so that, if one were to keep one's eyes open
> for these things and follow the track of the incidental re-
> mark or revelation, and then circumspectly draw the frag-
> ments together, he would be in a position to know most of
> the events of their lives. (Eunapios of Sardis, *Lives of the
> Sophists*, 454)

Eunapios is telling his reader which philosophers will *not*
be treated in his collection of biographies, and why. He is writing in roughly the year 400, nearly three centuries after Plutarch's death, in a world where Christian monks "live like pigs
in the holy places" (472). His task is to write the history of a
philosophical tradition that all around him he sees being swal-
lowed up in ignorance and superstitious bigotry. From his perspective, Plutarch stands in that tradition as "the grace and lyre
of all philosophy," a figure to be mentioned alongside that other
first-century sage, Apollonius of Tyana, who was "more than a
philosopher . . . something intermediate between gods and
men" (454).

Eunapios's flowery account of Plutarch's biography of his
teacher Ammonios and his own internal autobiography "scattered through his books" is a curious combination of inaccuracy
and insight. At best, it is a very great exaggeration, given the
received corpus of Plutarch, where some fifty references to Ammonios leave us almost completely in the dark about the events
of his life. Similar problems are raised by Plutarch's references
to his own life. They are abundant, certainly, but they refuse to
form a coherent picture; they are vivid pieces of a perverse
jigsaw puzzle, arbitrarily and irrelevantly constituted and de-

fined, very seldom offering a join, utterly oblivious to any larger picture that they might be assembled to form.

The reason, of course, is that Plutarch's subject was never Plutarch (much less Ammonios), but rather the world of his own experience, and that the literary style he invented for the representation of that world was insistently self-referential. Eunapios thus puts his finger on the single most extraordinary fact about Plutarch's accomplishment: his constant *personal* presence in everything he wrote. Whether the subject is Stoic physics or the life of Publicola, the evocation of the author's immediate experience—some casual remark by his father or grandfather or what he himself thinks of Domitian's extravagant and tasteless new temple on the Capitoline (*Pub.* 15)—may well enter the narrative, rooting the discourse in a consciousness made vividly present by the technique. Plutarch's prose invents its speaker without aspiring to define him and in so doing disrupts the space between the reader and that voice. The real content of Plutarch's prose is Plutarch talking about whatever Plutarch is talking about. He may even talk *to* the reader, dictating what to expect, how to react. But more often, he simply asserts his presence by an anecdote—something from his own life that intrudes to illustrate an ethical point or to establish some link between Plutarch's experience of the world and the life of some ancient general or statesman.

To be sure, these fragments, anecdotes, and impressions can be assembled, as Eunapios suggests, and some sort of lacunose picture will reluctantly emerge. But while we engage in this effort, we should bear in mind that the pieces are part of a puzzle that existed in Eunapios's imagination, but not in Plutarch's. To Plutarch, these glimpses of himself were simply the condition of his peculiar mode of expression. That they could be assembled into a single picture would have been of no more interest to him—indeed, perhaps of much less interest—than the fact, noticed by his contemporaries, that the lines and half-lines and formulae of Homer could be rearranged into poems of radically different meaning and content.

There is within the vast corpus, however, a substantial exception to this general rule that self-representation is a stylistic device rather than a goal pursued in and for itself. In the bulk of the major dialogues—the major creative commitment of his career as a writer—Plutarch remains a very elusive presence. Sometimes we do see him undisguised in the role of teacher of philosophy or elucidator of philosophical problems ("Slowness," "No Pleasant Life," "Against Colotes"). But of the three Delphic dialogues, *The E at Delphi* is narrated by an anonymous first person, presumably to be understood as Plutarch—although the "I" in *The Disappearance of Oracles* is eventually identified as Lamprias, Plutarch's brother. In the third, *The Delphic Oracles Not Now Given in Verse*, the authorial voice is perhaps to be found behind the mask of Theon, a name that Plutarch himself associates with an identity of convenience (*Roman Questions* 30, 271e; *Common Conceptions* 1061c, 1076a). In *Love*, Plutarch is a central character, but the frame distances the dialogue and its author from the reader, projecting it back into a remote past—the time of Plutarch's marriage, envisioned by a son of that marriage, now already grown. We have no way of knowing here whether Plutarch—the author whose doubly masked voice we read—is to be imagined as alive or dead at the moment when his decades-old conversation is brought to life.

Beyond these deliberate but coy self-portraits in the major dialogues, there is another body of autobiographical material in the *Table Talk* that is explicitly presented as belonging to the genre of the memoir (612e). However, these ninety-one interrelated mini-dialogues have in common with the more traditional sort of memoir little beyond the fact that they re-create or reinvent past experience—specifically, afterdinner conversations, in

Rome, in Athens or Delphi, in Chaeronea or some country es-
tate in Boeotia. The net effect is the creation of a genre that is a
sort of intellectual home movie. Although Plutarch supplies a
narrative thread and often represents himself as speaker, the
content of the work is the public but intimate sphere of the
symposium and the wit and wisdom of the participants. This
sort of home movie is the furthest thing in the world from a
lumpy, unedited video. On the contrary, it is edited down to the
frame, and the principal events are turns of phrase, evocations
of ancient poetry, and ingenious variations on thorny intellectual problems. Not that these questions are necessarily solved
or, for that matter, soluble—the ingenuity and elegance of the
attempts are what counts. Even the pursuit of meaning in the
inherently meaningless—the simply false or mistaken—is explicitly defended in one of the conversations (628b–d), and by
no less a figure than Philopappus, heir in exile to the throne of
Commagene in Syria, whose pretentious grave monument
dominating a hill adjacent to the Acropolis is even today one of
the archeological extravagances of Athens.

The alternative to repartee is silence, which is an offense
against good taste and good sense, an admission of the inad-
missible. In his characteristic manner, Plutarch brings this
home to the reader with an anecdote (644f): Simonides said to a
silent guest at a symposium, "Man, if you are stupid, you are
acting clever, but if you're clever, you're acting stupid." One
suspects that the anxiety implied here lurks behind every one
of these conversational vignettes, whether the subject that provides the pretext for the display of cleverness (*sophia*) is the
susceptibility of old men to drunkenness (3.3) or the relative
priority of the chicken and the egg (2.3). The range of these
discussions over wine that are here salvaged from the silence of
forgetfulness is extraordinary, with a relentless juxtaposition of
the trivial and the intriguing, the immediate ("Should the host

provide place cards?" [1.2], "Should symposiasts wear crowns of flowers?" [3.1]) and the remote ("Who is the god of the Jews?" [4.6], "Why do sailors on the Nile draw water before dawn?" [8.5]). Customs, physiology, behavior, history, natural history—all provide acceptable topics, as do science and philosophy, although at this end of the spectrum the limits are defined from the very first conversation (614f–615a): the "subtle and dialectical problems" of the philosophers are out of place; they escape the other symposiasts, who themselves retreat to a low level of conversation and storytelling, and in this rift, "the goal of symposiac sociability is lost, and Dionysus is outraged."

Even here in the *Table Talk*, literary precedents and norms sometimes shape what we might take for a confessional representation of reality (as the great philologist Wilamowitz, an enthusiastic reader of Plutarch, warned). Nevertheless, it is from these self-representations that we gain what insight Plutarch allows us into the social and intellectual world in which he lived and in which he chose to portray himself.

Sometimes, the scene is specified, but elsewhere we are left in ignorance of the time and place of the conversation reported. The symposium may go on, passing from one topic to another; or the end of one "question" and the beginning of another may bring an entirely new cast of characters. It is in contexts such as these that we learn, for instance, that Plutarch's father raised horses (642a), that he read the philosophers but might (at least in the symposiac context) defer to his son on the interpretation of a passage from Aristotle (656c–d). He also believed that the host of a symposium should supervise the assignment of places, reflecting age and rank (615e–616b). The old man is given, in these vignettes, a series of attributes that are remarkably vivid and define a social identity—a model of the country gentleman that has been imitated repeatedly down to the present in England and other European cultures with marked social stratification. The portrayal of the father even has the gently comic side that one might expect in this context. Plutarch has his grandfather observe (678e–679a) that Plutarch's father has recently given an overcrowded dinner party—one that ignored the priority of Space proclaimed by Hesiod (*chaos*, Theogony 116) and corresponded instead to Anaxagoras's cosmological claim that "all things were [crushed] together" (Anaxagoras fr. B1 DK). Looking beyond the *Table Talk*, we can flesh out this portrait of Plutarch's father. In a first-person anecdote characteristically inserted into a series of historical ones, Plutarch in *Precepts on Statecraft* (816d–e) recalls that when, as a young man, he was sent as half of a delegation to the Proconsul of Achaea and his fellow ambassador failed to perform the mission, his father took him aside on his return and told him in his report always to say "we" and not "I," to cover for his colleague and neutralize potentially dangerous resentment.

Notice that in all of these anecdotes Plutarch's father remains nameless. This is not a matter of reticence on Plutarch's part in naming family members. In telling of Antony's defeat at Actium (*Ant.* 68) Plutarch inserts an anecdote illustrating the hardships that resulted for the Greeks from the conscriptions and confiscations during those wars, and he introduces it with "My great-grandfather Nicarchos used to tell the story." And so we know the name of one of Plutarch's great-grandfathers (otherwise unattested). His paternal grandfather, Lamprias, is invoked earlier in the same *Life* for word-of-mouth evidence about Antony's dissolute life with Cleopatra (*Ant.* 28): "Philotas of Amphissa, the physician, used to tell my grandfather Lamprias how he was in Alexandria then, studying medicine, and got to know one of the palace cooks. " And this grandfather, along with his son and grandson, was often portrayed in the *Table Talk*, as we have seen.

Characteristically, Plutarch's father's name is an item of

information that Plutarch neither reveals nor hides. By general agreement, we have it recorded in the odd dialogue entitled *Whether Land or Sea Animals Are Cleverer,* which consists of two competing set speeches, constituting a debate on the question— a debate judged by Soclaros, another denizen of the *Table Talk,* along with a sweet old man named Autoboulos, who at one point casually refers to "my son, dear Soclaros, your friend" who teaches philosophy in the tradition of Plato (964d). This son can hardly be anyone but Plutarch. The deduction is supported, if not proven, by the fact that Plutarch himself had a son named Autoboulos, the narrator of the dialogue *Love,* presumably his eldest and so named for his paternal grandfather. If we may factor all that is said by Autoboulos in this dialogue into Plutarch's composite portrait of his father, we can attribute to the old man some strikingly idiosyncratic notions. The idea that animals and humans have similar—even the same—souls is as old as Pythagoras in Greek tradition, and philosophical vegetarianism has a history just as long. In Plutarch's time, the debate was broadening (as it has conspicuously in our own time) into a widespread concern with the proper relations between humans and animals. Plutarch's father (in the frame dialogue of the debate, which will pitch hunters against fishermen) is made to maintain (964e–965b) that animals are rational and also share with us other traits, including emotions, and as a result, justice and injustice characterize our relations with them. His solution: "Those who punish and kill animals that are savage and simply harmful do no wrong," nor do those who tame and exploit the gentle ones. We seem to be left with a sketch of a benevolent yet oddly judgmental ethical vegetarian who leaves room for killing (and even eating) predators, but never their prey.

I have taken time to explore the incidental but rich portrait of Plutarch's father, Autoboulos, as a sample of the texture of the pervasive internal autobiography so characteristic of Plutarch's writing. To do the same for all that he reveals about the rest of his family and especially himself would easily fill a book this size, and the bulk of what would be learned would be characteristically anecdotal, incidental, intimate, and liminal. The relatively few facts "of importance," in the sense that they might contribute to an article in a biographical dictionary, are these.

Plutarch identified the small town of Chaeronea in western Boeotia as his home and that of his ancestors, and he lived for extended periods of his life (*Dem.* 1–2), serving as some sort of administrative official there in his later years ("Precepts" 811c). He also lived for periods of time in Athens (*Dem.* 31; *Table Talk*), where he studied with Ammonios and went on to do further work in Platonic philosophy. He was an adopted member of the tribe Leontis (*Table Talk* 628a) and so an Athenian citizen. His anecdotes of experiences in Athens seem to require no extended period of residence after the completion of his education (presumably in the late 60s), because Chaeronea was no more than a day's travel from Athens, and frequent trips there were no doubt part of his routine while living at home. He traveled to Alexandria (*Table Talk* 678c) and perhaps to other cities in the east, as well as Rome. As an anecdote already cited indicates, his education and position in society resulted in his being sent on at least one diplomatic mission while still a "youth" (*neos*). That particular journey would not have taken him outside Greece, but later ones took him to Rome: "In the time I spent in Rome and Italy," he observes (*Dem.* 2), there was no time to perfect his Latin "because of political duties and those who came to me on account of philosophy." These journeys were divided, then, between official duties and lectures. We see him engaged in the latter activity in an anecdote in

Curiosity (522d); the message is that we should not be in a hurry to open letters:

> Once, while I was lecturing in Rome, Rusticus, whom Domitian later executed out of envy for his reputation, was in the audience, and a soldier marched in and handed him a letter from the emperor. There was a silence. I stopped speaking so he could read the letter. But he did not—nor even open it—until I finished my lecture and the audience went away. Everyone was impressed by his dignity on that occasion.

It is clear from this incident that Plutarch was in Rome in dangerous times for intellectuals and for critics of the imperial establishment—Rusticus was executed in 93—and clear as well that Plutarch's sympathies and associates were such that he might himself have been in danger. Beyond Rome, his travels in Italy took him as far north as the Po Valley (Brescello and Bedriacum, *Otho* 14, 18) and Ravenna (*Mar.* 2).

The remaining location of importance in Plutarch's self-presentation is Delphi, scene of three of his most widely read dialogues, where he held various offices, including a priesthood (*Table Talk* 700e). He undoubtedly spent periods of time there in these capacities, but again it is important to remember that Chaeronea was just a short day's journey away. Plutarch appears in the dialogues (in person or thinly disguised) as a fixture of the place, one who might be consulted about problems of interpretation of the monuments. The guides (*periegetai*) took care of the ordinary tourists, but Plutarch would seem to have been at least sometimes available as a higher resource for the more sophisticated inquirer into Delphic lore.

One thing that this autobiography lacks is a chronology, and it is a task of great delicacy to assess all of the casual givens, along with the gaps, and establish one. C. P. Jones has both done the groundwork—including epigraphic and prosopographic studies to supplement Plutarch's remarks—and provided an accessible synthesis of the results in his *Plutarch and Rome*. The large picture, not surprisingly, shows early years of rhetorical training and travel, succeeded by philosophical training and a life of diplomacy, teaching, and scholarship, bound increasingly in old age to Chaeronea and to Delphi. What is characteristically lacking in the autobiographical remarks are the honors that later sources tell us were paid Plutarch, first by Trajan (the *ornamenta consularia*, which have been thought to presuppose equestrian rank) and then by Hadrian, who appointed him to the high office of procurator of Achaea, though at an age (over seventy) when he could hardly have been expected to perform, as the holder of that office normally would, as the emperor's agent in overseeing the imperial property. There is no reason to doubt that he received these honors; nor is his silence on the matter any surprise, both because of the offhand nature of the remarks he does offer us and because, if this gentle philosopher hated anything, it was self-advertisement. He believed that excellence should be active, should be displayed ("Live Unknown"), but he found self-congratulation (e.g., Cicero's, *Cic.* 51 = *Comp.* 2) decidedly distasteful.

The Reader, the Writer, and His Books

For all his commitment to the active (as opposed to the contemplative) life, Plutarch read books and wrote books, two activities that in his time, as in ours, were inseparable from libraries. Exceptionally, Plutarch shares with his reader this aspect of his life and work, something foreign to the previous range of ancient literary representation:

For one who has undertaken to compose a history out of material that is not at hand and easily available, but is for the most part foreign and scattered here and there, one really *should* have "an illustrious city," supportive of the arts and populous, where he will have an abundance of books of all sorts [as well as knowledgeable people to learn from]. . . . I, however, live in a small city, and care for it and stay here so that it will not become yet smaller. (*Dem.* 2)

He read, and he kept notebooks (*hypomnemata*) that allowed him, for example, to pull out a substantial volume of material on a given subject when pressed for time (*Tranquillity of Mind* 464f). If we could deduce more concerning the nature and organization of those notebooks, we would know a great deal more about Plutarch's manner of composition. We may imagine, though, that to supplement the substantial private library he undoubtedly possessed in Chaeronea, he traveled— whether to Athens or to Rome—equipped to take notes and store up material from any library available to him.

His reading was surely voracious, and although he very often cites his source for an anecdote or a narrative, one senses a contrary impulse to avoid cluttering up his *Parallel Lives* with acknowledgment of his sources. Nonetheless, Gärtner's *index auctorum* to Konrat Ziegler's monumental Teubner edition of the *Lives* has about 275 entries (even setting aside such vague attributions as "certain Naxians say"), more than 230 in Greek and more than 40 in Latin—and that is for the *Lives* alone. A comprehensive survey of the corpus raises the number of authors to over five hundred.

In spite of what must at first sound like an almost pedantic insistence on sources, the *Lives* have nevertheless proven the richest of mines for the sort of research known in German (and in English, with a touch of irony) as *Quellenforschung*—source research. The scholar who would elucidate Plutarch's sources for a given *Life* will start from Plutarch's own acknowledgments. But those acknowledgments will account for only a small amount of the information imparted in the *Life* in question, and the scholar will have to proceed to ask, next, which other authors elsewhere cited by Plutarch are likely sources for the unattributed information and, finally, what other possible known authors he might have tapped. The nineteenth-century tradition of this research (which lived well on into the twentieth) was generally wedded to the notion that Plutarch must always have had a *Hauptquelle*, a principal source, for a given *Life*, an author whose account he followed, embellishing it with anecdotes and variants from others. In its most extreme form, this activity was bound up with a low estimate of Plutarch's genuine historical curiosity and knowledge, in the absence of which he would (supposedly) have worked exclusively from relatively recent syntheses, never troubling, for instance, to read Thucydides and Herodotus, but citing them for bits of information he found attributed to them elsewhere. This condescending view has lost favor in the past few decades, and Plutarch as a researcher has tended to recover some of the respect he had conspicuously lost since 1800. His method of writing does, however, make it very difficult to know whether he is citing an acknowledged source at first hand or only through an intermediary, even though he will not infrequently acknowledge that the latter is the case.

To take a single example, we know, by way of references in Plutarch and a handful of other authors, that one Hieronymos of Cardia, who served under several of the successors of Alexander in diplomatic and perhaps military capacities, wrote a history of his time (a period more interesting than one might wish for)—extending at least from the death of Alexander in 323 B.C.E. to that of Pyrrhus in 272. Hieronymos is said to have lived to be over one hundred years old, so all the events of this half-century fell within his active life, and he was eyewitness to many of the most important and most devastating of them. The wars of the successors of Alexander were hugely destructive and repeatedly redrew the political map of the eastern Mediterranean, and Hieronymos's voluminous history, presumably completed around 260, was also a remarkably *good* history—or so several modern historians have thought, although the judgmental Augustan critic Dionysius of Halicarnassos considered him unreadable ("On Literary Composition" 4, p. 94, 3–8 Roberts). We have not a single word of Hieronymos's book preserved—something likewise true of many of the other authors whom Plutarch taps—but one reason for believing that he was both more informative and more vivid than Dionysius gave him credit for is that the vast (and quite verifiably unreadable) *Library of History* of Diodorus Siculus (1st century B.C.E.) by general assent perks up considerably for the three books (18–20) where he is heavily dependent on Hieronymos. How does Plutarch fit into all of this? Plutarch mentions Hieronymos in all three of the biographies that fall in the half-century following the death of Alexander: *Eumenes, Demetrius Poliorcetes,* and *Pyrrhus.* In the first two, he is mentioned as an actor in the drama, also being identified in both instances as "the historian." In the *Life of Pyrrhus,* Plutarch cites Hieronymos as a source of relevant information (always on points of detail), but this is the tip of the iceberg. In the *Pyrrhus,* with its rich characterization and vivid battle narratives, and in the *Demetrius*—the portrait of a conqueror of sublime ambition whose only goal and reason for being was conquest, such that once imprisoned by his enemies, he obligingly drank himself to death—the lost narrative of Hieronymos can be glimpsed repeatedly. Thus it is more than likely that Plutarch actually read Hieronymos of Cardia—and Thucydides and Herodotus and hundreds of the other authors cited in the *Lives*—even if doubt often remains concerning his personal knowledge of a particular text or passage.

In the essays and dialogues, the issue of sources is radically different. That Plutarch read widely in philosophy no one can doubt. The study of philosophy in the tradition of Plato meant, in his time, reading Plato's dialogues, as well as the commentaries on the dialogues that had begun to accumulate centuries earlier. The ten *Platonic Questions* are short essays in this genre, attacking problems that arise from a single Platonic passage or a few related ones, disposing of (generally anonymous) existing solutions, and proceeding to a new explanation. We have only a single extended text of this nature from Plutarch ("Generation of the Soul," discussed below), and like the shorter ones, it addresses only a single problem in a single dialogue, but along with the *Platonic Questions* it implies a depth of knowledge of the dialogues and the history of their interpretation that should be no surprise, given Plutarch's education and intellectual commitments.

The citations bear this out. Plutarch quotes or echoes Plato incessantly—more frequently than any other author except Homer—and those reminiscences are drawn from thirty-plus works (several of them today considered spurious). Of the dialogues generally recognized as authentic, only three have not been detected (*Lysis, Ion,* and *Hippias Minor*), and these omissions are surely to be regarded as coincidental. The distribution of the passages evoked reflects in a general way the status of the various dialogues in Platonic education in Plutarch's time, and perhaps his individual priorities as well. The *Republic* and *Timaeus* get disproportionate attention, as do the *Laws*.

Plutarch mentions Aristotle by name more than two hundred times, and here again, the passages that he seems to evoke indicate a broad knowledge of the corpus. The logical treatises (known collectively as the *Organon,* or "tool") are sparsely represented, but this is to be expected: Plutarch does not write about logic, and it would be difficult to believe that logic was one of his philosophical strengths. The Aristotelian material in the corpus reflects Plutarch's own concerns. The biological treatises are richly represented—Plutarch mentions a huge amount of zoological lore that is also in the *Historia animalium*, and it is likely that he found much of it there (although an intermediate source has been suggested). It would be misleading to suggest that Plutarch gives evidence of a *deep* knowledge of Aristotle, but there is correspondingly ample evidence of *breadth*. He was, at any rate, at home with basic Aristotelian notions and able to use them as analytical tools. In one of the *Platonic Questions* he explores a problematic passage of the *Timaeus*, where Timaeus describes the demiurge sowing souls, "some in the earth, some in the moon, some in the other instruments of time" (*Tim.* 42d). Perhaps, Plutarch suggests, those "instruments of time" are bodies—conceived as instrumental in the manner of Aristotle, who called the soul "an entelechy [or "actualization"] of a body that is natural, instrumental, and has the potential of life" (*Platonic Questions* 8, 1006d). This is very close indeed to the wording of a pair of definitions in Aristotle's *De anima* (412a27–28; 412b5–6). The differences and omissions may be important for Aristotle's arguments, but they are not for Plutarch's, and his use of this basic definition suggests a remarkable sensitivity to precisely what Aristotle insists is the originality of his own approach to soul: that a soul must be conceptualized in terms of a body, whose life it constitutes. What we see in instances like this one is that Plutarch had a command of the philosophical literature that included texts, commentaries, and concepts, and that he moved freely in this difficult medium, and not in the manner of a thinker with only a second-hand knowledge of the texts.

The other two traditions of philosophy in which Plutarch

read—the Stoics and the Epicureans—present a whole new range of problems, because most of the texts to which he had access have been lost and the notions they contained must be recovered from quotations and paraphrases in later writers. In the case of the Stoa, Plutarch is among the most important of these sources, and he shares with several others (notably Cicero and Galen) a polemical hostility to Stoic explanations of the world of our experience. Positions stated to be refuted are often poorly stated, even when presented with the best will possible, and faced with Plutarch's many claims about what Chrysippus or Cleanthes thought, one often doubts that his formulation does justice to the text that lay before him.

Beyond history and philosophy, Plutarch had a knowledge of poetry—lyric, epic, and dramatic—worthy of one of the most educated, cultured individuals of his time. In the manner of the Greek prose of the Roman empire—a manner that Plutarch did much to create—he cites, echoes, and evokes poetry, poetic phrases, and poetic vocabulary on every page. The language of Plato and Lysias—the core of the canon of classical Attic prose—is built on a remarkably small vocabulary, small not certainly from poverty, but as a result of restrictive and exclusive selection, dictated by taste. Within the classical canon, certain words belonged in prose, many more in poetry, and although a common core of basic vocabulary inevitably exists, the distinction is nevertheless carefully maintained. Plutarch not only quotes poetry abundantly but mixes into his own prose, which in syntax broadly respects the models of ancient Attic, an abundance of poetic vocabulary, most of it from poems five hundred and more years old. For the student of Plutarch's Greek, it is an often repeated experience to go to the lexicon for the meaning of an odd word, to find that it occurs in Pindar, perhaps in Aeschylus, and then for the first time in prose in Plutarch, half a millennium later.

The poetry that he knew is varied but reflects an educational canon long in place. Homer, the three Attic tragedians, the lyric poets—if there is any idiosyncratic bias in Plutarch's poetic repertory, it is expressed in a patriotic fondness for the two Boeotian poets in the canon, Hesiod and Pindar. In the case of the former, Plutarch undertook a study of the text, although only fragments of his commentary survive, embedded in later ones. He lived within a few hours' journey of the valley, cut deeply into Mt. Helicon, where in his time a festival of the Muses was celebrated, tracing its origins to the bard of Ascra. Plutarch visited that shrine. It would be surprising to learn that there was any shrine in Boeotia he had not visited, but in this instance he eliminates any doubt by portraying himself there in the dialogue *Love*. This means that he also must have seen the most precious "historic" artifact displayed by the priests of the Muses: the tripod that Hesiod won in a contest with Homer. One of the surviving fragments of Plutarch's commentary reveals that he considered the passage in the *Works and Days* that mentions such a tripod to be inauthentic. He was too discreet to add that ancient shrines, like ancient poetry, are subject to manipulation and interpolation.

One of the most interesting and elusive aspects of Plutarch's reading is his acquaintance with Latin literature. The fact that he learned Latin at all singles him out from most of the Greeks who visited Rome as teachers or diplomats and who in all probability learned little more than the "restaurant Italian" of modern tourists. From the late republic through Plutarch's time and beyond, Latin was repeatedly described as a dialect of Greek, derivative (on phonetic grounds) from the "Aeolic" spoken by Evander's Arcadians, who had settled the site of the future Rome before the coming of Aeneas. As such, Latin was not *barbaros* ("foreign" or "non-Greek") from a Greek perspective, but both the language itself and the culture of which it was the vehicle were imagined as derivative, corrupted by non-Greek influence, and far from independently creative. There just was not very much written in Latin that most Greeks felt any need to read. The most striking exceptions are historical texts, because Greeks might well ignore the intellectual accomplishments of the Romans, but they could not ignore their military and political accomplishments. Plutarch, given the nature of his research on the *Parallel Lives*, had a more acute need of a wider variety of such texts than had most of his predecessors.

Plutarch is perhaps the first Greek to preserve for us something of his experience of learning Latin. In a passage cited in part above (*Dem.* 2), he explains why, in his parallel lives of Demosthenes and Cicero, he will not concern himself with comparing the two orators' styles. While in Italy he lacked time to study Latin. The result:

> I began to become acquainted with Latin books late, and at too advanced an age. It was an amazing thing that I experienced, but true: I did not so much grasp and become acquainted with the subjects through the words—I already knew about them one way or another—rather, it was through *them* that I was able to follow the words. To be sensitive to the beauty of Latin style and its quick rhythm, along with the metaphors, the arrangement of words, and the other ornaments of discourse is something I judge attractive and by no means unpleasant—but the study and practice required to develop such sensitivity are no easy matter, and more appropriate for those with more leisure than I, and whose age leaves time for such pursuits.

Even the nod to the "quick rhythm" (*takhos*) of Latin is precious testimony to how that language must have sounded to a Hellenophone: a spare, efficient language (or rather dialect), innocent both of the supposed mother tongue's luxuriance of expressive particles and of its precious definite articles, with their capacity to define grand, sweeping units of sense in a manner the Latin stylist could scarcely imitate.

Many of Plutarch's readers have detected excessive modesty in this account of his knowledge of Latin. We have seen that echoes of more than forty Latin authors can be found in the corpus, and his knowledge of the works of Cicero (along with Caesar, the only subject of a Roman *Life* whose writings constituted a significant part of his accomplishments) is remarkably extensive. He can hardly have absorbed the matter of Cicero's letters and speeches—the parts of his output most vividly reflected in Plutarch's *Life* —other than directly from Cicero's Latin. I doubt very much that he bothered with Latin poetry or philosophy (although he may have glanced at some essays and poems of Cicero's out of interest in their author, rather than in their style or content). They could hardly have seemed more than inferior and derivative products of a tradition Plutarch could engage at the source in the original language—the parent language, his own. Although numerous apparent echoes of Latin authors have been detected outside the *Lives,* actual citations of Latin authors are almost exclusively confined to the biographies.

These are not all the books that Plutarch read, but only a small sample at best. In looking at those he wrote, it will be necessary to give a more inclusive account. however large and complex the corpus. The sheer bulk of the preserved works is rivaled by that of no ancient non-Christian author, with the exception of the fourth-century C.E. orator Libanius.

Inevitably in a corpus of this size there are gray areas— missing works to which reference is made in surviving ones, as well as ancient pseudepigrapha that have crept in over the centuries. The earliest indications we have of what Plutarch wrote come from Plutarch himself, in the form of casual remarks closely comparable to the rest of the "internal autobiography" already described, and equally frustrating. Next, we have a list, the so-called Lamprias Catalogue of unknown date, listing 227 titles. It may be the shelf list of the Plutarch holdings of some ancient library, and scholars have tended to place it in the third, fourth, or fifth century. The corpus as we have it contains about half that number of titles, although fragments of many of the missing ones, in the form of quotations in later authors, confirm their existence and throw some light on their contents. The Lamprias Catalogue is by no means perfect. It omits at least a dozen surviving authentic works, as well as some pseudepigrapha that have survived in the manuscript tradition. What it alone can do, however, is to provide us with a late-antique perspective on the corpus and a sense of how much has been lost. Next after the Lamprias Catalogue, the corpus of Plutarch was defined critically about the year 1300 by the scholarly monk Maximus Planudes, whose editions, represented by outstanding manuscripts, effectively set the canon of the *Moralia* (see Appendix 1).

What survives is still a very great deal, and it is sharply divided. First, there are the *Parallel Lives*, the project that occupied Plutarch through much of his maturity and into old age and which since antiquity has stood as his major accomplishment. It consisted of twenty-two sets (one double) of biographies, of which twenty-one survive, each pairing a Greek military or political figure with a Roman. The project is as imposing in its symmetry as it is idiosyncratic (see below, Chapter 2). The parallels and comparisons take various forms. The biographies vary in style and manner with the development of the project and with the differences in the evidence available, starting as they do in the remote, mythified realm of the Bronze Age (*Theseus*) and ending with the end of the republic (*Julius Caesar*). They were probably written primarily for the young, and there can hardly have been a more influential account of Greece and Rome, before or since.

The *Parallel Lives* were not Plutarch's only project in biography, nor do they seem to have been his first. He completed a series of *Lives* of the emperors of Rome that culminated (to judge by the Lamprias Catalogue) in 69, the year that saw four emperors proclaimed, two murdered, and one a suicide. Plutarch was in his twenties at the time. That there is no indication of a *Life* of the next emperor, Vespasian, suggests that the series was completed under the Flavians (69–96) and did not include them. Of this series, originally comprising *Augustus, Tiberius, Claudius, Caligula, Nero, Galba, Otho,* and *Vitellius,* only *Galba* and *Otho* survive. Even here, there is reason to think that Plutarch's project was more complex than a simple series of eight lives. The Lamprias Catalogue treats *Galba* and *Otho* as a pair, and the two biographies as we have them in fact form a continuous narrative, the first opening with a characteristically Plutarchan series of anecdotes, along with general observations on the consequences of the death of a commander in chief (in this instance, Nero), whereas the *Life of Otho* continues without a break from the murder of Galba. The *Lives of the Emperors,* then—almost certainly to be dated before the *Parallel Lives*— may well have had some sort of idiosyncratic, perhaps binary, organization that anticipated the major series to come. Among the other biographies attributed to the most famous of all ancient biographers were a number of literary *Lives* (notably *Hesiod* and *Pindar,* both lost, but perhaps genuine), a *Life of Heracles,* and a surviving series of short lives of the ten canonical Attic orators that is very unlikely to be Plutarch's own.

Then there is the *other* Plutarch, the Plutarch of the poorly titled *Moralia,* or "Ethical Essays." This label accurately describes a small but influential minority of the nearly eighty essays, dialogues, compilations, and philosophical polemics that make up the collection so titled—such essays as *Tranquillity of Mind* and *How to Tell a Flatterer from a Friend*. From the Church Fathers to the Renaissance and beyond, these often attractive, rambling, anecdotal explorations of various aspects of human conduct, combined with advice on how best to live one's life, have found a vast number of appreciative readers. A great deal in the collection, however, has nothing whatsoever to do with ethics. The *Moralia* of Plutarch in fact constitute the bulk of the surviving documentation of the intellectual life of the period between Nero and Hadrian. Polemical pieces (e.g., *Stoic Self-Contradictions* and "Against Colotes") document for us the status of various philosophical controversies in Plutarch's time. Essays on every imaginable subject, from cosmology to table manners, define more clearly than any other body of writing the worldview of a thinker of the high empire and the intellectual engagement of an ancient Platonist with the world of his immediate experience.

Perhaps the most characteristically Plutarchan genre is the "question" (*problema*) or "cause" (*aition*). Plutarch did not invent it; it may well have had its origin in the classroom, and it is documented as a literary genre in the fourth century B.C.E. in a collection of "Homeric Questions" attributed to Aristotle. These consist of "problems" (*problemata*) and "solutions" (*luseis*), supposedly proposed or endorsed by Aristotle, relating to Homeric matters ranging from the meaning of a word to the apparent contradictions in Homeric narrative. The problem-solution format became a constant of ancient literary scholarship, richly reflected in the marginal notes (*scholia*) of manuscripts, but many other sorts of *problemata* are found in the Aristotelian corpus as well, most conspicuously in the massive Peripatetic collection of "Why?" (*dia ti;*) questions known as Aristotle's *Problems*. By its nature, the collection was infinitely expandable, and the collection of Aristotle's *Problems* that we have may well be much later even than Plutarch. Whether Plutarch knew such an "Aristotelian" collection is unknown, but this semiliterary genre had its own norms, reflected in the questions attributed to both authors. These questions are most frequently answered by another question—an indirect, even coy way of suggesting a solution. The possibility so introduced is then supported by evidence or argument.

The fragmentation of inquiry is the basic principle here, driven by Plutarch's constantly restless curiosity as he inquired into everything, interrogated everything in the world around him. The *Table Talk* reflects on one level this way of relating to the world, creating as it does a refined mode of discourse that is an end in itself, and those elegant inquiries are sometimes appropriately given the title "Symposiac Questions" (*symposiaka problemata*). The collections of questions may be notebooks of a sort, jottings that record a brief intellectual engagement. Plutarch's are classified in groups and reach us as *Greek Questions, Roman Questions, Platonic Questions*, and *Natural History Questions*. All demand to know *why* something is or was the case, to assemble a net of causality to account for some phenomenon in the world. Not surprisingly, it is impossible to read very many at a stretch.

At the other end of the scale of readability within the *Moralia* are the major dialogues. The obvious and explicit precedents are the dialogues of Plato, that mode of intellectual drama in which he so excelled that it might seem his private intellectual property. This impression is at least in part an accident of transmission. Aristotle wrote dialogues, and even the Socratic dialogue was a genre with many practitioners, including Xenophon as well as Plato—as was the subgenre or set piece "Socrates' Defense Speech" (*Apologia*), multiple imaginative re-creations of which circulated in fourth-century Athens.

We have only two surviving corpora of Greek philosophi-

cal dialogues, however, Plato's and Plutarch's, bound together
in a complex relationship of imitation, evocation, and nostalgia.
Plato's dialogues have retained their fascination in part because
they so deliberately disorient the reader, demanding a response
that is simultaneously esthetic and intellectual. These qualities
of the older corpus are increasingly appreciated, making it time
to look again at Plutarch's contribution with that in mind. Plutarch's dialogues are surely, along with the *Parallel Lives*, the
major focus of his literary activity, the genre he practiced with
the greatest seriousness.

In a sense, the questions and the dialogues are two manifestations of the same intellectual and literary orientation. The
dialogues, whether concerned with the traditions of Delphi,
with cosmology, or with the interpretation of Plato, dramatize
inquiry. The genre serves Plutarch as it served Plato: as a vehicle to present some of the basic givens of intellectual life and,
most importantly, the imperviousness of the world to virtually
all of our attempts to reduce it to chains of causality. Even more
than the essay—which, because Montaigne reinvented it by
creating for himself a literary persona in imitation of Plutarch's,
tends to be seen as Plutarch's characteristic medium—the dialogue with its polyphony allows Plutarch to present multiple
solutions to a given question and to keep them in balance, in
tension with one another, without conceding that they are mutually exclusive. The result is, like the dialogues of Plato, a
primarily esthetic object, a protreptic, proclaiming simultaneously the seductive necessity of inquiry and our remoteness
from both certainty and truth.

Plutarch the Thinker

We have seen that, however we might choose to designate
him, Plutarch must surely have defined himself primarily as a

philosopher and teacher of philosophy, even though his philosophy committed him to an active public life, and the voluminous corpus that reaches us does not contain the systematic elaboration of a philosophical position. As with the account that Plutarch gives us of his life, so the account of his intellectual commitments must be recovered piecemeal from texts whose goals lie elsewhere. The task is by no means an impossible one, however, in spite of the obstacles posed by internal contradictions and poetic, or simply vague or confused, formulations. It will be useful to organize this capsule intellectual self-portrait around a few central problems—problems that Plutarch himself did not treat in isolation but which recur constantly throughout his writing.

MAN IN THE UNIVERSE

What is a human being in Plutarch's understanding—or perhaps it would be better to ask, in his imagination?

Any answer we can give will be characterized by a radical dualism—as one would expect, given Plutarch's Platonic commitments—but it is a strangely modern dualism when set against the Platonic foil, one that looks forward not simply to Descartes but to Beckett and Artaud. In one of the most beautiful formulations, the mind (the *nooun:* "that which knows," "the knower") is imagined as the ultimate cause, *within* the person, of movement and so of action (and as we shall see, the knower is so located only very provisionally and with significant qualifications). This knower is "shaken" by a "thought" (*noethen*), whose source lies beyond both the knower and the individual. That interaction in turn sets "soul" (*psuche*) moving—imparting motion to it by a mechanism that can be expressed only in similes. It is like the twist of the feeble steering oar that turns a great cargo ship or like the light touch of the potter's fingers that makes the well-made wheel spin. Compared to these inanimate, dead objects, though, *psuche* is a vastly more sensitive thing, perfectly susceptible to the motion imparted by way of the knower in us, by the thought from beyond.

> Here are the sources of the passions and impulses, drawn tight and stretching into the *knower*, and when this is shaken they are pulled, and in turn pull on the person, and impart tension. It is in this process that we are best able to grasp the tremendous power of thought: insensitive bone and tendon and flesh, glutted with fluids—this inert, immobile, ponderous mass—as soon as there is communication between soul and mind, and soul receives an impulse in that direction, that mass leaps up with all its parts in tension and rushes into action as if it had wings. (*Socrates' Sign* 589a)

Not quite an angel on a bicycle, but a sack of bone and tissue and humors, provisionally endowed with a knower, through which our "life" or "soul" (*psuche*) maintains contact with the objects of thought, out beyond the limits of the material universe.

The status of this knower and the nature of its connection to the sack of tissue can, of course, never be resolved. The implied metaphor of the "impulses" as puppet strings extending from immaterial mind into the flesh remains just that, a metaphor, a trope, and one that would be difficult to shore up with syllogisms. Plutarch's Stoic adversaries would have found it trivial, if not laughable, committed as they were to the commonsense notion that nonmaterial things cannot exert force upon material things. But as Plutarch imagines it, our *life* is a nonmaterial thing, but one deeply mired in the physical universe, and our *mind* (*nous*) is something linked to the distal end of that life, insulated by it from the material sphere and at the same time linked through it to the sack of tissue.

Plutarch's notions about these matters are expressed in a range of styles, from analytic (though rarely rigorously and never dully so) to mythic, the latter characterized by bolder, sustained metaphors and comparisons. Projected onto the cosmic plane (and a few steps farther along the imaginative cline), the mind is sun-stuff, and its ultimate dissolution will take the form of a return to the sun, but in the process it will leave behind, first, the flesh that will decay into earth and then the life that has been bound to that flesh (*Face in the Moon* 944–45). This "second death" occurs on the moon, the frontier and mediator between the universe of the eternals and the sublunary realm of change. The moon itself is quintessential soul-stuff, into which our lives decay after abandoning the sack of tissue here below. This last death, when mind has fled back to the sun, and the soul is dissolving into the moon, is a process of everfading reminiscence and dreaming—one that may be dangerously and unnecessarily prolonged if our lives have been deeply implicated in the flesh and have left it only reluctantly.

In the "myth" of *Socrates' Sign*, a visitor to the oracle of Trophonios at Lebadeia, named Timarchos, is treated to a somewhat different vision of the structure of the universe and the relation of soul to matter. After a blow on the head, what he sees when he looks up (realizing the metaphor of "seeing stars") is a sea with floating islands of light. Eddies and currents convey the planets against the background of the fixed stars, with abysses of blue-black and broad paths of white shoals. This spectacle fills him with joy, but when he looks down, vertigo is mixed with fear and trembling:

> What lay before his eyes was a huge circular chasm, like half of a bisected sphere, terrifying and deep, filled with

darkness that knew no peace but was constantly agitated and boiling up. From it were heard the roars and howls of vast numbers of beasts, and the wailing of countless infants mingled with the cries of men and women and all sorts of vague murmurs and noises, cast up from the abyss—and all of this upset him deeply. (590f–591a)

Down there as well, flecks of light can be seen, but these lights sink into the groaning darkness of the abyss and appear out of it. A disembodied voice explains:

"What you are looking at," the voice said, "though you do not realize it, is the spirits (*daimones*) themselves. This is how it is: every life has its share of mind and there is none that is wholly irrational or mindless. But as much of every life as is immersed in the flesh and in the passions is changed and diverted by pleasure and pain into irrationality. Not every life is immersed in the same way: some sink completely into the body and live out their time in a totally disordered state at the mercy of the passions, whereas others are partially submerged, keeping their purest part outside, where it is not dragged down but, so to speak, floats on the surface, attached to the head of the person who has sunk into the abyss and holding afloat around it as much of the life as obeys it and is not overpowered by the passions. The part that lives submerged in the body is called "life" or "soul" (*psuche*), and people generally call the other part that is beyond decay "mind" (*nous*) and conceive of it as located within themselves—just as reflections in mirrors make objects themselves appear to be located there. Those, however, who have correctly solved this puzzle refer to mind as an external spirit (*daimon*). (591d–e)

This, then, is the process represented by the lights floating in the abyss, sometimes disappearing into it and sometimes reappearing. They are the little flames of mind-stuff (which is also sun-stuff and star-stuff) that accompany every soul that enters the groaning abyss. Some are dragged under and lost. Others resurface, or even manage to remain afloat throughout the ordeal of the life's experience of the material universe.

This vision, like that of the "myths" of the Platonic dialogues that lie behind it, comes about through the adoption of an imagined perspective beyond the physical universe: Timarchos, after his knock on the head, "looked up and didn't see the earth anywhere" (590c). Matter, from this perspective, is the murky twilight at the limit of the light, something beyond (and below) being, the substrate and condition of a realm of experience where being as such is remote to the point of inaccessibility, replaced by coming-to-be (*genesis*) and destruction (*phthora*).

This vision is not the perspective of our everyday lives, here in our sacks of tissue. Its truth is the truth of the imagination, an imagination that imagines itself as transcendent, able at least provisionally to formulate and comprehend the limits of its own condition. Its other aspect is very much of *this* world, and validates the sphere of immediate experience in the realm of *genesis* and *phthora* as powerfully as the transcendent perspective evokes our tragic alienation from that realm of being.

A famous and often imitated passage from the essay *Tranquillity of Mind* illustrates this well. The translation here follows that of Thomas Wyatt (1528), whose rhythms are difficult to surpass (even if he found Budé's Latin translation easier to follow than the sometimes forbidding Greek).

Yes, and if we be wise, then [each day is] a most gladsome holiday. For this world is a certain most holy temple and

most meet for God. Into this temple man is admitted when
he is born, not to behold carven images wanting senses,
but the sun, the moon, and the stars, from which cometh
moving and the first principles of life, which providence
hath given unto us to behold that they should be sensible
images and followings of intelligible things, as Plato says.
Besides these, the floods that bring forth always new wa-
ters, and the earth producing food both unto trees and
unto all kind of beasts. With this goodliness and prospect
beginning truly our life, it must be full of surety and over-
spread gladsomeness. (477c–d)

What from the perspective of eternity is the groaning abyss
beyond being is, viewed from within, "a most holy temple"
composed of "sensible images" of *noeta*, that is, of things apprehended not by the senses but by the mind. These radical
formulations, which superficially viewed must surely seem
mutually exclusive, turn out to be complementary, and the link
between them is a relation of interpretation, of expression in a
new (and alien) medium. This world in which we live is, from
the imagined perspective of eternity, an abyss of pain, of that
coming-to-be whose inevitable complement is decay and destruction, but it is simultaneously the expression, in the defective medium of matter, of that same eternity.

For Plutarch, time is already that "moving image of eternity" that it was to be for later Platonists. His world is already,
by implication, that "best of all *possible* worlds" (in the ago-
nizingly inadequate Platonist formulation ridiculed in Voltaire's *Candide*), and it is such by virtue of expressing in the
medium of time, space, and change that which is eternal, immaterial, and immutable.

A century and a half after Plutarch's death, the first major
thinker of the later Platonist tradition, Plotinus, followed this

line of argument in his defense of the world against those his circle knew as "gnostics"—thinkers, including at least some Christians, who saw this world as the creation of an evil demiurge, a place of punishment characterized by unalloyed evil, this last a principle inherent in matter and inseparable from it. In Plutarch's time, such thinkers had not yet emerged as an object of attention for philosophers (the term, in his time and place, could only mean "thinkers in the Greek traditions of philosophy"). In the essay *Tranquillity of Mind*, Plutarch is writing not against a philosophical (much less a religious) position but against a morbid and neurotic disorder of the psyche. Still, the positions are, mutatis mutandis, quite similar, and it is Plutarch (as so often) who provides us with insight into the antecedents of the major philosophical debates of late antiquity.

COSMOGONY AND COSMOLOGY

There are few areas of philosophy in which we can see Plutarch self-consciously exploring new territory and providing new explanations. As we have seen, his idea of doing philosophy consists largely of interpreting existing texts and entering into dialogue with thinkers who were long dead. The positions he endorses are largely those of the Platonist tradition he embraces (or at least they are what Plutarch understood to be such, and we seldom have solid evidence to test his claims). And the positions he rejects are those of the two so-called materialisms, the Stoa and the school of Epicurus.

On one matter, however, we have evidence of his status as a deliberately tendentious Platonist—or, to put it differently, as a lucidly original interpreter of Plato. His position in this instance was fortuitously to assure him prominence in the debate on creation that in his time was in its infancy but which would assume critical importance as Christianity aspired to philosophical respectability. The essay *The Generation of the Soul in the Timaeus* characteristically supplies the reader with an account of its own creation. It presents itself as a synthesis of observations, both oral and written, that Plutarch had made at various times about Plato's notion of the soul, a synthesis that was needed because Plutarch's ideas on the matter were both complex and idiosyncratic, or, more specifically, "in contradiction with most of those who have followed Plato" (1012b). This account of Plutarch's position is addressed to two of his sons, once again deliberately mixing the most public of relationships—the teacher of school philosophy to the student—and the most intimate.

The *Timaeus* had, by Plutarch's time, assumed a prominent position in the philosophical schools as the keystone of Platonism. It is one of the dialogues largely occupied by a single speech. After a dialogic frame, which looks back to the discussion that makes up Plato's *Republic,* Timaeus, described as "our best astronomer and one who has concentrated on learning about the nature of the universe" (27a), accepts the others' invitation to give an account of what he has learned. He starts from the distinction between "that which exists permanently" (*to on aei*) and "that which is forever becoming" but never can participate in the being of the eternal things (*to gignomenon men aei, on de oudepote,* 27d). The former category of entities is perceived by mind, the latter by the senses, and since the cosmos is clearly a thing apprehended by the senses, Timaeus claims that it must have had a beginning and therefore a cause (28c). The goodness of the created cosmos points to the goodness of its creator (29a) and to the notion that this good "maker" (*demiourgos*) must have done his work while contemplating a model in the realm of the eternals, a model therefore exclusively perceptible to mind. The epistemological implications of this are made explicit: "As being is to becoming, so is truth to belief" (*pistis* 29c).

The realm of being, then, is the realm of truth, and radically divorced from the cosmos of becoming that is the world of our immediate experience, a realm in which we can aspire only to beliefs (or "opinion" [*doxa*]). The most we can hope for in giving an account (*logos*) of this realm and its creation is that it be the most "likely" (*eikos*) account available (29b–d).

This paraphrase of Plato might seem to take us far from our goal of understanding the thought, not of the fourth-century philosopher, but of Plutarch, half a millennium later. What one must never forget about Plutarch's engagement with the world, however, is that Plutarch expresses that engagement almost exclusively in terms of centuries-old formulations. This is not at all to say that he engages only texts, divorced from experience. Nothing could be further from the truth; he is constantly evoking lived experience and often, in the "myths" of his dialogues, stretching the imagination to accommodate some sort of account of what it is to live in such a world as Plato envisioned— which is also the world as Plutarch conceptualized it. Plato's text is, by and large, implicit in Plutarch's. He takes upon himself to elucidate the interaction of that text with the world of experience and does so, not as someone resurrecting old notions, but as someone who is in possession of such a powerful expression of his own beliefs, embodied in an ancient text, that to explore the world is to explore that text as well. It is in this sense that there is a broad analogy between Plutarch (along with the other later Platonists) and believers in scripturally based revealed religions—Jews, Christians, and Moslems. The analogy is potentially misleading, however, and there are striking differences between the two situations. The dialogues provided later Platonists with an account of the world and an intellectual focus of extraordinary power, but one that was not coercive, neither credited with superhuman authority nor exploited by a priesthood. Still, a reader of Dante utterly ignorant of the

New Testament reads a different book than does the reader who brings to the *Commedia* that essential background, and to read the New Testament in the service of understanding Dante will deliver a body of story and ideas that were an essential part of Dante's world, things that he might generally have stated as his own beliefs. In much the same way, Plato is the substrate on which Plutarch builds his own descriptions and analyses of what it is to experience this world, and in reading Plato to illuminate Plutarch we are likewise turning to texts that are so intimately bound up with Plutarch's own experience that the line between the two can be difficult to draw.

Plutarch begins his essay with a problematic paragraph from Timaeus's long speech (35a–b), where the subject is the demiurge's creation of soul, specifically the world-soul, or that by virtue of which the cosmos is alive and self-moving. This soul is a mixture, we are told, of indivisible being (or "sameness") and the fragmented realm of becoming (also designated "difference"). It is, then, in essence a tertium quid, an intermediary entity, encompassing in an unexplained way the two realms of the primary dichotomy but separate from them. This is a theme on which Plutarch delivers endless variations: the soul as intermediary and as mediator—the soul as analogous to the moon, positioned between the realm of being and that of birth and death and in some obscure way uniting characteristics of each. The *Timaeus* passage introduces an even more bewildering variation, in which this compound, mixed together by the demiurge as if he were mixing wine and water in a bowl, is then parceled out in an assortment of ratios that in some sense constitute the mathematical harmonies that govern the composition of the universe—or, rather, of its animating principle, here under construction.

It is at this point, before the strange discourse on fractions and harmonies, that Plutarch steps back and surveys the opinions of earlier Platonists, right back to Xenocrates, who knew Plato, and his student Crantor, and in so doing reveals something fascinating about his own relation to the tradition and about the tradition itself (1013a–b):

> All of these interpreters uniformly agree that the [world-] soul did not have a beginning in time and was not subject to generation, but that Plato gave an account that said it was both created and a mixture because it has multiple capacities, which he singled out for the sake of analysis. They think, moreover, that he thought the same thing about the cosmos—that it was eternal and ungenerated— but seeing that it was difficult to grasp how it was constituted and organized without postulating a beginning for it and an initial assembling of the generative elements, that is the path he took.

This passage exposes unexpected continuities in the tradition of the interpretation of Plato in which Plutarch situates himself. It is a commonplace of later Platonist readings of myths—including the myths of Plato and those of Homer—that they reveal to the properly trained interpreter static and permanent truths about the universe. These principles are spun out in stories, with one event succeeding another, only for the sake of our weak and discursive intellects, in deference to which the "mythoplasts" have dilated into narrative their accounts of complex truths not easily grasped in their entirety. This tradition of interpretation is richly represented in the fifth century of our era in Proclus's commentaries on the dialogues of Plato, and might well appear to be a late-antique aberration were it not for this passage of Plutarch's, where precisely the same interpretive strategy is shown to have been in use among readers of Plato's myths from the time of their composition.

If, according to these early readers of Plato, the myth of the

Timaeus told of the creation of the world only to throw light on what Plato himself knew to be eternal and uncreated, Plutarch, while he relates to us this orthodoxy of interpretation, will have nothing of it. He presents himself as a literalist: if Plato said first the world-soul and then the world were created, that is what he meant. Plutarch tells us that he has written about this elsewhere (1013e)—perhaps in the lost work the Lamprias Catalogue calls "According to Plato, the World Was Created"—and so he gives only a sketch of his position here. He nevertheless makes it clear how much is at stake: Plato uses creation to demonstrate the existence of the gods and the priority of soul over body. If we dismiss the *Timaeus* story as an analytic allegory and read the sequential narrative as simply a way of rendering a complex, eternal synthesis more accessible to the mind, we lose those arguments as well, and Plutarch is not prepared to pay that price or to concede that Plato would have done so.

Within his own tradition of philosophy, then, this is where Plutarch stands on the origins of the cosmos. On the matter of its organization, his position is most clearly expressed in the dialogue "The Face in the Moon," where he upholds a Platonizing account against a Stoic one. We will have a closer look at this dialogue in Chapter 3, but at this point it will serve to bring out something of what is at stake in the confrontations of Platonism with the Stoa in Plutarch's dramatizations.

The dialogue opens with a mutilated discussion of the possibility that the image (the "Old Man") we see on the face of the moon is the reflection of the earth, surrounded by the great ocean. This line of questioning is soon abandoned, however, in favor of an exchange among the narrator (Lamprias, Plutarch's brother), Lucius, and a Stoic named Pharnaces. What we learn is that the Stoics claim that the moon is a "mixture of congealed mist (*aer*) and soft fire" (921f) and that the image we see is formed of ripples beneath the surface. It would be presumptuous to assume that this belief was generally held among Stoics, or even by any particular Stoic at any given time. The principal motive for the claim here would seem to be a commitment to the notion that the universe is governed by an orderly series of rules that "naturally" keep things in their places—the heaviest of them at the bottom (in the center of the earth) and the lightest farthest from that point. For all its orderliness, the system is vulnerable to a number of objections, including the problem that the model does not account for any fuel that might sustain this supposed fire, as well as some doubts about just how to define up and down and about the centrality of the earth.

Lamprias at this point is concerned primarily about defending the notion of a solid, earthy moon, made of a substance analogous to that of our world. His demolition of the Stoic system (which, in his analysis, turns out to be unable to account for a significant percentage of the phenomena) is less impressive than his formulation of an alternative, teleological account that asserts that the moon is what it is and where it is because of providence (*pronoia*), which organizes everything "for the best" (*epi to beltion*, 927d). Nature (*physis*)—or the deterministic network of forces that the Stoics, according to Lamprias, designated by that word—has nothing to do with it. What makes an element of the universe appear to be located and functioning "according to nature" (*kata physin*, a Stoic buzzword, 927c) is that it is functioning for the "preservation, beauty, or function" of the whole, which it does when it seems to occupy its "natural" location or to have its "natural" movement or disposition (927d). Take man—

> the outstanding example of a creature that has come to be "naturally": the heavy, earthy parts are at the top, mostly in the head, and the hot, fiery ones are in the middle. Some

of his teeth grow up, and some grow down, but neither set
is "unnatural." Nor is the fire that shines out above from
the eyes "natural," and the fire in the guts and the heart
"unnatural," but each is placed appropriately and usefully. . . .

    The same is likely to be true of the cosmos, given that
it is a living being, with earth in all sorts of places and fire
and water as well, and air (*pneuma*) not where it is "ex-
pelled by necessity" but where it is placed in an arrangement governed by reason (*logoi*). (927e–f, 928a)

This, then, is what is at stake: a moon that stays in the sky
because it belongs there (as an optimal part of an optimal, and
incidentally animate, whole) and not because its weight—
heavier than the celestial fire but lighter than earth—has inevitably lodged it there. In fact, the Stoics talked of *pronoia*—
providence—every bit as much as the Platonists did, but Plutarch's account makes it clear that from a Platonist perspective,
or at least from *his* Platonist perspective, they were defective in
their teleology. They failed to understand the scope and freedom of the rational divine order in everything, organizing it
"for the best."

ETHICS

    The umbrella title—*Moralia*—given to the nonbiographical
works of Plutarch is sufficient indication that their author was
long perceived as a thinker whose major contribution was in
the field of ethics, but few of the narrowly ethical essays are
read today. This was far from true in late antiquity and in early
modern Europe. Such essays as *How to Profit by Your Enemies*
and *Virtue and Vice* were among the first polytheist works to
attract Syrian Christian translators, and they have doubtless

been mined for many thousands of sermons in dozens of languages. This is in fact the greatest obstacle to reading these essays today: they read like sermons. At best, they are colorful and, as we would expect from the author of the *Parallel Lives*, illustrated with well-selected anecdotes. But they participate in the genre of the sermon in all too many ways: they tend to be facile, obvious, and sadly lacking in surprises.

If Plutarch made a contribution to ethical thought, it was the contribution of an educator and a popularizer, yet there are some interesting and important aspects of even this ancillary role. First, of all, these essays constitute a new genre in the preserved philosophical literature in Greek. The surviving precedents in Latin—notably in such essays of Cicero's as *De amicitia*—no doubt had close Greek comparanda in their time, but virtually nothing of the Greek literature of the two centuries before Plutarch survives intact. In a striking number of instances, titles of lost essays of Chrysippus and other Stoics resurface in Cicero and Plutarch. We may conclude that Plutarch's originality in these ethical essays is only apparent. He did not invent the Greek literary consolation or the sermonlike admonitory essay any more than he invented the Greek tradition of biography, but the accidents of transmission have left him at the source of all these traditions in the preserved literature.

The terms in which classical Greek ethical thought was framed were already in place in Plato. The goal and its formulation were nonproblematic. *Eudaimonia*—quaintly but misleadingly translated as "happiness"—designated the state one hoped to reach. A colleague of mine used to tell undergraduates that it meant the condition of being "well-off, in the view of a third party," and that is a very helpful formulation. *Eudaimonia* is a form of success that can be assessed—or experienced—only from the outside. It stands for the fully realized life. The ethical thought of Plato consists largely in assessing the role of various accomplishments or excellences (*aretai*, again quaintly and misleadingly, "virtues") in attaining that state of being well-off. The ethical treatises of Aristotle begin in this tradition but, with a characteristic liberality, expand the discussion to a wider range of human behavior.

In the reductive summaries of the doxographers—popularizers who summarized the salient opinions of the philosophers and philosophical schools—the debate over ethics in the Hellenistic period turned, once again, largely on the criteria that formed the basis for the judgment that an individual was "well- off." Did the traditional and largely nonproblematic "excellences" suffice—self-restraint, doing right, piety, wisdom—or were certain externals required, health, for example, and if not wealth, then at least the absence of dire poverty? The Cynics with their outrageous street theater shocked their audiences into an awareness that much of what society thought shameful or polluting was in fact "indifferent"—it made no difference. Stoics took the extreme position: only the excellences mattered, and those could be achieved only by the wise man, and all at once, in a kind of epiphany, or not at all. The Stoic ideal of *apatheia* ("absence of emotion") was contrasted with the Peripatetic praise of *metriopatheia* ("moderation of emotion"), conceived as a more humane goal, one conceding to human nature a need to grieve the loss of a loved one, for example.

This last instance indicates a change that is important for Plutarch. Classical ethics put the emphasis on objective criteria—to describe oneself as *eudaimon* could only be hubristically pretentious and nonsensical. But in the Hellenistic world we see a shift in the direction of an internalized ethics, one in which what it feels like to be a certain sort of person is matter for discussion, analysis, and evaluation. There were antecedents, of course. In the fifth century, Democritus had written about *euthymia* ("tranquillity" or "contentment"), which he postulated as a goal, distinguishing it carefully from pleasure (*hedone*); and Socrates' contemporary Aristippos of Cyrene was cited as an antecedent of Epicurus in assigning value to pleasure.

In what is perhaps the most attractive of the ethical essays, entitled *Tranquillity of Mind* (*euthymia*), Plutarch places himself in that tradition of Democritus, appropriating even his title (as did Seneca, writing about the same time). Plutarch distances himself from his model early on, however, for he believed, rightly or wrongly, that Democritus thought a public life to be incompatible with peace of mind, a price, says Plutarch, that is simply too high (465c). (In the essay entitled *Is "Live Unknown" a Wise Precept?* Plutarch responds to his own rhetorical question regarding that Epicurean maxim with a resounding no, pointing out that Epicurus himself formulated the question to attract attention: excellence attracts notice and inspires memory, whereas obscurity breeds nothing but mold [1129d].) The thrust of Plutarch's string of prescriptions and anecdotes is this:

> Each individual has the stores of tranquillity and discontent within, and the jars of goods and evils do not lie "on the threshold of Zeus." This is made clear by the range of our experience: the foolish overlook and neglect even the good things right in front of them, because they always keep their minds focused on the future, whereas the wise, by memory, keep vividly present for themselves even the good things that are gone. (473b–c)

Peace of mind is not the inevitable accompaniment of any particular way of life, although it is an undisputed desideratum. It is the result of certain dispositions, certain qualities of character. Plutarch cannot tell us how to achieve it, but he can provide models of it and communicate vividly what it is like. This is the quality of the ethical essays that often raises them above the level of the many sermons that have mined them and degraded them. Plutarch is too good a writer to sink into such dullness.

Plutarch the Educator

Plutarch did not have a profession in our sense of the word; rather, he had an identity. He was heir to the oddly elitist notion so pervasive in Greek society that the only product of a fully realized life was a fully realized person. To paraphrase a treatment of the matter from the generation after Plutarch's death (Lucian's *Dream*): to be, for instance, a sculptor—even a Phidias—was to coat yourself with grime and marble dust, to reduce yourself to a tool for the production of a beautiful artifact. The higher goal—or so Lucian maintained—was that of the epideictic (or display) orator, the intellectual performer, whose discourse was the full realization of his fine-tuned education, the highest expression of the cultural refinement of his time. The display orator's performance, his product, was himself.

We have good reason to believe that Plutarch, presumably in his youth, displayed the fruits of his education in this way. A small minority of the pieces transmitted in the *Moralia* (*The Fortune of the Romans, The Fortune of Alexander, The Fame of the Athenians,* and a few others) seem to belong here and probably predate his further philosophical education in the late 60s and perhaps the 70s.

Education thus had a complex role in Plutarch's life, and it is certain that he in turn taught others. We have seen that he lectured on philosophy in Rome. It would be satisfying to know whether those lectures resembled *The Generation of the Soul in the Timaeus* and *The Principle of Cold* or, rather, *Tranquillity of Mind*—that is, whether he offered his audiences school philosophy in the form of his comments on the texts and the earlier commentators and examinations of problems of physics, or polished exhortations to live their lives as pleasantly and as fully as possible. The audiences were in any case composed of adults (on the evidence of the anecdote cited above). We also see Plutarch engaged in philosophical discussion with others who seem roughly his own age and sometimes, by mutual agreement, lecturing to them ("Against Colotes," "No Pleasant Life"). There is a certain amount of evidence to suggest, however, a long-term commitment on Plutarch's part to the education of the young, and that is what will concern us here.

The essay that traditionally has taken first place in editions of the *Moralia* is a discussion of the upbringing of the aristocratic young man that begins with the boy's conception and ends with his marriage ("Education"). That it is rhetorical to the point of archness and glib to the point of fatuousness does not necessarily prove that Plutarch was not its author, but it has generally been treated as inauthentic ever since the first modern editor of the complete *Moralia*, Daniel Wyttenbach, in 1810 devoted thirty-five pages to meticulous argumentation (in Latin) to proving it so. His approach throws light on a notion of Plutarch and his activities that is attractive, persistent, and founded on very little. In the manner of the scholarship of his day, Wyttenbach (who was, incidentally, one of the giants of classical philology) felt that he must supply a complete scenario for the production of the text he denied Plutarch: "It therefore seems likely to me that the author of this book was a young man (*adolescens*) educated in the rhetorical schools, first by other teachers and then by Plutarch, but not long enough to acquire from him much color or style—a recent addition, then, to Plutarch's rhetorical school, and in philosophy still a raw beginner or utterly ignorant, and scarcely imbued with the first principles and protreptics" (vol. 6.1, p. 62). Wyttenbach went on to conjecture that Plutarch had set the students the exercise

"What might one be able to say about the education of upper-
class boys, and what would give them good character?"

To his credit, Wyttenbach presented his scenario as conjec-
tural, but it is conjecture based on as deep a knowledge of this
corpus as one could find anywhere. The hard evidence that
Plutarch maintained such a school is slight, however. Introducing the dialogue *The E at Delphi* (385a), Plutarch casually mentions that the subject of this puzzling Delphic dedication had
come up often "in the school," but that he had steered around
it. His language implies knowledge on his addressee's part of
some sort of school where Plutarch presided. Beyond this, the
evidence consists of the rhetorical pieces in the corpus (evidence, presumably, that Plutarch studied rhetoric, but hardly
proof that he taught it) and the dialogue *Whether Land or Sea
Animals Are Cleverer* where, as we have seen, Plutarch's father
and his friend Soclaros act as judges in a debating contest that
pits praise of land animals (and hunting) against praise of sea
creatures (and fishing). The school of Plato and the school of
Aristotle both mixed rhetoric with philosophy, and the argument (as Wyttenbach developed it) is that we see in this idealized, quasi-bucolic scene a literary representation of Plutarch's life in Chaeronea, where young men would be sent to
him to perfect their rhetorical skills and become initiated into
philosophy.

Whether or not this helps us to imagine how Plutarch's
time in Chaeronea was occupied, the two essays that follow
"Education" in the traditional order of the *Moralia* offer ample
evidence that Plutarch gave serious thought to pedagogic matters, evidence reinforced by many studied digressions on pedagogy elsewhere (e.g., *Cato Min.* 1). *How the Young Should Listen
to Poetry* is framed as a letter to a contemporary of Plutarch's
(otherwise unknown) who, as we learn, has a son the same
age—perhaps twelve—as one of Plutarch's sons. Plutarch offers

this father advice on the use of poetry in education. The two boys have finished their primary education and can read and write. That they should now encounter the poets is inevitable, but not without pitfalls. Poetry is inseparable from pleasure and therefore always hazardous, always potentially misleading and addictive. The boys will therefore need supervision; they will need to be supplied with certain hermeneutic principles and prejudices that will neutralize the dangers of poetry and maximize its value as a propaedeutic to philosophy. The first such principle is summed up in the proverbial observation that "poets tell a lot of lies" (*polla pseudontai aoidoi,* 16a). Some of these lies are deliberate and a function of the seductiveness of the poetic art, whereas others stem simply from the poets' ignorance or misinformation. One way or another, the young reader must be taught distance, skepticism, and, most of all, judgment. Beyond this, he must be predisposed to find edifying messages in the poems selected for him. He must watch closely for signals of the poet's judgment of his characters and their actions, understanding that some are exemplary and others are not, and finally. he must use the seductive fictions as tools for the sharpening of his own ethical judgment.

This essay airs some hermeneutic principles that are not without interest, especially given that Plutarch's constant search for meaning and explanation is such a salient aspect of his identity as a writer. Plutarch interrogates myths (*Isis and Osiris*) and artifacts ("E") in ways that are surprising and decidedly idiosyncratic. What we see in those instances is a series of interpretive strategies closely bound up with Plutarch's ontology. These symbols that give intimations of the eternal—the gods, the realm of being—are in his conception necessarily polyvalent. They are subject to multiple, sometimes incompatible, but never mutually exclusive interpretations simply because they are signs within this sublunary realm of fragmentation, birth, and decay—signs that designate something beyond that realm. They represent that transcendent truth but can never participate in its unity, and so, to our fragmented perceptions, they will reveal multiple aspects of that truth, sequentially.

If Plutarch's understanding of myths and artifacts is thus paradoxical, uncanny, and remote from our own notions, what, then, about the interpretation of texts? Like most ancient writers, Plutarch has relatively little to say about the interpretation of literary texts, and in this sphere his hermeneutic strategies are largely pragmatic. What certainly underlies them is his rhetorical education, where he will have learned that meaning (*dianoia*) was a largely nonproblematic element of texts—at least in comparison with their persuasive powers, the primary focus of the art. Clarity may be threatened by such tropes as irony, sarcasm, and allegory, all of which achieve their effects by saying something other than what is meant. These can open up a disjunction between sign and signifier and, if abused, may result in frigidity, obscurity, and failure of persuasion.

We are indebted to Plutarch in this essay for one of the most precious pieces of evidence we possess regarding the history of the hermeneutic dilemma raised by such indirect expression (whether a strategy of the poet in question, as generally claimed by the interpreters, or not). The subject is those passages in Homer (notably the "Deception of Zeus" [Il. 14. 153–351] and the "Song of Ares and Aphrodite" [Od. 8.266–366]) that because of their uncharacteristic sexual explicitness, even obscenity, had for centuries been singled out for criticism by Homer's detractors. The problem arises, we are told, because of Homer's characteristic restraint with regard to explicit judgment of the characters and actions he portrays:

> In Homer, this sort of instruction is tacit, but he leaves the option of a sort of reexamination that is useful in the case of

the stories that are most criticized. Some people forcefully distort these stories, using what used to be called "hints" (*hyponoiai*) but now are called "allegories" (*allegoriai*), and claim that the Sun reports that Aphrodite is in bed with Ares because the conjunction of his star [Mars] with hers [Venus] brings about illegitimate births—but when the Sun turns around and catches them, these do not go unnoticed. They want Hera's adornment to seduce Zeus and the aphrodisiac magic of the scarf to be some sort of purification of the air [*aer* as *Here, Hera*] by contact with fire—as if the poet did not himself supply solutions. For in what he says about Aphrodite he teaches the attentive that vulgar music and obscene songs and pornographic stories produce licentious behavior and people fixated on luxury, self-indulgence, and sex. . . . And in the story about Hera he has not only shown perfectly that sex and pleasure achieved by drugs, aphrodisiacs, and deception are ephemeral and quickly sated and unsure but even that they are transformed into enmity and rage when the pleasure is gone. Look at what Zeus says to her:

Just see if fawning and sex do you any good—
after you came from the other gods and tricked me into
   bed! (19e–20b; Il. 15.32–33)

This passage has often been understood to show that Plutarch "rejected" allegorical reading (or teaching) of Homer, but clearly the issue is not so simple. He does reject as violent "distortions" of Homer's text an astrological allegory and a "physical" allegory of a sort familiar from the scholia, where (with the help of an implied etymological wordplay on Hera's name) an obscene episode was transformed into a cosmic allegory depicting the interrelations of the physical elements. What he replaces these with, however—announcing that these are Homer's own answers to the criticisms—are in effect moral allegories, mes-

sages he asserts are implanted in the text but are in fact articula-
tions of his own tendentious and moralizing readings.

It is true, nevertheless, that Plutarch, the persistent and
often idiosyncratic hermeneut, neither praised nor extensively
exploited the traditions of allegorical interpretation of literary
texts—particularly Homer—that had long been a mainstay of
pedagogy and commentary. Rather, he neutralizes obscenity
with moralizing paraphrase and musters dubious evidence to
show that Homer meant to provide negative exempla in those
delightfully pornographic stories and that this intention can be
recovered from elsewhere in Homer's text. Like most, if not all,
allegorical readers, he claims to have recovered the true intention of the author.

Despite this insistence on the articulation of authorial intention, the pedagogic hermeneutics of this essay leave room
for an active reader. In a passage that constitutes a very rare
breach of the pervasive intentionalism of ancient literary interpreters, Plutarch observes:"Chrysippus has correctly demon-
strated the application of the poet's words to things beyond
what is explicit, showing that one must transfer and extend the
useful observations to similar situations" (34b). The examples
provided are trivial. Hesiod said, "You wouldn't lose your ox if
you didn't have a rotten neighbor" (*Works and Days* 348), and
this amounts to saying the same thing about your dog, your
jackass, and so forth.

Notice that Chrysippus—a Stoic—is credited with this
"correct" notion, and not only is Plutarch generally hostile to
Stoics, but the enemies of the Stoa tell us again and again that
the Stoics were tendentious, intellectually dishonest readers
who habitually made outrageous claims—notably in the form
of physical allegories of the sort cited—to convince the world
that the early poets were Stoics before the fact (Cicero, *De nat-
ura deorum* 1.41). It is in fact probable that a lot of Stoic ped-

agogical notions underlie this essay, because the Stoics were among the first ancient thinkers to explore systematically the problem of interpreting texts. What we see here is a principle that might explain some of the mistrust expressed by non-Stoics regarding Stoic readings, although in its pedagogic context Plutarch presents it as inoffensive and even helpful. Like the decipherment of the trope of allegory, this hermeneutic principle is ultimately a matter of rhetoric: the author, we are told, chooses one illustration of a sound principle but by a sort of metonymy uses that instance to point to a whole range of other examples, and it is the job of the interpreter—or at least of the teacher of poetry to the young—to make explicit some of those implied instances.

Plutarch clearly gave long and serious thought to the education of the young. The essay that follows this one in the traditional order, *Listening to Lectures*, was written to advise a somewhat older boy on his continuing education. In *How Progress in Virtue Might Be Perceived* he argues—this time explicitly against the Stoa—that real progress toward excellence (and so, education imparting *arete*, "virtue") is both possible and perceptible. When we turn to the *Lives*, we will have to ask whether that huge project was likewise undertaken in the service of the ethical progress of the young.

All of the essays discussed above address the practicalities of education and self-improvement in the context of Plutarch's own society. In comparing the educational programs of Lycurgus and Numa (*Numa* 26 = *Comp.* 4), Plutarch gives us a surprising glimpse of his broader ideals. Numa failed; he missed his opportunity to put in place an educational system to shape the young "so that there would be no differences or disturbances in their character, but sculpted and molded right from the start, they would travel a common path of excellence together." This echo of Socrates in the *Republic* describing the education of the guardians is a reminder that even this gentlest of Platonists had a weakness for Spartan social engineering and education for uniformity. If this ideal lies somewhere behind Plutarch's pedagogic practice, it is nevertheless remote from the tenor of his practical advice and what we can recover of his educational activities.

Plutarch the Priest at Delphi

Nearly a century before Delphi was excavated, a French envoy to the court of Ali Pasha of Ioannina visited the sleepy little village that stood on the site of the ancient oracular shrine. Pouqueville enthused over the wealth of inscriptions he saw: "marble slabs, pieces of walls, interiors of caves . . . covered with dedications and decrees that should be studied and carefully copied" (*Voyages*, 2d ed., iv, 113). He himself copied and published only one, which might be translated as follows (CIG 1713):

EMPEROR CAESAR
SON OF THE GOD TRAJAN
PARTHICUS, GRANDSON
OF THE GOD NERVA, TRAJAN
HADRIAN AUGUSTUS:
THE AMPHICTYONS
[ERECTED THIS STATUE]
UNDER THE SUPERVISION FROM DELPHI
OF MESTRIUS PLUTARCHUS
THE PRIEST

The Amphictyonic League was composed of the states that contributed to the maintenance and administration of the Delphic shrine, and its council consisted of delegates from those states. As a prominent and respected Boeotian, Plutarch served in this capacity, but in this inscription he is specifically called priest (*hiereus*), the highest official of the shrine and a position of considerable responsibility, both fiscal and liturgical. A characteristically casual reference to his "fellow priest (*suniereus*) Euthydemos" (*Table Talk* 700e) confirms this, and several passages in the essay *Whether an Old Man Should Engage in Public Life* throw further light on Plutarch's activities in Delphi. In one of these (785c) he indicates obliquely that he has held the positions of agonothete (presiding over the Pythian Games) and president of the Amphictyonic Council, as well as Boeotiarch, and in the other (792f) he declares himself unwilling on account of age to retire from his duties (specified as sacrificing, marching in processions, and dancing) "after serving Pythian Apollo for so many years." The Pythian Games were pentaeteric, like the Olympics, and so a Pythiad, like an Olympiad, was the period of four years between celebrations of the games. It has been reasoned, no doubt correctly, that Plutarch would not have said "many" (*pollas*) Pythiads unless he meant at least five, and so he here declares himself to have served the shrine for at least twenty years, perhaps more. The activities evoked, especially sacrifice, sound like those of a priest (and not just a delegate or even an agonothete), and so it has been argued, though less conclusively, that he was actually one of the two perpetual priests for at least twenty years, and perhaps over thirty. The inscription guarantees, at any rate, that he was priest in the late teens of the second century, because Hadrian became emperor in 117, and Plutarch is unlikely to have lived on long into the 120s.

What exactly did it mean for Plutarch to hold this priesthood, and quite likely for such an extended period? He and his colleague were the principal leaders of the ritual activity of the shrine, which must have been considerable. Plutarch never depicts himself in such a role, however, and although he writes more about Delphi than any other surviving author does, we look in vain in the midst of all his Delphic lore for any hard facts about ritual or about the mechanisms of consulting the oracle in the late first and early second centuries. The inscription tells us that while priest he had administrative duties as well, such as overseeing the preparation and installation of a statue of the new emperor.

The literature of the ancient world is singularly lacking in accounts of what the modern world has called religious experience. Apuleius, who was born a few years after Plutarch's death, is often held up as the exception that brings out the truth of this generalization. At the end of *The Golden Ass* his protagonist is returned to articulate human existence by conversion to the religion of Isis, and although the rich fantasy of the novel creates a texture deliberately divorced from everyday experience, the transformation represented by that final conversion is rendered all the more powerful by that fantasy.

If Plutarch ever experienced anything comparable, there is no trace of it in the huge corpus. This may well reflect only a compartmentalization of experience, a deliberate silence. Indeed, it is a commonplace of Greek literature from its beginnings that the secrets revealed to initiates in the various mystery cults were excluded from literary representation, and so this entire sphere—of central importance to many generations of polytheists—remains a major blind spot in our understanding of their lives. Even so matter-of-fact a figure as the second-century travel writer Pausanias avoids violating restricted sacred space by his prose: he tells us that he was forbidden in a dream to describe anything within the sacred enclosure at Eleusis.

The prohibition was so much a fact of life, behavior, and discourse that it was proverbial. This is dramatized in the conversation on the chicken and the egg in Plutarch's *Table Talk*, when one of the speakers says "with a laugh":

Moreover, I'll "sing to the knowers" the sacred Orphic discourse that not only makes the egg prior to the chicken but comprehensively attributes to it absolute priority over all things. Let the rest of that "remain in silence" (as Herodotus says), because it is reserved for the initiate, but the fact remains that the world contains a vast range of living creatures, but every class of them participates in generation from an egg. (636d–e)

Plutarch repeatedly skirts this silence, this blacked-out area. In the *Consolation to His Wife*, he invokes as a guide for her "the secret symbols of the mysteries of Dionysus, knowledge of which we initiates share with each other" (611d). This veiled reference adds little to the rhetorical force of its immediate context and so can probably be taken at face value as an indication that both Plutarch and his wife had in fact undergone such initiation. In a discussion of the nature of the gods of the oracular shrines, one of the speakers in *The Disappearance of Oracles* (Cleombrotos) excludes the Mysteries from the discussion in these terms: "As far as the initiations, in which the greatest manifestations and intimations of the truth about the gods are to be found, let them 'rest in silence,' as Herodotus says" (417b–c).

If Plutarch believed in the truth of what he has Cleombrotos say about the Mysteries, then we must assume that he did seek out initiation when and wherever it was to be found. It is likewise no surprise that all such material is excluded from the theological essays.

In the long and analytical *Isis and Osiris*, however, we find no indication of the proximity of barriers or of prohibitions against making public the hidden meanings of myths, ritual, and symbols—even though Plutarch asserts that Osiris and Dionysus are identical and calls on his addressee as witness to this, because she was initiated into both cults (364e). The prologue to that essay is a celebration of the goal of learning the truth about the gods: "The impulse toward truth, and especially truth concerning the gods, is a desire for divinity," one that Plutarch associates both with Isis herself (etymologized as a Greek word meaning roughly "knower") and with the gods in general: "If you take away knowledge of reality and thought, immortality would not be life, but just passing time" (351e).

Plutarch thus believed in the existence of the gods he served, and he repeatedly asserts his belief in their benevolent providence as well. They were not the remote, impassive, and indifferent divinities of Epicurus, nor were they the fiery *logos* of the Stoics, pervading the material universe and shaping and animating it. Why did he choose to believe in these providential, eternal, benevolent beings? It is difficult to say. In the dialogue *Love*, he has his father put on the persona of Tiresias in Euripides' *Bacchae* to object to a proposal that the divine status of Eros be critically examined:

> You seem to be to be broaching an imposing and dangerous matter, Pemptides, or rather to be shaking the unshakable beliefs that we share about the gods, if you ask for an account and defense of each divinity. Our ancient, ancestral faith is sufficient, and you could not name or discover a clearer indication, "Not if the subtlety were devised by the sharpest intelligence" [*Bacchae* 203]. Rather, this faith is a common foundation and basis for piety, and if its security and traditional authority are disturbed or shaken on one point, the whole is damaged and becomes subject to doubt. (756a–b)

This is not so much traditional piety as pious traditionalism, and it may well be that Plutarch himself could do no better in defense of his "faith." The position looks forward to the holistic notion of polytheist tradition developed in the third century by the emperor Julian, in that it implies a commitment to the notion that the edifice of custom that comprehends Greek thought, literature, and identity is inseparable from the traditional cults. Piety is a social virtue, and respect for the gods is respect for the values that give coherence to society. One of the speakers in *The Disappearance of Oracles* finds unacceptable on two counts the explanation that oracular shrines failed because of the deaths of their respective prophetic *daimones:* the explanation is "too bold" and "too barbarous" (*barbarikoteron,* 418e).

If Plutarch's theological inquiries are largely an attempt to know more clearly the traditionally defined, benevolent forces that rule the universe, his attitudes toward belief are defined by a polarity of modes of error: superstition and atheism. The essay *Superstition* (*deisidaimonia*) pits these two against each other in a relentless and rhetorically exaggerated confrontation. The subject is perverted religion, a relationship with the "blessed and eternal" that is corrupted by fear—and in fact the term *deisidaimonia* really means "fear of divinities" and has nothing to do etymologically with the English word "superstition," which is a makeshift translation at best. It might seem paradoxical that the essay presents *deisidaimonia* is a far worse thing than atheism. The latter is an error (the belief that there are no "blessed and eternal" benevolent beings), but the former is an emotion that stems from an error (the crippling terror that arises from the belief that such beings exist but are harmful or hostile rather than benevolent). Atheism is a lack—a blindness to a source of joy and help—but "god fearing" is a far more destructive force that manifests itself in paranoia and compulsions, stemming from the notion that divinities, whether vengeful or simply hostile, are responsible for the ills we experience. One of Plutarch's examples of such behavior takes the form of a tableau, difficult to tie down historically, in which Jews observing the Sabbath sit inactive while their city is taken by siege (*Superstition* 169c). Plutarch elsewhere takes an interest in Jews—a *Table Talk* conversation moves from Jewish dietary laws (4.5) to the identity of their god (4.6)—but he never mentions Christians. There is little doubt, however, that he would have seen both religions as pervasively characterized by the qualities that this essay warns against. In the *Lives*, the most vivid depiction of the consequences of *deisidaimonia* is the portrait of Alexander in his last days, obsessed by omens and portents, dividing his time between sacrifice and drunkenness (*Alex.* 75).

The target of *Superstition*, however, is neither Jews nor Christians, nor alcoholic Macedonians. The Lamprias Catalogue seems to call this essay *Deisidaimonia, Against Epicurus* and although only passing reference to Epicurean errors is made here, the issue that Plutarch addresses is one close to the core of the appeal of Epicureanism. Epicurus's gods do not interfere, benevolently or maliciously, in the affairs of humans; indeed, they have no existence beyond our mental images of them. They are, in other words, at most a focus of contemplation and, at the very worst, harmless, and never a focus of fear or anxiety. Some Epicureans (including Philodemus, the philosopher of Herculaneum) advised participation in traditional religious observance, but the first principle of Epicurean theology was the remote indifference of the gods. They simply do not care. To Plutarch, these thinkers who denied the gods the tasks of both creation and providence must have seemed virtual atheists. What he shows in the essay on *deisidaimonia* is that traditional theology, properly—that is, Platonically—understood, can provide exactly the confidence that Epicurean theology offered: freedom from fear of divine anger or punishment. In the dialogue *The Slowness of Divine Justice*, where an Epicurean objection to the notion of providence is countered, we see a rather different Plutarch, upholding the idea conspicuously muted here that the gods do punish wrongdoers. If called on this apparent contradiction, Plutarch would of course have replied that divine justice is benevolent and corrective, and so not to be feared.

Plutarch's priesthood at Delphi raises many questions that he refused to answer. That he erected the statue of Hadrian, with its titulature proclaiming the divinity of the imperial family, makes us wish he had been more candid about his perceptions concerning this new, and very public, class of gods. We may postpone, for now, a closer examination of the four dialogues set in Delphi, but they, along with the other essays on theological matters and the titles of some that are lost—*The Daedalic Statues of Plataea, The Kestos of the Mother of the Gods*—suggest that Plutarch the priest devoted a great deal of his energy to articulating the mysteries of cultic symbolism, both in his own shrine and elsewhere. There were guides to do this at Delphi—the "periegetes," to whose activities Plutarch himself is the best witness (395a). The term *periegete* is broader than it might seem at first glance; the hierarchy of periegetes in the ancient world included both the tourist guides of a site like Delphi and travel writers like Pausanias, who went from shrine to shrine compiling collections of lore. To judge by the dialogues, Plutarch himself—as mentioned earlier—served as an expert periegete, discussing thorny issues of Delphic theology and symbolism with the more serious and inquiring visitors, those who shared his commitment to pursuing the truth about the gods.

II PLUTARCH'S PAST

The Project of the Parallel Lives

ALTHOUGH PLUTARCH HIMSELF BECAME A ROMAN CITIZEN, and many of his friends and acquaintances were Roman citizens, the intellectual, literary, and philosophical culture of Plutarch and his circle owed almost nothing to Rome. The Greek world was reorganized by Rome; its social and economic dynamics were transformed, along with its material culture. But philosophy and rhetoric, as well as literature, advertised their conservatism and their direct continuity with the Greek past. In these areas, it was the Romans who consented to be hellenized, rather than the reverse. The process had begun as early as the third century B.C.E. and had continued for longer than three hundred years when Plutarch was writing the *Parallel Lives*.

This conventional view of the cultural relations of Greece and Rome is unlikely to meet with much protest. Nevertheless, this sort of cultural mythmaking obscures real differences. We can perhaps entertain the notion of a philosophical tradition withdrawn into an ivory tower to such an extent that the economic and social transformation of its environment might leave it unscathed, although it is difficult to imagine how such a tradition might continue to provide a satisfactory account of the world to its adherents. Greek literature was retrospective from the beginning, but although it often devalued the present, it hardly denied it or blocked it out—rather, it commented on the present indirectly by way of representing the past.

The decidedly idiosyncratic project of the *Parallel Lives* represents a distinct phase in the evolving process of cultural accommodation that made it possible for Greeks and Romans to coexist in a world where the imbalance of military, economic, and political power was so great. It involves claims about the Greek and Roman past quite distinct from those voiced in the second and first centuries B.C.E., the period that saw the development of the picture of the relative prestige of Greeks and Romans that was given powerful and influential expression in the *Aeneid*, particularly in those familiar lines addressed by the dead Anchises to his living son, who has intruded among the dead:

Others will inform bronze to breathe more gently,
Of this I am sure, and draw living faces from the marble.
They will plead a better case, measure the journeys
Of heaven with the stick and tell the rising stars.
You, Roman, concentrate on the rule of peoples by might.
These will be your arts: to civilize peace,
Spare the defeated, and persevere to defeat the proud.
  (6.847–53)

Those "others" to whom excellence in sculpture and rhetoric was conceded needed no further identification. Virgil's reader would have immediately identified them as the Greeks.

We may think of that Hellenistic and Augustan formulation as the first imaginative romanization of Greece. A century after the death of Virgil, Plutarch gives us the first substantial indication that it was being superseded by a second romanization, one that envisioned in a new way the relationship of Greeks—especially Athenians—to Romans.

The reconceptualization of the relationship of Greeks and Romans for which Plutarch provides evidence involved the belated realization of a very old Athenian project: an Athenocentric Greece. It was not Italy or even Latium that conquered the Mediterranean; it was a single city, Rome, and the Latin speakers who traveled to the limits of that empire as administrators and civil servants identified themselves with the destiny of that single city. Greek culture had developed very differently, and intense competition among the poleis had prevented any one city from achieving enduring dominance over the others. Beginning with Herodotus or even earlier, an Athenocentric tradition of historiography had emerged that viewed Greek history from an Athenian perspective, but in fact the situations of Rome and Athens had little in common.

Democratic Athens had aspired not only to cultural but also to political and military dominance of the Greek world. In the fifth century and then, after one major defeat, soon again in the fourth, the Athenians had pursued a program to extend the scope of their own institutions (and their courts in particular) and win for them the status of Panhellenic institutions, serving (and served by) their "allies." But all of those aspirations became irrelevant in the fourth century with the rise of Philip and the extension of Macedonian power throughout Greece, to be supplanted, after more than a century of grouping and regrouping, by the power of Rome.

At the time when Athenian aspirations to political and military dominance of the other Greek states were fading, however, the literary accomplishments of fifth- and fourth-century Athens were being placed on a pedestal. Of the authors who received the attention of Hellenistic scholarship in Alexandria and elsewhere, a disproportionate number were Athenians. Athens had even appropriated Homer. It was probably the Pisistratids in the sixth century who had made a home for the *Iliad* and *Odyssey* in the greatest of the Athenian festivals, the Panathenaia, a celebration of Athenian identity and cultural hegemony far more blatant than the Dionysia with its dramatic presentations. From at least the third century, the poems were

widely considered to be Athenian cultural property, and scholars asserted that Attic was the dominant element in their poly-
dialectical poetic idiom.

The cultural accomplishments of Athens survived the
city's imperial aspirations, and because it served the interests of
the conquerors, Athens was allowed prominence in a sphere
where that prominence, far from threatening them, was to their
advantage. The Greek culture that was homogenized for export
by the Macedonians was largely Athenian. In their hands, it
crossed the ethnic boundary and became an international high
culture. The Romans inherited that cultural property by conquest and knew how to make still better use of it than the
Macedonians had—although of the two accomplishments, that
of the Macedonians in freeing Greek culture from its ethnic
matrix may be seen as the greater, or at least the prerequisite for
what the Romans were to do.

All of this is familiar enough, and with different emphases
can be seen in most, perhaps all, modern accounts of the relations of Greece and Rome. But something that happened
shortly after Plutarch's death, in the time of Hadrian, was far
from a linear development out of these historical trends. In 130
(or thereabouts) Athens became the center of the Greek world—
not because its orators and playwrights were the most admired
and not because Attic sculpture and architecture had been
treated as exemplary—but because Hadrian (or those responsible for Hadrian's cultural programs), in rethinking the concept
of Greekness and the history of the Greek world, had placed
Athens in a position within that world closely analogous to the
position of Rome in the universal empire. By a single imperial
gesture, Athens, long the capital of Greek eloquence, was made
the seat of the Panhellenic Council—the council that was to be
the arbiter of Greekness itself and the forum for discussion of
the issues relating to Greekness. The imperial policy that put

Athens in that prestigious position should be seen against the background, not of the well-known model of Greek-Roman interaction sketched by Virgil, but of the decidedly idiosyncratic portrayal of Greece and Rome that was the best-known accomplishment of the most prominent Greek intellectual of the generation before Hadrian: Plutarch.

Plutarch's *Parallel Lives* constitute the principal document in the high empire's reinvention of Classical Greece. What emerges, of course, is a vision of the Greek past as diptych, face-to-face with and mirroring the Roman past. Some of the implications of this bizarre project seem to have been too little appreciated, both in relation to the radicality of the distortion of Greek realities introduced by Plutarch's box of mirrors and in relation to the implications of those distortions, not just for imperial Roman conceptions of Classical Greece but for all subsequent conceptions as well.

The process of rethinking the Greek past in terms of a contemporary reality dominated by the military, political, and cultural power of Rome was centuries old by the time Plutarch made his contribution. The powerful model that shaped Polybius's history can reasonably be taken as normative for the second and first centuries B.C.E. Here, the growth of the Roman people and Roman power take firm hold of center stage. Greece is rethought as marginal. Delphi may be the center of the world, but the center of power is Rome, and it is only in relation to the irresistible expansion of that power that the experience, interaction, and history of the Greek states can find its legitimate place in the larger scheme of things. As I have already suggested, this picture of history is quite compatible with the cultural myth presented in the *Aeneid* and with the attendant deference to Greece in the arts and rhetoric.

Seen against this background, the radical ahistoricity of the *Parallel Lives* and some of the implications of that ahistori-

city emerge more clearly. Not only do the *Lives* distance themselves from history in the most obvious senses, the ones Plutarch himself insists on—that the biographer in the interest of the depiction of character reserves the right to elaborate on or suppress the raw data at his disposal, and so forth—but more importantly, the *Lives* abstract their subjects from history in the Polybian sense. The box of mirrors provides the new context, the substitute for history, but in its odd way it amounts to a recreation of history along new lines, elevating Greece from its marginality and asserting a very peculiar equation of entities that are in some sense to be seen as equals.

The individual pairs of *Lives* are quite disparate. In some instances, the component biographies hardly seem to complement each other at all or even to provide interesting comparisons. In others (e.g., *Phocion* and *Cato the Elder*), salient qualities justify the pairing. Frequently the juxtapositions are simply of exemplary figures (Pericles and Fabius Maximus) or the opposite (Demetrius and Antony), whose stories are presented as complementary because in them similar virtues or vices are seen in different historical contexts. Plutarch's comparisons (*synkriseis*), where we have them, are generally unsatisfying. They tend to emphasize and reiterate details of circumstance in the two careers in question that either resemble or contrast with each other, details placed one after the other, without building to any coherent conclusion. They often remind us of the curious affinities of the whole project with rhetorical training as Plutarch catalogues facts and arguments that might serve, first, to praise Caesar at the expense of Alexander, then Alexander at the expense of Caesar. Yet these comparisons are the glue, the equals sign in the equation. Factitious though they may be, they allow the massive juxtaposition to stand, asserting a parallelism that exists only as a function of Plutarch's idiosyncratic imagination.

One of the most interesting deformations in this hall of mirrors lies across the representation of Athens. Plutarch's little piece that usually goes under the Latin title *De gloria Athenien-sium* has been an embarrassment to some of Plutarch's admirers. It has been qualified as a rhetorical exercise, tendentious, no doubt the work of a young man still far from the skills of the mature biographer and thinker. Its Greek title poses the question "Whether the Athenians were more famous (*endoksoteroi*) for War or for Intellectual Accomplishments (*kata polemon e kata sophian*)." The author's emphatic thesis is that the military accomplishments of Athens far outweigh its intellectual ones in their contribution to its fame. That this seems so outrageous to us is a function of our predisposition in favor of the Hellenistic and Augustan (Virgilian) model of the relations of Greece and Rome outlined above. And whether the piece is rhetorical juvenilia or not—that is, even if we must imagine that young Plutarch the display orator was equally prepared to deliver a companion piece arguing the opposite position—the answer it offers to the question posed is entirely consistent with the presentation of Greeks and Romans in the *Parallel Lives*. The Athenians, like the other Greeks juxtaposed with Romans, were all men of action. In fact, the selection of Greeks overall tends to focus on periods in the histories of various cities when they were growing, or reaching a peak of accomplishment, or when, at the very least, a great deal was at stake.

This matter can be traced deep into Plutarch's most consistently held philosophical principles. He regularly values political engagement over contemplative withdrawal and portrays the philosopher as an adviser to the powerful and a guide for society. This writer, whose esthetic appeal is surely his most salient feature, was no esthete, and he was not predisposed to reinforce the Hellenistic and Virgilian picture of the relationship of Roman military and political accomplishment to a Hel-

lenism distinguished primarily for its esthetic accomplishments.

What has just been said does not relate exclusively, of
course, to Athenians. But the centrality and dominance of the
Athenians among the Greek lives, and the repeated and quite
misleading juxtaposition of Athenians and Romans, should be
seen in this peculiar light. The simple numbers say a great deal:
on the one hand, roughly twenty-four Roman lives; on the
other, ten Athenians, four Spartans, two Macedonians, two
Thebans (one lost), and finally, to complete the Greek side, a
scatter of five randomly distributed figures. Thus we have a
fairly complete series of Athenian lives, representing the
founding, early growth, and imperial aspirations of the city, the
last resistance to foreign domination (*Demosthenes*), and, exceptionally, a single figure who represents the best qualities of
Athenian statesmanship in the period of Macedonian rule (*Phocion*). The Spartan series is restricted to highlights: the founder-
figure (*Lycurgus*), two leaders from the peak of Spartan international success at the end of the fifth century and early in the
fourth (*Lysander, Agesilaus*), and two paired figures from the
period of reform and brief expansion in the third (*Agis and
Cleomenes*). Thebes is represented only by the two leaders of its
greatest period (*Pelopidas* and *Epaminondas*), and even this degree of visibility is undoubtedly to be attributed to Plutarch's
streak of Boeotian nationalism. No other Greek city has more
than a single representative, but a significant number of the
remaining Greek lives cluster in the period of the wars of the
successors of Alexander, a period when Greeks and Romans
saw military action against each other (*Pyrrhus*) and which was
therefore perhaps the most suggestive and useful period for
Plutarch's purposes.

If the numbers leave any doubt about the nature of the
comparison, the pair that stands at the head of the traditional

order of the lives, *Theseus and Romulus*, makes Plutarch's perspective clear. In this Greek world rethought in terms not of art
but of action, Athens stands in a position analogous to that of
Rome in the empire. Greek (and principally Athenian) men of
action are juxtaposed with Roman men of action—men who
embody, each in their own context, the political and military
excellences (*aretai*) at the center of Plutarch's enterprise.

   Perhaps the most amazing fact about this idiosyncratic
Plutarchan equilibrium is that it became an orthodoxy. The
twentieth century saw the dismantling of the diptych, and the
Parallel Lives are no longer read in pairs, as Plutarch created
them. We have lost the rhetorician's taste for contrast and comparison, for balanced periods and balanced portraits, and in the
absence of that taste, the architecture of Plutarch's project became meaningless. From our perspective, an effort of imagination is required to appreciate the power exercised by the *Parallel
Lives* in earlier ages. The eccentric contemporary of Tacitus
seemed in the Renaissance to need no apologies. Indeed, his
shaping intelligence was the principal optic through which Renaissance and early-modern Europe viewed classical antiquity.
Plutarch also had an enormous and well-documented impact
on his contemporaries and subsequent generations. There is
probably no single intellectual figure whose influence is found
more pervasively in the literature of the Roman empire from
the second century through the fifth. From Aulus Gellius,
whose birth must have occurred within a few years of the death
of Plutarch, to Eunapios, and beyond into the Christian centuries, Plutarch was echoed, cited, and praised more than any
other Greek author of the Roman period. Eunapios himself,
two and a half centuries after Plutarch's death, provides us
with the judgment that the *Parallel Lives* were still viewed as
"the finest of his writings" (*Vit. Soph.* 454).

   Plutarch's diptych served a multiple function. Against the

background of the Hellenistic-Augustan cultural mythology, it reasserted the political and military, and not merely esthetic, excellence of Greece. Against what I have characterized as the Polybian model of the military and political marginalization of Greece in the face of the inevitable rise of Rome, it restored—or rather invented—a balance in which, in the status quo of the Pax Romana, it was possible to pretend that a kind of partnership of equals existed. In this process of cultural mythmaking, Athens was moved to the center of the Greek world to mirror Rome, the center of empire. Hadrian might, of course, have done what he did, with or without the powerful literary precedent Plutarch had provided him. But that lover of dramatic and even of whimsical symmetries, who included in his benefactions both the Pantheon and the Temple of ROMA and AMOR, can hardly have been insensitive to the power of the conciliatory vision of a dynamic, ahistorical equilibrium between Athens and Rome that the *Parallel Lives* offered. And no one knew better than Hadrian how to translate such symmetries into institutions and monuments.

The Lives *and the Function of Biography*

If Plutarch's re-creation of the past of Greece and Rome has had decisive importance in shaping later perceptions of antiquity, he nevertheless embraced some positions that remain decidedly unpopular. Conspicuous among these is his assessment of the "father of history," Herodotus. In a polemical essay so violent in its language that its authorship has been challenged, Plutarch denounces Herodotus "on behalf both of my ancestors and of the truth" as a falsifier of facts, a toady of the Athenians (although he badmouthed them as well), a lover of barbarians, and, most of all, a denigrator of great men generally and of the accomplishments of Thebes and Corinth specifically (*The Mal-*

ice of Herodotus 854f). Even the title of the essay loses something in translation: the *kakoetheia* that it attributes to Herodotus might better be rendered as "malignancy," or, in plain language, "rottenness." Plutarch's sparse references to Herodotus in the *Lives* in fact fall in line with the major criticisms of the essay: he cites Herodotus for (among other things) two anecdotes portraying Themistocles extorting money from allies (*Them.* 7, 21) and for the claim that the only Greeks who actually fought against the Persians and the medizers at Plataea were the 169 who died there (*Arist.* 19). Plutarch will have nothing of this disparagement of that "finest" of victories (*Cato Maj.* 29 = *Comp.* 2), and to counter it he turns to epigraphic evidence, citing the self-congratulatory rhetoric of the altar dedicated by the victors for what they represented as their Panhellenic victory (*Arist.* 19).

The demonstration hardly suggests a circumspect use of historical evidence on Plutarch's part, but it makes clear what is, in Plutarch's book, Herodotus's great crime: he is a naysayer, a belittler. This is his principal failure as a historian: he exposes the reprehensible, sometimes sleazy side of men and accomplishments that deserve admiration. We might think it more important that, according to Plutarch, Herodotus falsified the historical record and distorted the facts in the process, but the odd priorities expressed in the essay are not unique to Plutarch. In recent years, the study of the Greco-Roman past has seen an increasing divide between those who endeavor to recover that past (historians) and those who study ancient accounts of it (historiographers). The latter have brought home to us again and again the inescapable conclusions that, first, the demands and expectations of ancient readers and writers of history were distinctly different from our own, and, second, that rhetoric— particularly the rhetoric of praise and blame—shapes ancient historical writing to its very foundations, often at the expense of what we like to think of as the facts. Plutarch's position is extreme here, and I do not mean to imply that his arsenal of deprecation does not include deriding Herodotus's alleged falsehoods—the appeal to truthfulness as a criterion for judging historical writing is always available—but what is striking is that Plutarch is more offended by Herodotus's "slander" than by his falsifications of the record.

This unexpected judgment is important to bear in mind when we turn to the way Plutarch distanced his own enterprise as a biographer from that of historians. We must not assume that Plutarch's criteria for "historical" writing coincide with our own. In one of his programmatic passages (which tend to occur in the rhetorically rich prologues to the first of a pair of lives), he draws the distinction in these terms:

As I undertake to write the life of King Alexander and that of Caesar by whom Pompey was destroyed, in consideration of the vast number of deeds in question, I will in preface say only one thing: I beg my readers not to hold it against me if I have not managed to work in every single one of the famous acts reported of these men, but rather have cut most of them short. The reason is that I am writing *Lives*, not *Histories*, and the revelation of excellence or baseness does not always occur in the most conspicuous acts. Rather, some little thing, a witticism or a joke, often displays a man's character more clearly than battles with thousands of casualties, huge military formations, or sieges of cities. Just as painters carefully reproduce the face and the elements that contribute to the expression, where character is revealed, and pay very little attention to the other parts of the body, in the same way you must allow me to explore the indicators of the soul (*ta tes psuches semeia*) and to use these to portray each life while I leave the great accomplishments (*ta megethe*) and the battles to others. (*Alex.* 1)

If the biographer is like a portrait painter, then what would provide the corresponding comparison for the historian? If we were to violate the deliberate asymmetry of Plutarch's highly rhetorical formulation, we could do worse than to insert the sculptor, the creator of heroic, full-length portrait statues in the medium that appropriately commemorates the "great accomplishments and the battles" at the cost of the psychological subtlety and depiction of character cultivated by the portrait painter and the biographer. My point is that both modes of writing about great men of the past are, as Plutarch represents them, concerned with the exemplary value—the value as exempla—of their subjects. Plutarch may claim the right, as a biographer, to deflect attention from traits, characteristics, and actions that are at odds with the sort of person he is painting (*Cimon* 2) and that would destroy the harmony of the portrait. It would be rash, however, to assume that Plutarch would not extend the same liberty, the same obligation, to the historian. At stake is less a distinction between biography and history than one between the representation of the past as glorious and a provider of models (in the tradition both of epic poetry and of the exempla learned in the schools of rhetoric) and its opposite. Some indication of this opposite pole can be seen in the understating or undercutting of greatness for which Plutarch criticizes Herodotus—a mode of representation that, in the Aristotelian scheme of the genres of discourse, impinges on the space of lampoon and comedy. The representation of figures of the past as worse than men as we know them, or simply worse than they were, had no place in Plutarch's notions of biography *or* history.

With the conspicuous exception of the prominent pair of negative exempla—Demetrius Poliorcetes and Antony, whose stories are articulated in a tragic mode—the *Lives* are largely portraits of various modes of being well-off, of *eudaimonia* (cf. *Dem.* 1). A few other pairs (notably *Pyrrhus and Marius*) reiterate the characteristic failure of alpha males to enjoy what they do accomplish or to reach a state of equilibrium and thus escape from their compulsion to conquer yet more. If these are failings that vitiate success, they nevertheless presuppose that success (in the eyes of the world) and use it as a foil for a more philosophical assessment. The question of the intended function of these exemplary portraits is left characteristically open, although Plutarch does provide us with some suggestive hints regarding his ideal audience and his designs on that audience.

It is in his convoluted introduction to the negative pair of *Lives,* where his tone is momentarily defensive, that Plutarch states most explicitly the function of his biographies. He refers there to the *Lives* as *paradeigmata* ("patterns, models, paradigms") and justifies through an anecdote the inclusion of the intemperate, bellicose, erotic, extravagant Demetrius and Antony, both of whom came to bad ends. A Theban flute teacher named Ismenias, we are told, took his students to hear bad performers as well as good so he could say to them, "This is the way to play the flute, and this is the way *not* to play it." Plutarch concludes, "It likewise seems to me that we will be better spectators and imitators of the better lives if we are not uninformed about the bad and legitimately condemned ones." (*Demetr.* 1)

The relation of implied audience to text is, then, one of contemplation and imitation—hardly a surprise coming from a teacher of Platonic philosophy and a reader of the *Republic.* But given that paradigm, as well as the pedagogic anecdote that accompanies this discussion, we may well suspect that these *Lives* are addressed primarily, though not exclusively, to the young—that is, to the sort of aristocratic young men whose education was a concern to Plutarch. This is not to say that the examples the *Lives* offer would be useless to an adult, but only that a young, flexible, growing mind would be far more likely to make the best use of them.

Nothing is simple in Plutarch, however. Beyond this implied audience lie two more. The first was imposed by the social and literary conventions of Plutarch's moment in history. The addressee of the project as a whole (and of the *Table Talk* and an essay) was Quintus Sosius Senecio, well connected in the elite of Trajanic Rome and himself twice consul (in 99 and 107). To judge by his appearances in the *Table Talk*, he and Plutarch were friends for a long time. They may have been students together in the 60s. He seems to have been the sort of man of action and intellect Plutarch respected, and as such, whatever other audiences the text may imply, this one is not to be lightly dismissed as a pro forma dedication. It is unlikely that Sosius Senecio was still a young man when Plutarch began sending him pairs of *Lives*, but our last bit of evidence in any case leaves no doubt that Plutarch envisioned mature readers in addition to young ones. The project of the *Lives*, he tells us in the prologue to *Aemilius Paulus*, was begun "for others": "But I have persisted and developed a fondness for it for my own sake as well, trying one way or another to use history as a mirror and to fashion my own life according to the kinds of excellence it displays and to assimilate them to that life" (*Aem.* 1).

Plutarch talking about his subject is, as we have seen, Plutarch's true subject. Plutarch the reader of Plutarch, absorbed in contemplation and imitation, sits among Plutarch's projected audience.

The Mythic Limits of History

If the grand scheme of the *Lives* is a denial of history, at least in the Polybian sense, Plutarch nevertheless stands out among ancient authors for his perspective on the past and his sense of the sublime in the vistas of time. The historically ear-

liest lives are played out at the limits of knowing. This is both a
practical and an esthetic matter, a function, on the one hand, of
the nature of the information available, but informed as well by
a familiar Plutarchan concern: savoring the distance that separates us, as knowing subjects in the imperfect, sublunary world
of time, from the truth. In that it calls into play the limits of
knowledge, this perspective is inevitably tinged with irony,
along with nostalgia. One result is that Plutarch's introduction
to *Theseus and Romulus* strikes something close to the tone of
Thomas Mann introducing the Joseph novels ("Deep is the well
of the past . . ."):

> Just as the writers on geography, Sosius Senecio, push the
> things that are beyond their knowledge out to the margins
> of their maps and put such labels there as BEYOND LIE
> SANDY WASTES FULL OF WILD BEASTS, or UNEXPLORED
> SWAMPS, SKYTHIAN FROZEN BARRENS, or FROZEN SEA, so I
> might do well—now that in the project of the *Parallel Lives* I
> have explored the period that is within the range of plausi-
> ble accounts and accessible to inquiry that sticks to the
> events—to say about the rest: BEYOND LIE WONDERS AND
> FICTIONS, THE HAUNTS OF POETS AND MYTHOGRAPHERS,
> WHERE NOTHING IS CERTAIN OR CLEAR. (*Thes.* 1)

This pair of lives, the earliest chronologically, falls about a third
of the way in the sequence of composition, to judge by the
complex of tantalizingly casual cross references. Plutarch goes
on to say that he has already written *Lycurgus and Numa* and
now proposes to venture still further out into those sparsely
and fabulously populated regions of the map of the past that
elude proper historical inquiry:

> I decided to set the founder of lovely, far-sung Athens
> alongside the father of undefeated, glorious Rome and to
> compare them, and so may I succeed in refining the mythic

material so that it will accommodate itself to my story and
take on the appearance of history, but where it shows will-
ful contempt for credibility and remains impervious to reason, I shall need an audience that is both generous and
disposed to accept accounts of the remote past (*arkhaiologia*) without excessively rigorous scrutiny. (*Thes.* 1)

This is one of the pairs of *Lives* where symmetries are proclaimed both at the beginning, in the dedicatory preface, and in
a comparison at the end. The comparisons are not particularly
enlightening, although the taming of the mythic to a rationally
defensible discourse is explicitly at work from the start: "Both
were of lowly birth and obscure background, but both acquired
the reputation of having been born from the gods" (*Thes.* 2). The
only substantial reason for their juxtaposition lies in the factitious equation of the "two most illustrious cities" of which
Romulus "founded" (*ektise*) the one and Theseus "assembled"
(*synoikise*) the other.

Given that he must work here with untractable and implausible mythic material, Plutarch in fact does establish a com-
positional symmetry between the two biographies that is less
developed in other pairs. Each has an extensive topographic
section in its center, such that the physical reality of the cities
themselves is linked to the stories of their founders. Each begins, like many other *Lives*, with the ancestry, childhood, and
education of its subject (a pattern that once again points to
Plutarch's pedagogic concerns in the *Lives*), then relates the
founding of the city, its violation at the hands of invaders, and
its recovery. Both founders subsequently find themselves at
odds with their fellow citizens. Theseus dies in exile, whereas
Romulus is murdered by the patricians. Theseus is given a
hero's honors by the Athenians (especially after his epiphany at
the Battle of Marathon), whereas Romulus is immediately pro-

claimed a god by his hypocritical murderers (so that the plebeians will give up the search for his body).

Plutarch's retelling of these two stories from the mythified extremities of the historical record has a striking omission: although he clearly knew the Romans claimed that their city was founded in the sixth Olympiad (i.e., around 753, *Rom.* 12) and that the synoicism of Theseus must have occurred over a half millennium earlier, he says nothing to situate the two events in time relative to one another. As a result, they are allowed to be experienced as contemporary, suspended in the timelessness of the discourse of *arkhaiologia*. It is true that several details mark the remoteness of the time of Theseus: in his days, the Greek countryside was infested with thieves and murderers, awaiting the civilizing catharsis brought by Theseus himself and by his older cousin and model, Heracles (*Thes.* 6–11); the wisdom of his time was pre-philosophical, expressed in the *gnomai*, or proverbial utterances of the early sages, who included Pittheus, Theseus's grandfather (*Thes.* 7). Plutarch even identifies one of the many *gnomai* preserved in the Hesiodic corpus as the creation of Pittheus (*Thes.* 3)—"Let the wage set with a friend be adequate" (*Works and Days* 370)—although from our perspective the notion that such proverbs might have identifiable authors is implausible. Finally, there is a tantalizing reference to artifacts that bridge that gulf of time. Plutarch claims (quite anachronistically) that Theseus struck coins—the first Athenian coinage—and that they displayed a bull (*Thes.* 25). It has long been noticed that the statement offers a peculiar combination of numismatic accuracy and folly. The earliest Athenian coins, the so-called Wappenmunzen, do include coins depicting bulls, but they date from the Pisistratid sixth century, not from the Bronze Age. It is impossible, moreover, to say with confidence that Plutarch actually saw such heirloom coins or had firsthand knowledge of them and their supposed origins. The whole business—along with the reduction of the Minotaur of myth to a brutal Cretan general named Taurus ("Bull") with a soft spot for Pasiphaë—may well be derived from the fourth-century atthidographer Philochoros, the acknowledged source of much of the material Plutarch recycled into the *Theseus*.

Philochoros's rationalizing paraphrase of the story of Theseus and the Minotaur (where the Labyrinth was just a prison, and the hostage Athenian boys and girls were destined to be prizes in the funeral games for Minos's son Androgeos, treacherously murdered in Attica) represents the sort of accommodation of myth to historic or biographical narrative that Plutarch envisions in the prologue (*Thes.* 16). Even more striking is the euhemerizing paraphrase of the story of Theseus's and Perithous's descent to Hades to steal Persephone, an adventure that Plutarch situates after the founding of the city. The fabulous version of the story, populated by gods and featuring the traditional motif of the hero's triumph over death, was recounted in a poem attributed to Hesiod and now lost. This attribution means that the poem passed for being as old as anything in Greek tradition. Plutarch's version (unattributed, but we may well be hearing Philochoros again) is as follows (*Thes.* 31). Theseus and Perithous stole Helen, who went by lot to Theseus. Then the two set out to northwest Greece to find a wife for Perithous. There they encountered the Molossian king Aidoneus ("Hades"), a possessive father with a beautiful daughter named Kore ("Maiden," the euphemistic alternate name for Persephone in myth and cult) and a wife named Persephone. Loath to see Kore married, Aidoneus was accustomed to force her suitors to wrestle with his hound Cerberus—Molossian hounds were proverbially big and fierce—and that was the end of Perithous. But this pair of heroes had a history of forcibly abducting girls, and Aidoneus smelled treachery, so he locked Theseus up as well. Theseus's extended absence gave his political enemies a

foothold—he had had the poor judgment to turn his new com-
munity immediately into a democracy—and Menestheus, "the
first demagogue" (*Thes.* 32), became the city's leader. When
Heracles in turn came to visit King Aidoneus, he used the
power of a guest's prayer to secure Theseus's freedom, but
Theseus was unable to seize power back from Menestheus and
died in exile on Skiros.

Less of this sort of debunked myth is found in *Romulus,* a
function of the nature of the traditional material tapped and of
Plutarch's more immediate sources. Both Dionysius of Halicar-
nassus and Livy draw from Fabius Pictor, a third-century Roman historian who seems to have first assembled (in Greek)
what came to be the well-known traditions about the prehistory
and early history of Rome. Plutarch may well have gone directly to Fabius Pictor, and he would have us believe that he
went even further, to Fabius Pictor's own source, a Greek
named Diocles of Peparethos. There are fabulous and folkloric
motifs enough in this material—the phallus growing from the
king's hearth, the exposed twins suckled by the she-wolf—but
Plutarch has no trouble dismissing the former as "grotesque"
(*muthodes*), and he observes that *lupa* ("wolf") is used in Latin to
refer to a prostitute, suggesting that the wife of the swineherd
Faustulus who raised the twins may have had a poor reputation. The method, again, is that of Plutarch's sources, but their
love of alternate accounts and of juxtaposing the fabulous, savored for its imaginative appeal, with the down-to-earth is his
as well.

The pair of antiphonal topographic passages already mentioned is unique to this pair of *Lives.* Theseus's new city is soon
invaded by the Amazons (responding to his earlier invasion of
their land and his carrying off Antiope), and the description of
their camp and of the battle lines inscribes the ancient war
on the familiar city and its monuments (including "Amazon

tombs" that still preserved the memory, *Thes.* 27). Plutarch's
manner here smacks both of Hellenistic epic and of the travel
writer Pausanias (who wrote perhaps a generation after Plutarch's death). Similarly, when Romulus's new city is invaded
by the vengeful Sabines (here, descendants of Spartan colonists), we are given the familiar story of the treachery of Tar-
peia, who gave her name to the Capitoline (the "Tarpeian
rock"). The battle ranges across the Forum as the "Lacus Curtius" receives its name, and the Romans start to flee to the
Palatine before they are "stopped" at the location where the
temple of Jupiter *Stator* was to stand (*Rom.* 17–19). Plutarch's
sources for all of this Athenian and Roman topological lore are
less interesting than his manipulation of it, moving the cities
themselves to the center of their founders' stories and bonding
those stories to the monuments.

In the elaborate symmetries of the *Comparison* of these two
lives, Plutarch is hard pressed to produce any ethical messages
of substance. The figures are imposing, but hardly inspiring or
worthy of emulation, and the greatness of the cities they
founded cannot easily be located in their own stories. The *Comparison* is little more than a list of points on which Theseus gets
"the vote" as the better of the two men, followed—after a discussion of some areas in which both are reprehensible—by a
parallel list of the superiorities of Romulus. Not surprisingly,
the middle section of the *Comparison* is the more interesting,
particularly in its account of the political failure of both founders. Both initially maintained the status of "regal" leaders (the
basilikos tropos), but both lost power, and for diametrically opposite reasons that point to a pattern of more general application. The effective ruler can fail in one of two ways: by relaxing
or democratizing his authority (Theseus) or by intensifying it
and becoming tyrannical (Romulus). The former failing stems
from fairness or generosity, the latter from selfishness and se-

verity, but the effect is the same. The leader's success is measured by success, and neither Romulus nor Theseus was able to
sustain the polity he created (*Rom.* 31 = *Comp.* 2).

Here, at the limits of history and biography, Plutarch is re-
creating two remote figures whose characters were scarcely exemplary, although their stories could be made to be so. As such,
they become vehicles for a rather awkwardly superimposed
political message and for a message about the fate of souls that
is difficult to read as anything but a thinly veiled criticism of the
cult of the imperial family. Both Theseus and Romulus were,
not surprisingly, elevated retrospectively to superhuman status
by the cities they founded. In Theseus's case, Plutarch reports
the history and details of the cult without comment and with
apparent approval (*Thes.* 35–36). The story of Romulus, on the
other hand, is fraught with difficulties. In an account very close
to Livy's, Plutarch offers alternative versions, making it clear
that the story of his instant divinization (as Quirinus) was immediately perceived as a patrician subterfuge to cover up his
murder. These suspicions were put to rest by a patrician named
Julius Proclus, who swore publicly that he had met the di-
vinized Romulus, who gave him instructions for the establishment of his cult. Plutarch observes only that "these things
seemed plausible to the Romans" (*Rom.* 28) and that some sort
of divine influence seemed to come over them, for no one contradicted Julius. But then Plutarch compares the story to a number of Greek stories or fables (*mythologoumena*) that "implausi-
bly divinize that which is by nature mortal" and concludes with
a resounding passage that marks a rhetorical shift:

> Utterly to deny the divinity of human excellence is im-
> pious and low-minded, but to mix earth with heaven is
> ridiculous. . . . And hence we have no business sending the
> bodies of good men along with them to heaven, contrary to

nature. Rather, we should believe that their excellences and their souls, perfectly naturally and according to divine justice, are carried upward from mankind to the heroes, from the heroes to the *daimones,* and from the *daimones* (if they are totally purified, as by an initiation, and sanctified, leaving utterly behind them mortality and the life of the senses) to the gods, *not by virtue of a civic law,* but truly and most credibly, achieving the finest and most blessed of ends. (*Rom.* 25, my emphasis)

Plutarch's account of Romulus has generally been read as positive and sympathetic. Certainly his major crime, fratricide, is blurred by the suggestion of his innocence (*Rom* 10, 34 = *Comp.* 5), and the rape of the Sabine women is put in the best possible light (and compared favorably to Theseus's outrageous record of sexual assault, *Rom* 14–16, 35 = *Comp.* 6). But Plutarch took his theology seriously. Even if he will go no further than to acknowledge that quite a few of the Athenians at Marathon "believed they saw" Theseus leading them into battle (*Thes.* 35), the hero cult of Theseus fits comfortably within his clearly articulated notions of the relations of human and divine. The cult of Romulus/Quirinus, however, does not. It was founded on what Plutarch exposes as a lie: the claim by the patricians that he had been absorbed, body and all, into the ranks of the gods. That this is explicitly equated with "legislated" deification, in contrast to "genuine" deification, has implications that neither Plutarch nor anyone else in the high Roman empire chose to explore in detail, at least in public.

The order adopted by modern editions of the *Parallel Lives* generally follows the historical sequence of the Greek subjects (see Appendix 1), which throws into relief a marked hiatus between the opening three pairs and the other twenty. This is in harmony with the received notion that the combined efforts of the fifth-century historians Herodotus and Thucydides mark a watershed in our knowledge of the events of the ancient Greek world. For the sixth century and before, we have only shreds of information, anecdotes, and chronologies constructed retrospectively from disparate information, some of it sound and some quite untrustworthy. It is doubtful that the Greeks themselves had much more, for as archivists they had nothing comparable to the king-lists of Egypt and Mesopotamia, which form the basis of all chronologies for the region that extend back beyond the second half of the first millennium B.C.E. True, the Greeks claimed to know the names of the Olympic victors back to the founding of the games in 776, but that fine thread of history (itself subject to doubts [*Numa* 1]), supplemented by oral traditions, marked the limits of their knowledge of the past.

The situation for Rome was even more desperate. Plutarch's claim that Romulus learned to read (*grammata, Rom.* 6) while in the swineherd's care is doubly implausible. The first, slim evidence for written Latin dates over two centuries after that mythic moment. Writing itself came late, and then whatever state archives existed were destroyed when the Gauls invaded in 390 (cf. *Numa* 1 and *The Fortune of the Romans* 326a, based explicitly on Livy 6.1.2). When Fabius Pictor, nearly two centuries later, was writing his account of early Rome, it is unlikely that he had much reliable information from before that invasion.

There is a certain historiographic logic, then, in the pairing of Themistocles and Camillus as the fourth (chronological) pair of lives. Themistocles, from early in the fifth century, and Camillus, the savior of Rome from the Gauls early in the fourth, each represent a significant threshold of history in their respective traditions.

Next in sequence after Theseus and Romulus (but composed earlier) we have the lives of two undatable lawgivers from the remote past, the Spartan Lycurgus and Numa, the second king of Rome. Both were demonstrably figures of the culture-hero type, honored by their cities for fundamental legislation that shaped those cities' identities and defined their differences from others. Most of the institutions and most of the notions of right and wrong, of legality and crime, with which those lawgivers were credited must in fact have developed over long periods of time, but their retrospective attachment to a powerful founder figure in the remote past served to slow this development and to legitimate the status quo. The Spartans' projection of the founder of their self-consciously unique and fiercely conservative form of culture and society to the eighth, ninth, or even tenth century B.C.E. is manifestly at odds with the archeological record, which indicates considerable accumulation of wealth during the archaic period, along with fine pottery and luxury goods. The Romans, again retrospectively, dated Numa, to whom many primitive laws and institutions were credited, to the years 715–673 (with misleading precision), but Plutarch lays out the chronological problems from the start: Numa was said to have been influenced by Pythagoras, but the historical Pythagoras lived a century and a half after the dates attached to Numa.

Plutarch's parallel accounts of the lawgivers are far more complex in pattern and message than those of the two founders. There is in fact no question of framing a narrative of Lycurgus's life, as Plutarch's opening sentence announces: "There is, generally speaking, nothing to be said about Lycurgus the lawgiver that goes undisputed" (*Lyc.* 1). What he gives us is sketchy and hesitant. Lycurgus stepped aside from kingship; he traveled; he legislated; he exacted an oath that the Spartans would observe his laws until he returned, then visited Delphi for confirmation that his state was well founded, and either starved himself to death or otherwise made sure the Spartans would have no excuse for getting around their oath. That is his story. His character is sketched with scarcely more nuance in a simple anecdote: a young aristocrat assaulted him with serious bodily harm and was subsequently handed over to him to do with as he pleased. Lycurgus made him his servant, and exposure to his "gentleness, the freedom of his soul from passion, the austerity of his lifestyle, and his tirelessness" turned the assailant into a follower (*Lyc.* 11).

Beyond this, the *Life* is not about Lycurgus but about the Spartan state he created. Plutarch had at his disposal at least five accounts of "The Constitution of the Spartans," of which only one (Xenophon's) survives today. (Such essays, in which laws and institutions of individual cities are described, have their origins in the school of Aristotle, and although few survive, their fragments quoted in later authors are precious evidence for the facts about the organization of the Greek poleis.) More important, however, he had the *Republic* and *Laws* of Plato, along with an explicit conviction that "Plato, Diogenes, Zeno, and all the respected writers on these matters" took as their model what Lycurgus actually accomplished, and subscribed to his basic principle "that just as in the life of an individual, the full success of a city lies in excellence and in harmony with herself. And he organized and harmonized his state to this end, so that the citizens might remain free and self-sufficient and sound in their wisdom for the longest possible time" (*Lyc.* 31). This sounds like a paraphrase of the *Republic*, and indeed it is: Plato (as Plutarch understood him) articulated and recorded what Lycurgus had accomplished in fact, even though Lycurgus had explicitly refused to commit his laws to writing. There were limits, however. Plutarch knew and indicated the nature of Plato's reservations about Lycurgus and his constitution and even defends Lycurgus against Plato (*Lyc.* 28).

It requires an effort of the imagination to enter into the utopianism of Plutarch, although many will find it a more accessible fantasy than the more complex one of Plato (or, rather, of the Socrates of the *Republic*), of which it is a belated and esthetically refined reflection. Both of these aristocrats found a peculiar satisfaction in the idea of a human society rationally structured, by a benevolent and self-effacing lawgiver, on the basis of strict material egalitarianism and meritocratic administrative structures. As Plutarch tells it, Lycurgus's redistribution of wealth, the senate he created to mitigate the danger of tyranny from above and of democracy from below, and the egalitarian, enforced common messes were, along with the educational program that made these institutions durable, the basic building blocks of the Spartan state.

The extraordinary thing about Plutarch's re-creation of Lycurgan Sparta is his insistence on the "gentleness" (*praotes*) of that state and of its founder. And yet it is Plutarch himself who, citing the authority of Aristotle, provides us with the most excruciating details we possess of the domestic terrorism practiced by the Spartans to keep the serfs who produced their food—the helots—in line. This *Life* is the principal window we have into the chapter of Aristotle's lost "Constitution of the Spartans" where the institution of the *krypteia* was described (*Lyc.* 28). Some—probably not all—young Spartiates were sent out into the countryside for a period of time to live off the land and to hide by day and ambush and murder helots by night. Plutarch's paraphrase of Aristotle seems to indicate that the selection of victims was random, although he also says that in at least some instances the raiders killed "the strongest and the best" of the helots. This, Plutarch says, explains Plato's ultimately negative judgment of Lycurgus and his constitution, a judgment we may easily identify with the unattributed one

stated just before: "Some charge that Lycurgus's laws are adequate to produce courage but not justice" (*Lyc.* 28).

Plutarch's defense of Lycurgus marks the remoteness of
his utopian vision. No, he says, both Plato and Aristotle were
wrong. Lycurgus's Sparta was founded on the principles of
gentleness and justice. The cruel and unjust institutions and
practices for the oppression of the helots can be dated (*pace*
Aristotle) to the great earthquake and helot revolt of 464. They
are a corruption of the gentle justice of the authentic Lycurgan
state. The "negative historicism" (Karl Popper's term) opera-
tive here is deeply Platonic: everything enters this world in its
peak condition—it is as good as it is going to get—only to decay
over time through a natural process of contact with the sublunary realm. Lycurgus's Sparta, as Plutarch imagined it, was no
exception.

Lurking below the surface of Plutarch's account of Lycurgus's state is a criticism raised in the same texts of Plato and
Aristotle that Plutarch obliquely echoes and answers. In the
Laws, the Spartan state is repeatedly said to be deficient in that
it is organized primarily for war and conquest (cf. Aristotle
Politics 2, 1271a41–b7), but Plutarch denies this and insists that
Lycurgus envisioned not empire but self-sufficiency. This is an
important aspect of Plutarch's revisionist portrait of the Lycurgan state, and one that proves to have special relevance to his
parallel treatment of Rome's early lawgiver Numa.

Numa was a Sabine, and the Sabines were (according to
Plutarch) colonists from Sparta (*Rom.* 16). We might anticipate,
then, that the philosopher-king of early Rome would contem-
plate the (purified) Lycurgan model as he set out to legislate for
the new city. Nothing could be further from the truth, but the
tacit parallels between Plutarch's Lycurgan Sparta, purged of
the aggressive militarism and domestic repression that were to

become Sparta's salient characteristics, and his vision of the
nascent dominatrix of the world, Rome, under the sway of a
Pythagoreanizing pacifist for forty-three years, are nevertheless fascinating.

Born on the day Rome was founded, Numa stayed in his
Sabine town through much of the reign of Romulus, although
he became the son-in-law of the Sabine co-regent Tatius (*Numa*
3). In his youth, he was already a paradigm of excellences and
had conquered the passions and "the violence and acquisitiveness that are respected among barbarians." On his wife's death,
he became reclusive and spent his time wandering the countryside, giving rise to the story (which Plutarch debunks on
theological grounds) that he had a goddess named Egeria for a
lover. Among his Pythagorean traits Plutarch counts this cultivation of a portentous, mythified persona, as well as a certain
calculated sententiousness combined with obscurantism.

The scene in which envoys from Rome persuade him to
leave his peaceful, rustic life of study and "warless affairs" is
a rhetorical tour de force consisting of two antithetical set
speeches (*Numa* 5–6). Numa sings the praises of the life of
contemplation; the ambassadors speak of duties before the
gods. This owes much to the discussion in Plato's *Republic* (7,
517–520) of what it will take to persuade the philosopher to
rule, but the arguments have been streamlined and the rhetoric
inflated. The result is the sort of scene that Renaissance libret-
tists readily transformed into opera.

This much suffices for biography and characterization (beyond some closing remarks on self-serving claims made regarding Numa's progeny [*Numa* 21]). The rest of the *Life* is a
collection of descriptions of early Roman institutions, conspicuously excluding all those related to war. Numa established the
pontifexes, the Vestal virgins, the round temple of Vesta imitat-
ing the shape of the cosmos, and temples without statues, be-

cause he believed with Pythagoras that the bodies of the gods are "invisible, uncreated, perceived by intellect" and not by sense (*Numa* 8). The list of Numa's contributions, it must be admitted, is cluttered with antiquarian lore that accumulates with little shaping or consideration for the reader—deficiencies utterly foreign to Plutarch at his best, but the scholar and obsessive cataloguer of odd and little known religious traditions sometimes distracts or eclipses the rhetor. We learn a great deal more than seems necessary about Numa's calendar reforms, for example. Still, one theme—peace brought to a society born of war and violence—is sounded repeatedly, such that it dominates this *Life* and, retrospectively, the pair. The temple of Janus and its history resume the theme within the *Life:* Numa locked up war inside the temple for forty-three years, and. a few minor aberrations aside. the doors stood open for the next seven hundred years, until Octavian / Augustus closed them again in 31, after the Battle of Actium.

If the paradox of the peaceful kingdom of Numa at the origins of Rome, sandwiched between the wars of Romulus and seven subsequent centuries of bloody conquest and expansion, is the theme of *Numa,* the *Comparison* raises the stakes. Here, Plutarch makes explicit the questions that should have been asked by the attentive reader of the pair of biographies. There is the usual list of symmetries: Numa tuned Rome down, whereas Lycurgus tightened the strings of Sparta; Lycurgus loved and instilled bravery, whereas Numa loved and instilled justice. Although Plato's and Aristotle's criticisms of Lycurgus are more prominent and less lightly dismissed in the *Comparison* than in the *Lycurgus,* the Spartan lawgiver clearly has the greater claim on Plutarch's admiration. Numa should have done as Lycurgus did and nip acquisitiveness (*pleoneksia*) in the bud, before the gulf between rich and poor tore the state apart. And again, Numa missed his chance to create an educational system integral to the state, which would have perpetuated his constitution. As a result, Lycurgus's laws were observed for five hundred years (a little less if we factor in the repressive measures against helots, from 464). As soon as Numa was gone, his pacifist justice collapsed, and the Romans went back to fighting wars.

This is where the latent theme of Spartan military training and its relation to empire (as opposed to independence) has its payoff, and this is where Plutarch uses the rhetorical question to make the reader understand the sort of interrogation these pairs of lives demand:

> "Wait a minute," someone will say. "Has Rome not advanced to a better state through her wars?"—a question that will require a long answer if that answer is directed to people who define a "better state" in terms of wealth, luxury, and empire, rather than security, gentleness, and independence with justice. (*Numa* 26 = *Comp.* 4; cf. *Lyc.*31)

This statement is extraordinary, coming from a Greek thinker of the high Roman empire. The century had had its Seneca and its Tacitus to sound the familiar and characteristically Roman complaints of "decadence" and deviation from the noble values of the republic. But the hard fact that the history of Rome was the history of the continuous, centuries-long military expansion of a single city to world domination, at a cost of millions of lives and unimaginable destruction, was one the Romans always veiled in some other rhetoric. It might be the sanctimonious whitewash of the "civilizing power" of Rome, or it might be the self-serving notion of manifest destiny as served up by historians, politicians, or poets. But to ask, simply, "Is Rome better off because of all those wars?" required an outsider. And to answer in a manner so rhetorically indirect, yet so explicit and damning, required an outsider like Plutarch,

resting on the good conscience of a hegemonic, Greek philosophical discourse that even emperors (at least most of the
time) allowed to shake its finger at them.

It would be a fruitful exercise—one that has not been attempted
in some time—to give a sympathetic reading to each of the
twenty-two surviving pairs of lives and to try to see the pairs,
rather than the individual lives, as the basic units. I suspect that
only such a reading could bring out the contemporary reso-
nances of these biographies. We tend to see the comparisons as
mechanical, even trivial, and it is certain that their rhetoric is
not that of our time. But as we have seen in the two pairs
already discussed, the earliest in the narrative sequence, much
of what Plutarch has to say to the reader emerges only from
such an integrated reading. The following two sections will
take the same approach to a sampling of pairs of lives from eras
closer to Plutarch's own.

Conquerors

If we were to belabor Plutarch's refusal explicitly to answer
his own question about whether Rome reaped benefits from
militarism, we might interpret his silence as follows: If he was
speaking to an audience whose values are those that prevail in
the theater of power, the philosopher would have to say, "No,
Rome did not go from a worse to a better state through its wars,
but I will have to explain why." If he was speaking to philosophers, if any answer were needed, he might simply and quietly
say, "No, of course not."
    What did he say in general, then, of conquerors? The *Lives*
constitute, as we have seen, representations of various forms of
success, of *eudaimonia*. Virtually every figure Plutarch presents
is, by some criterion of judgment, a success, although some are

individuals who rose to great power only to come to a bad end. We will not find Plutarch passing judgment on conquerors for conquering—rather, the career of a conquering general is a career, and just that. It can be lived well or badly, and it may be characterized by success or by failure; moreover, the successful career may be lived by a man who is far from admirable, and the unsuccessful one by a good man plagued by misfortune.

A relevant paradigm for this odd conception of the relation of moral identity or personhood to the facts, the accomplishments, and failures of a life can be found in the Myth of Er at the end of Plato's *Republic*. The problematic myth with which Socrates closes the long dialogue on justice was, not surprisingly, very much present to Plutarch's mind. Nearly twenty citations or echoes of the passage have been noted in his works, but even without those verbal echoes his concern with this most famous of Plato's myths would be evident in the imitations and elaborations present in Plutarch's own dialogues. What Socrates reports is the near-death or out-of-body experience supposedly recounted by a slain soldier who revived on his funeral pyre. The report pretends to represent the fate of souls and the structure of the universe as firsthand, eyewitness experience, and the extravagance of the fantasy that such firsthand knowledge might be possible lies near to the heart of its complex ironies. Er witnesses the souls of the deceased experiencing judgment, reward, and punishment and ultimately being brought before the Fates to be equipped for the next round in their cycle of incarnations. What the Fate Lachesis holds in her lap is both lots (with a nod to her name, which sounds like "Allotter") and lives, or, more specifically, "patterns of lives" (*bion paradeigmata*, *Rep.* 617d, 618a); the phrase is repeated by Plutarch (*Cato Maj.* 4), and is almost identical to one that he uses to refer to his biographies at *Demetrius* 1. The lots determine only the order: each "soul" must choose a "life" for itself. Socrates tells his interlocutor Glaukon that this moment of choice is crucial in the existence of the soul; it is the real test of the soul's moral judgment and self-restraint (fruits that might be anticipated as benefits accrued from the philosophical life). What interests us here is the description of these "patterns of lives":

> They were of every sort, lives of every variety of beast and man: there were tyrannies, some lasting the duration of the life and others cut short and ending in poverty and exile and homelessness; there were lives of men who were famous, some for their bodies, because of their beauty or strength or competitive success, others for their family and the glories of their ancestors; and there were lives of obscure men as well, and of women. (Plato *Rep.* 618a–b)

In this peculiar model of human identity and responsibility, the component parts are defined in a way that is deeply counterintuitive, and yet something like this model is clearly at work in Plutarch's *Parallel Lives*. The important point is that character is emphatically *not* destiny. Rather, character is character ("soul" or, in the Myth of Er, an attribute of soul), and destiny is destiny (a "pattern of life"). The two are somehow juxtaposed—the Myth of Er indulges the fantasy that the former chooses the latter, but that is to make a point about free will and its limitations to which Plutarch is not committed. But Plutarch's oddly schematic enterprise can be seen taking shape right here. He explores and relates what he himself calls "patterns of lives"— and on the whole expresses few judgments that imply that the individual might have acted otherwise or that a difference of character could have caused a change in the pattern of life. There are missed opportunities, as we have seen, but not of a sort that shakes the broad outlines of the life. Rather, Plutarch documents and evaluates the "souls," the characters of the men who lived those lives, the ways they were or were not tested by

the pattern allotted to them, and the qualities they demon-
strated as a result. This is not to say that Plato's myth exhausts
the possibilities open to Plutarch—it is, after all, not a psychology but a myth, a reductive, colorful illustration. There is room
for initiative and its praise in the *Lives,* along with reprehensible
failure; and character is by no means something preformed that
enters the world with the individual—it can be molded by education. Finally, character and patterns of life interact: power, for
instance, corrupts. But for all this, Plato's myth does serve to
illuminate some of the strangeness of the psychology that underlies Plutarch's enterprise and to explain why judgment is
sometimes suspended when we might expect praise or blame.

Plutarch's conquerors, then, are conquerors, and we will
not find him passing judgment on them for that. One can be a
successful conqueror or an unsuccessful one. The career of conquest can continue to the end of the life, or it can be cut short by
failure; or the successful conqueror may survive to retire to a
life of another sort. His *eudaimonia* (properly and philosophically assessed) will primarily be a function of the character that
he brings to his pattern of life, although it may be difficult to
characterize as successful some patterns marked by extreme
misfortune.

Several pairs of lives might serve as examples here. *Lysander and Sulla* is an attractive choice, in part because both of
those conquerors took the city with whose fortunes Plutarch
most identifies himself, Athens, and so might be expected to
emerge as villains. Their treatment of Athens is in fact a factor
in their comparison, but even this remains paradoxical. Sulla
seems to have trampled on everything that Plutarch most valued. He cut down the groves of both the Academy and the
Lyceum for timber for his siege engines. He commandeered the
treasures of Delphi (*Sulla* 12), which he eventually returned at
the expense of Thebes (19). Plutarch's melodramatic descrip-

tion of the slaughter that Sulla perpetrated when he took the rebellious city in 86 B.C.E. (14) does not prepare the reader for the judgment in the *Comparison* (*Sulla* 43 = *Comp.* 5) that because he restored the democracy after the sack, he treated Athens more generously than did Lysander, the victorious Spartan general at the end of the Peloponnesian War in 404, who imposed on the defeated Athenians the tyrannical oligarchy of the Thirty.

Both Lysander and Sulla were outstanding for their brutality and butchery. Both were "harsh" (*thrasus*), and there is no room here for the "gentleness" or "moderation" (*praotes*) that is praised repeatedly in *Lycurgus and Numa*. Sulla betrayed friends, and Lysander's harsh treatment of conquered cities gave Spartan power a bad name (*Lys.* 13). The larger armies and superior military technology of the Roman general produced casualties on an order unthinkable in the wars of Athens and Sparta three and a half centuries earlier. Much of the fighting between Sulla and the "barbarian" armies of Mithridates of Pontus, who challenged Roman hegemony in the eastern Mediterranean early in the first century C.E., took place near Plutarch's home in Boeotia. What he relates, then, may come from local or family traditions, as did tales of Antony's more recent wars in Greece (*Ant.* 68). Of a Pontic army of 120,000 that faced Sulla at Chaeronea, 10,000 survived (*Sulla* 20, 22); and shortly thereafter, at nearby Orchomenos on the Copaic Basin, he defeated another: "As they died they filled the marshes with blood and the lake with corpses, so numerous that even today many barbarian bows, helmets, shreds of steel breastplates, and swords are found buried in the mud, even though nearly two hundred years have passed since the battle" (*Sulla* 21). There is no doubt that Plutarch and his intended reader take pleasure in this vivid, if somber, gore. The atrocities—whole cities slaughtered for harboring Sulla's enemies, proscriptions

on an unprecedented scale—are narrated in a tone of grim re-
portage, interspersed with anecdotes, not judgments or expres-
sions of indignation.

Lysander, whom the Spartans sent out again and again as
general in the last decade of the fifth century, is presented on
the whole in a more positive light. For one thing, he was shaped
by the city that Plutarch idealized as a self-perpetuating ethical
training ground, whereas Sulla emerged from the Rome of the
end of the second century, where the concentration and disparity of wealth, along with armed factions, had already destroyed the integrity of the state. Competitiveness was instilled
by Lysander's upbringing, along with a sense of duty to Sparta.
His faults, however, include deviousness and contempt for
oaths. His mass executions—three thousand Athenian pris-
oners of war after Aegospotami (the decision was that of the
Council of Spartan allies, *Lys.* 13) and "many slaughters" to
keep defeated enemies and dubious allies in line—fell far short
of Sulla's.

In spite of this, in the *Comparison* (*Sulla* 43 = *Comp.* 5),
Plutarch once again avoids a facile judgment or dismissal. Monsters of ambition, courage, and resourcefulness like Sulla command his reluctant admiration. Lysander, after all, achieved
what he did with the full support of the Spartan state. Sulla had
to contend with other Roman seekers after power, including
Marius, who was every bit as dangerous as he, and who under-
mined his support in Rome. Sulla's response, the seizure of
power and dictatorship by force of arms, emerges not as laud-
able, certainly, but as nevertheless impressive. What most inspires Plutarch's explicit admiration is his continued fidelity to
Rome in such conditions, when Mithridates would have offered security and an alliance. Finally, the pattern of life of a
conquering general must be judged by the criterion of success.
Sulla won more victories. Lysander ended his career and his life

with a tactical blunder. The Spartan is ultimately the more admirable for self-mastery and moderation (he was immune to the attractions of wealth, although the rich booty he brought home infected his city), but the Roman was admirable for his generalship and bravery. By all the values that Plutarch elsewhere praises, this should make Lycurgus the greater success, but as we have already seen, there is a thread of admiration for the sublimely ambitious in the *Lives*—we will see it again in the *Life of Demetrius Poliorcetes*.

Alexander and *Julius Caesar* form the most impressive pair of conqueror lives, and familiar themes are at play. They lack a *Comparison* (as does the pair *Pyrrhus and Marius*, the natural companion of *Lysander and Sulla*), and after a look at the two lives we may ask ourselves just what that absence means for our experience of the texts. The pair seems to be mutilated: *Alexander* ends abruptly and without the flourish and coda we expect, and *Caesar* begins equally abruptly and lacks the account of Caesar's upbringing that would have come in the opening pages. In its present state, however, *Alexander* is the longest *Life* we have, more than twice the length of most of the others, and *Caesar*, if in fact it has lost a few pages, would have been about the same length.

These two lives occupy a special position in Plutarch's diptych not only for their length but because in the parallel presentation of great Greeks and Romans, Alexander represents the moment in history when the balance of power just might have tipped the other way. Plutarch's views of these matters will not be found in the *Lives*, and the rather unsatisfactory evidence we have comes from two rhetorical pieces, presumably to be dated decades earlier, known as *The Fortune of the Romans* and *The Fortune* [or *Excellence*] *of Alexander*. Both have their origins in the debating exercise and are therefore of little value as evidence of genuinely held beliefs. The speaker is prepared to use his rhetorical powers to "prove" either the premise or its opposite. The exercise in question takes this form: "Was the success of X due to chance (*tykhe*) or excellence (*arete* [*virtus*])?" The encomiastic piece on Alexander presents both arguments but improbably paints Alexander's unblemished excellence as primarily philosophical. The piece on Rome, as we have it, presents only the case for chance, although its existence guarantees the existence of the antithetical argument for excellence—whether it came from Plutarch or from someone else hardly matters. It breaks off, in any case, in the middle of an elaboration on what chance did for the Romans in removing Alexander from the world in 323 at the age of thirty-two, before he could turn westward to confront Rome. Plutarch's overblown text goes only so far as to anticipate the grand clash of "unsubdued spirits with invincible arms" (326c), but the longer, intact, and similarly rhetorical passage in Livy (9.17–19) on which Plutarch's seems to depend contains a detailed examination of the question of whether Alexander, had he survived, would have conquered the small but dramatically expanding Roman state. Livy patriotically concludes in the negative, but context suggests that Plutarch was arguing the other side. What both texts prove beyond doubt is that the question (in essence a past condition impossible of realization) was a debating point in the first century of our era— perhaps even a rhetorical commonplace. This rhetorical exercise had roots in earlier historiography: Polybius (e.g., 1.3–4; 6.2; 8.2) had pondered whether the huge success of the Romans was due to fortune or to their specific excellence (political organization). This may remind us that a new era in the relationship of Greeks and Romans had been ushered in by the Pax Romana, an era in which not-so-ancient conflicts, real and imagined, were neutralized and revitalized as literature. This state of affairs lies in the background of Plutarch's juxtaposition of the founders of Greece's relatively short-lived empire and of Rome's enduring one.

Although multiple memoirs, documents, and an official history all issued from the campaigns of Alexander, all of these primary sources are lost to us. They were tapped and utilized, paraphrased and occasionally quoted, in the surviving accounts by Diodorus Siculus and Quintus Curtius, Plutarch, Arrian, and the "Callisthenes" who takes credit for the so-called *Alexander Romance*, the most fabulous and so most popular account of all. These are the major narratives of Alexander's career, spread over more than two centuries, although the earliest of these authors, Diodorus, wrote about three hundred years after Alexander's death.

Among the biographers of Alexander, Plutarch is the one who tells us the most about his sources, incident by incident. He names no fewer than twenty-four authorities, at least five of whom were eyewitnesses. The effect is by no means peculiar to this life. On the one hand, we are distanced from the events by having our attention drawn to Plutarch the scholar as intermediary, sifting and selecting the telling anecdotes (*Alex.* 1). But at the same time, we are brought closer to those events. We are told, for instance, that it was Callisthenes—the official historian, who fell from favor, was accused of participating in a plot, and did not survive the expedition—who recorded that ravens guided Alexander's party across the Libyan Desert to Siwa and even called back with their croaking those members of the party who went astray in the night (*Alex.* 27). An eyewitness account of such a wonder leaves the reader in just the sort of hermeneutic limbo that Plutarch often cultivates.

With its exceptional length and wealth of anecdotes, *Alexander* is unlike most of the other lives not only quantitatively but qualitatively as well. It is a richer story, spun out with more detail. It shares with the others, of course, the emphasis on the specific excellences of its subject as illustrated in specific acts and statements. But in spite of the opening disclaimer, this biography (like its companion) does in fact constitute a substan-

tial account of the campaigns of its subject, along with a representation of his character. It is also a dynamic portrait: we witness the changes that take place in Alexander toward the end of
his short life. If power, by its nature (or by human nature),
corrupts, then the man who took the Persian empire by force of
arms and sat on the throne of the Great King took risks of an
order beyond the military risks that were all too familiar to him.
It is striking that the *Life* as we have it never makes this point
explicitly, but it illustrates the point repeatedly. Here, we miss
the lost *Comparison,* where Alexander's increasing adoption of
the trappings of oriental despotism must have been played off
against Caesar's manipulative flirting with the symbols of a
kingship he so wanted to openly embrace.

That Alexander will undergo such a change at the end may
help to explain why Plutarch chose to present him, somewhat
surprisingly, as a figure preeminently characterized by self-
control (*enkrateia, sophrosyne*). We are far from the two-dimen-
sional, implausible philosopher-conqueror sketched in the rhetorical exercise discussed above, but this more vivid and more
believable Alexander still displays this most philosophical of
virtues from youth, just as he retains "philosophical" theological notions (*Alex.* 27). It is specifically with reference to pleasure
that the young Alexander shows his command of himself,
while his youthful energies make him quite driven in other
ways (*Alex.* 4). "Pleasure and wealth" were never his targets,
but rather "excellence and fame" (*Alex.* 5). The qualities that he
brought to those quests were daring (*tolme*) and proud ambition (*megalophrosyne*). These are ambiguous qualities at best,
and in his first great exploit—the sack of Thebes shortly after
inheriting Philip's kingdom at the age of twenty—they produced mixed results.

Philip's murder in 336 predictably sparked rebellions
among the peoples, both Greek and non-Greek, that he had

subjected. The young king's advisers pressed for caution and gentleness. He responded with the opposite and in the process made an example of rebellious Thebes: six thousand dead, thirty thousand sold into slavery (*Alex.* 11). Was this an aberration, a loss of characteristic self-control? Plutarch does not say as much, and in fact such grand gestures, whether of generosity or of military daring, express precisely the characteristics that made Alexander a world conqueror. What Plutarch does say is that Alexander himself felt immediate remorse for his treatment of Thebes and himself linked his sack of Dionysus's city with later aberrations and misfortunes (*Alex.* 13).

A number of themes, variously treated in the traditions of biography of Alexander, come into play here, most prominently Alexander as the new Dionysus, conquering India in the footsteps of the god, and Alexander as the barbarous (specifically Macedonian) heavy drinker who brought on his own early demise. Plutarch's position on this last matter is unique among the surviving biographies. He acknowledges that Alexander had a reputation for heavy drinking but denies the truth of the claim: Alexander loved conversation and so proposed over wine complex subjects for discussion, requiring long sessions (*Alex.* 23, cf. *Cato Min.* 6). Now, we know both that this claim had been made centuries earlier (Aristoboulos in Arrian 7.29) and that Plutarch knew of considerable evidence that could be mustered to counter the position he takes in the *Life* (*Table Talk* 1,6; 623d–624a). It remains, nevertheless, his position: Alexander's characteristic self-restraint extended to drinking as well—but there were lapses, increasingly so toward the end.

At Samarkand, in Central Asia, during a drunken party, Alexander ran his friend Cleitos through with a spear (according to some [Arrian 4.8], a sarissa, the Macedonian long spear that contributed very substantially to the military success of Philip and Alexander, *Alex.* 50–51). Many versions of this story circulated. All apparently acknowledged that Cleitos had offered extreme provocation, and a few, including Arrian's and Plutarch's, put the emphasis on Alexander's immediate and suicidal remorse. Other authors refer the drunken incident to the anger of Dionysus over an omitted sacrifice, but the link to lingering divine anger over the destruction of Thebes seems to be shared only by Plutarch and the obscure Ephippos (FGrHist 126, fr. 3 = Athenaeus 10, 44). The latter seems, in turn, to have written a hostile account of Alexander with emphasis on his depradations in Greece (cf. Lionel Pearson, *The Lost Histories of Alexander the Great*, 61–68). This Ephippos is not mentioned by Plutarch, but the likelihood that the biographer was acquainted with such anti-Macedonian versions of Alexander's story is great. The motif that Plutarch shares with Ephippos serves him, however, in the orchestration of his own eulogy of Alexander. Alexander's lapse in killing his friend, no less that the army's ultimate refusal to cross the Ganges, were linked in Alexander's mind to his offense against the divinity of Thebes (*Alex.* 13). The virtues remain intact (if violated); the drunken act and the ultimate reversal of fortune become part of that larger tissue of events manipulated by powers that we may appease or offend but which remain ultimately beyond our control. These were part of his pattern of life, the series of situations that his remarkable character faced and was tested by.

There is no doubt that Plutarch shows us an erosion of that character after Alexander succeeds Darius on the throne of the Great King. In one sense, that throne is just where he belongs. Everything about him is great (*mega*), from his generosity (*megalopsycheia, megalodoria*) to his ambition (*megalophrosyne*), and although the vocabulary does not echo the qualities so conspicuously, here should be listed as well his benevolent humanity (*philanthropia*) and his generous treatment of women, especially those of Darius's household, once they have fallen into

his power. Here we find one of Plutarch's most plausible illustrations of Alexander's combination of sheer expansiveness
of character with self-restraint. When Alexander does take his
place on that throne, the reader is told nothing of its impact on
him—rather, he becomes a spectacle for others, specifically for a
weepy old man from Corinth, who opens up an abyss of historical perspective by observing that "all the Greeks who died
before seeing Alexander seated on Darius's throne had been
deprived of a great pleasure" (*Alex.* 37, inexplicably repeated at
56; cf. *Ages.* 15). That moment is the culmination of Alexander's
quest to the extent that what he undertook was (at least in
pretext) the completion by counteraggression of the war that
the Persians had undertaken against the Greeks a century and a
half earlier. The aborted burning of the palace at Persepolis
(*Alex.* 38) leaves the theme of revenge (or historical reciprocity)
in a characteristically Plutarchan limbo. Alexander's only concern in victory, in any case, is to reward his followers with a
generosity that stretches their capacities for self-restraint and
then to get on with conquering the world.

Although Plutarch recounts Alexander's decline with
vivid anecdotes, he is sparing in explicit criticism. That he can
do this is in part a function of the deep literary traditions he
taps—including Aeschylus's *Agamemnon* and the *Iliad* itself—
where the trappings of oriental monarchy are inescapably
bound up with hubris, the disastrous and criminal loss of sense
of self that comes with great success and power. The biographical tradition had various ways of accounting for Alexander's
folly in coming to believe he was a god, but Plutarch underplays all of this, even denying that Alexander suffered under
any such delusion (*Alex.* 28). He paints an Alexander whose
fate was a concern to the gods. The few sentences that he commits to the legend that Alexander's father was not Philip but
rather Zeus Ammon could easily be turned to debunk the fable,

but that is not Plutarch's purpose in telling it. The story says something about the conqueror's relationship to the powers that govern the universe; it is part of his story.

The principal episode that illustrates the impact of regal hubris on Alexander is that of the *proskynesis*, or prostration, and it is striking that in this context the related issue of divine honors for the monarch—*proskynesis* to a god is natural and means simply "worship"—is passed over in silence. Here again, Plutarch taps a deep tradition of political representation in Greek literature. Prostration before superiors, and a fortiori before the Great King, was one of the most powerful symbols of the difference between "free" Greeks, on the one hand, and barbarians, who were "slaves" to their superiors. Plutarch's representation of Alexander's dilemma is remarkably evenhanded. As the successor of Darius, he was now a hybrid creature, torn between the systems of symbols of two and even three cultures (*Alex.* 45). The unlikely hero of the *proskynesis* episode is Callisthenes, Aristotle's nephew, who along with the atomist Anaxarkhos emerges as an individual here from the swarm of "teachers and flatterers" (*sophistai kai kolakes*, 53) who traveled with Alexander's army. Callisthenes is hardly idealized. Even Aristotle is quoted to the effect that his nephew was powerful with words but had no sense (*nous*, 53), which in this context surely designates the tact that intellectuals must exercise in order to communicate with and influence the powerful, who hold their lives in their hands. Such tact was a matter of immediate concern to Plutarch, whose ideal of the engaged philosopher, curbing and directing the power of the great, depended on the development of such skills ("Flatterers," *That Philosophers Ought Especially to Talk with Rulers*). On that score, Callisthenes was a failure and paid with his life (leaving room for the story, dismissed by Plutarch, that Aristotle was behind the poisoning of Alexander—using water from the Styx, *Alex.* 77). Still, there

was heroism of a sort in Callisthenes' frank and efficacious de-
nunciation of *proskynesis*—he averted a great "shame" both for
Alexander and for the Greeks (54). We are left to believe that the
matter was dropped.

What are we to think of this world conqueror, forced to
turn back by the failure of nerve of his armies and increasingly
beset by the ills of power—plots, jealousy, delusions, and finally
superstition (*deisidaimonia*, 75)? He executes inept advisers at
home and hangs numerous Indian sages for advising the rajahs
to resist him (59). At the same time, he pardons and rewards ten
of these same "gymnosophists" who show their wit and wisdom in an interrogation in which their lives are at stake (64). He
treacherously breaks a truce in order to rid himself of some
troublesome Indian mercenaries—a treachery duly noted as a
"blemish" (*kelis*) on his otherwise admirable record of military
decorum. There is a hallucinatory quality to the closing chapters. For the first time, we start to see the world from Alexander's perspective, and the spectacle is terrifying. He contem-
plates the violated tomb of Cyrus and its inscription:

> MAN, WHOEVER YOU ARE AND WHEREVER FROM,
> FOR I KNOW THAT YOU WILL COME,
> I AM CYRUS WHO WON THE PERSIANS THEIR EMPIRE.
> DO NOT BEGRUDGE ME THIS BIT OF EARTH
> THAT COVERS MY BODY

These things moved him deeply as he grasped the uncertainty and instability of existence. (*Alex.* 69)

From this point on, all sense of scale is lost. The contented
gymnosophist Calanus, who has followed Alexander from India to Persia, peacefully incinerates himself when ready to die,
announcing that he will soon see Alexander in Babylon. In response to Calanus's injunction to all to "get drunk and be

happy with the king," the companions enter on a gargantuan
drinking contest that leaves forty-two dead of drink (*Alex.* 69–
70). When Hephaestion dies in Ecbatana—Alexander's homo-
erotic side has been discreetly underplayed—Alexander is portrayed as a new Achilles mourning Patroclus: he crucifies the
physician and conquers and slaughters an entire nation, calling
it Hephaestion's grave offering (72). We are told of projects that
express his hubris more effectively than any possible reality: an
architect proposes sculpting Mt. Athos into a statue of Alexander holding a city of ten thousand in one hand (72). There are
warnings about entering Babylon, and again we are allowed
inside the conqueror's head. He has become "apprehensive
toward the gods and suspicious toward his friends" (74). The
latter are terrified of him, as he is of them. As he descends into
"god fearing" (*deisidaimonia*), he is "agitated and paranoid,"
turning everything into a "monstrous portent" (*teras kai se-
meion*). In this state, he takes to constant drinking, develops
fever, continues to drink, and dies (75). Plutarch does not take
the many poisoning stories seriously. Alexander's fate was
sealed by a power far greater than Aristotle's or Antipater's,
and it is impossible not to conclude that the character he
brought to it, for all Aristotle's training, failed in the end. The
sophrosyne and self-mastery of his beginnings are negated by
the paranoid delusions of his last days.

The cumulative portrait is rich in contradictions that Plutarch leaves unresolved, whether by design or because we have
lost part of his text. If we have any key to those missing or
silenced judgments, they will be found in the companion life of
Julius Caesar.

Plutarch's sources in writing about Caesar were almost
exclusively Latin authors, most prominently Caesar himself,
along with Cicero, Asinius Pollio, and Livy. Some of the material may have been available to him in Greek—Cicero wrote

letters in Greek, other late republican authors published in both languages, and some Latin histories were translated—but for most of the material that Plutarch actually cites, the likelihood is that he read it in in the language he learned, by his own account, late and imperfectly. His difficulty with the sources has been detected in some odd turns of phrase, apparently stemming from imperfect understanding of the Latin before him, and in some errors of fact. For all that, what is remarkable is Plutarch's ability to move easily through the the complex rivalries of the Roman strongmen of the first century B.C.E. and to convey both the splendor and the enormity of their wars and the theatrical daring of their politics. If, as I suggested above, Plutarch felt at least an esthetic nostalgia for a world where a great deal was at stake, it was preeminently in the Rome of Marius and Sulla, then of Caesar, Pompey, and Cato, that he found what he needed.

As we saw, Plutarch quite surprisingly made self-restraint the salient virtue of Alexander, and Caesar's portrait correspondingly emphasizes his cultivation of a gentle, generous, sensitive public image. There is tension between this public image and the reality of Caesar's all-consuming ambition, but Plutarch does not present him as hypocritical—once his victory is complete and his ambition satisfied, his gentleness will emerge as more than simply an expedient political strategy. As a rising politician, he spent far beyond his means to buy the goodwill and loyalty of the people, so much so that his rivals did not take him seriously (we are repeatedly reminded that they would have done well to recognize his potential and eliminate him early on). Generosity is a theme that runs throughout this life as it did Alexander's. During the campaigns in Gaul, we see Caesar recrossing the Alps each winter to hold court in Luca, securing support through gifts and distributions of wealth from his wars (*Caes.* 21). As a young politician, he could get the rich

Crassus to cover his debts, but as the *Life* develops, Caesar's admiring armies become tools for the production of the enormous wealth required to keep an entire nation in his debt.

Again, as a young man, he delivered a funeral oration for his second wife, Cornelia—something not customary, Plutarch emphasizes, on the death of a young woman, and which further improved his public image as a "gentle man of great character" (*Caes.* 5). In the trial of the Catilinarian conspirators convicted by Cicero, his speech against invoking the death penalty rings "fair and generous" (*philanthropon*, 8)—although suspicions remain that he himself was implicated in the conspiracy. And his policy throughout is one of aggressive reconciliation—*after* victory—even to a fault, as in the case of Brutus. Once the Civil War was over, Plutarch tells us, Caesar was blameless—he pardoned enemies, restored Pompey's statues, refused a bodyguard, made gifts to the people and to his soldiers—and the Temple of Clementia was the fitting dedication to his gentleness (*praotes*, 57).

If this thumbnail sketch is familiar, there are at least two possible reasons. The first is that the portrait is not inconsistent with Caesar's own self-presentation, which Plutarch largely follows. The other is that Shakespeare depended heavily on this *Life* in his own *Julius Caesar*. He understood the theatrical qualities of the biography and adapted speeches and tableaux from it.

Nowhere else in Plutarch is the contrast between the salient qualities—the excellences—of the subject and the objective facts of a career exploited to such effect. We have already seen, in *Sulla*, Plutarch's technique of juxtaposing the grim facts of the destructiveness of Roman warfare with the qualities of the men who lived their lives in the context of the brutal competition for supremacy that was the late republic. His *Julius Caesar* is the culmination of that development.

Caesar as a young politician cultivated the gentle, generous image described above, but what drove him was a clearheaded fixation on supreme power. At the opening of *Alexander*, in introducing the pair of lives Plutarch identifies his subjects as "King Alexander" and "Caesar by whom Pompey was destroyed" (*Alex.* 1). The descriptive phrase has the primary function of distinguishing Julius Caesar from Augustus, whom Plutarch also designates simply as "Caesar"—but it does more than that. It is complemented by the anecdote (apparently unique to Plutarch) of Caesar as propraetor and his party riding over the Alps to Spain in 61. They pass a wretched little Celtic alpine village, and someone makes a lame joke: " 'I wonder if there's competition for office even there, and rivalry for dominance and mutual jealousy among the powerful.' Caesar responded, deadly serious: 'As far as I am concerned, I would rather be first among them than second among the Romans' " (*Caes.* 11).

The ultimate conflict for supremacy with Pompey is assumed, then, from the start to have been the focus and goal of Caesar's pattern of life. Caesar's relentless ambition and his rise through the *cursus honorum* are narrated vividly and with very little elaboration or judgment. The campaign in Spain prefigures the spectacular successes in Gaul. Alexander reemerges here as Caesar's explicit model—Caesar reads in Spain of Alexander's conquests and weeps that the Macedonian had done so much in the span of life that he himself had occupied doing so little. So, in Spain he raises armies, fights wars, legislates, and leaves for Rome rich and with his soldiers well rewarded and proclaiming him imperator (*Caes.* 12).

When back in Rome, he sets to work constructing what came to be called the First Triumvirate—a Gang of Three consisting of Pompey, Crassus, and himself and devoted to nothing but the accumulation of power in their hands. Plutarch immediately marks his distance from the values they represented. The triumvirate's true goal was to destroy the senatorial aristocracy and themselves rule the people, and to that end Caesar in his first consulship passes legislation "worthy not of a consul, but of a radical tribune of the plebs" (*Caes.* 14; cf. *Cato Min.* 32). Plutarch's political values are on the surface here. Lycurgus's brilliance, we remember, was to establish a council—meritocratic in his utopian proto-Sparta but, in the real world of the societies that Plutarch knew, the equivalent of an oligarchic, aristocratic assembly—to ward off the evils both of tyranny and of democracy. The First Triumvirate was the negation of those values, an alliance to squeeze out the Senate, leaving behind only rulers and ruled. Plutarch says enough to establish his negative judgment of this part of Caesar's career, which was characterized by a self-serving populism built on shameful alliances. But he moves on quickly to Gaul and the Caesar he admires.

In 58, Caesar took up his inflated proconsular province (consisting of Gaul on both sides of the Alps as well as Illyricum to the east) and for the next nine years traveled on "a new path of life and of new exploits" (*Caes.* 15), showing himself to be the greatest military commander of all time. All the others mentioned for comparison are likewise Romans. In this sphere as well, Caesar displayed his "fairness and gentleness" (*epieikeia, praotes*) to captives, but the decisive mark of his success was the success itself: "[He excelled] all others in fighting the most battles and killing the most enemies. He fought less than ten full years in Gaul and took by force of arms more than eight hundred cities, subdued three hundred peoples, fought pitched battles against three million men, killed one million of them in combat, and enslaved that number again" (*Caes.* 15).

Plutarch's fanfare for Caesar's "new life" seems intended to ring loud and clear. It is true that the Romans dealt out

honors measured in enemy corpses—five thousand enemy casualties in a campaign was the minimum for a triumph to be
celebrated in the capital. But with one million dead Gauls Caesar had enough for two hundred triumphs.

Plutarch turns directly from the vertiginous grimness of
these statistics to a rapid series of anecdotes illustrating the
extraordinary acts of courage that Caesar inspired in individual
soldiers. The shift of scale is deliberate. Caesar achieved triumphs on the basis of statistics, but his real accomplishment in
Plutarch's eyes was the loyalty and superhuman performance
he inspired in his soldiers. The principles and methods are in
part the same we saw at work in his populist politics—generous
rewards to make each soldier feel a personal stake in the campaign—but in the theater of war Caesar backs this technique by
sharing the risks and labors of his men (in spite of poor health
and epileptic fits) and by serving as an example, as Alexander
had done less successfully with his companions, of tireless la-
bor (*Caes.* 17).

Plutarch's narrative of the Civil War again follows Caesar's own. If Caesar the conquering general was admirable
where Caesar the politician, the populist enemy of the Senate,
was not, the strongman who crossed the Rubicon with his army
to crush Pompey and seize absolute power in his own country
is closer to the former than to the latter. *Sulla* has prepared us
for this suspension of judgment. The power struggles of these
ruthless alpha males inspire awe, as do the qualities of will and
determination and the military skills deployed. Little is said of
motive or its judgment. Necessity is often invoked.

As Caesar crossed the Rubicon into Italian territory, where
he had no legal right to go as commander of his legions, the last
pretense that the Roman empire was governed by the Senate
collapsed. Pompey fled Rome, and most of the senators followed him in terror. Caesar chased his rival to Brindisi but

could not follow him across the Adriatic for lack of ships. This much is in Caesar's own account (*Civil War* 1.29). Plutarch adds that he had taken the whole of Italy in sixty days without bloodshed (*anaimoti*, 35). The observation is nevertheless coupled with an anecdote that reminds us what sort of man accomplished this "bloodless" coup. In Rome, the tribune Metellus tries to bar Caesar from the treasury. Caesar threatens to kill him unless he gets out of the way and adds, "And you know, boy (*meirakion*), that it's more difficult for me to say this than to do it" (35).

His consolidation of power from this point is anything but bloodless. Rushing from one end of the empire to the other, he secures armies, killing or routing (and then invariably pardoning) all those loyal to Pompey. In his account of the eventual fighting between Caesar and Pompey in Epirus and Thessaly, Plutarch's emphasis is once again on the fidelity of Caesar's veterans—now tired from a lifetime of warfare—and on Caesar's skills as a tactician. At Pharsalus, in June of 48, though badly outnumbered, Caesar put an end to Pompey's career (*Caesar* 42–45). In this war, Caesar was leading his legions not against barbarians but against other Roman legions; rather than belabor the point, Plutarch turns it into a tableau and lets Caesar describe it in the guise of a self-justification:

> When Caesar was inside the pale of Pompey's camp and saw the corpses of the enemy and others still dying, he groaned and said, "This is what they wanted. They forced me to this, to the point where I, Gaius Caesar, who fought the greatest wars, would have been indicted and condemned if I had given up my legions." (*Caes.* 46)

The opposition did not die with Pompey. Caesar celebrated his last triumph in 45, in celebration of victory in a brief war in Spain against Pompey's two sons. Plutarch, shifting the judgment of this action to the Romans, treats this as reprehensible:

> Nothing he did gave such pain to the Romans as the triumph he celebrated for this. When he had defeated no foreign lords or barbarian kings, but rather totally annihilated the children and the line of the most powerful of the Romans after fate had turned on him, it was not right for Caesar to celebrate a triumph over his country's misfortunes, priding himself on things that have no defense before gods or men except that they were done of necessity— and this, when previously he never sent a messenger or a public communication concerning a victory in the Civil War, but would have been ashamed to win fame by them. (*Caes.* 56)

Like the *Life of Alexander*, *Julius Caesar* accelerates toward the end, but the tone is very different. The lapse of his final triumph behind him, he settles into the dictatorship that he has received for life, an "acknowledged tyranny" (*Caes.* 57). He is still tireless in healing wounds, in generosity, in grandiose plans—plans free of the element of the feverish grotesque that characterizes those of Alexander. He still dreams of marching his legions in Alexander's footsteps to the ends of the world (58). He reforms the calendar and refounds the greatest of the cities that Roman expansion had leveled, Carthage and Corinth (57, 59).

His victory, however, was poisoned from the start. He had a passion (*eros*) for kingship, achieved that goal, and flirted with the symbols of regal power (*Caes.* 60–61). But this in turn generated malicious envy (69). The senatorial aristocrats, now hardly admirable as they stalk their patron, their savior, to whom many of them owe their fortunes or their lives, execute him on the (preannounced) Ides of March. There are omens, but no paranoia. Caesar responds to his wife's fears and to the genuinely alarming events by staying home, so the conspirators have to trick him into attending the Senate.

The brief concluding remarks return us to the theme sounded explicitly in the *Alexander* at the Tomb of Cyrus: what we might (with Walter Kaufmann) call "man's radical insecurity." Caesar's whole life was devoted to becoming first among the Romans. His formula for success (the triumvirate) worked where others had failed. Fate took care of Crassus, and he was left with only Pompey for a rival—Pompey, whose goals were no different from his, and whose ruthlessness equaled his own. Their "friendship" and cooperation in the period of the triumvirate had worked: it had destroyed the republic by reducing the other competitors for power to insignificance. But Caesar survived Pompey by only four years. He gained absolute power (*arkhe, dynasteia*) only at the end, so that he received no advantage from them before he was toppled by jealousy in league with fate (*Caes.* 69). Plutarch leaves us with an odd coda, in which "Caesar's great *daimon*" is said to have successfully avenged him—by killing every one of the conspirators, along with some who only wished they'd had the courage to be conspirators. Wonders abound: the comet of 44, the dimming of the sun and the failure of crops for a year, along with apparitions appearing before Brutus. Alexander left the world besotted by superstitious fantasies; Caesar left wonders behind him to trouble and amaze the world.

Plutarch's conquerors shaped their world, which became Plutarch's world. To Plutarch the ethical thinker, there was clearly an underlying pathology that constituted the common thread of their several existences—we might even think of it in terms of the Myth of Er as the common trait that caused each of these souls to choose the pattern of life he embraced. We have already seen this expressed in *Julius Caesar*, but we will have to

look beyond that *Life* for a statement of the more general principle. In *Antony,* Plutarch returns to the issue of Caesar's motiva-
tion and argues, against Cicero (*Philippic* 2.22), that Antony was
in fact not a decisive factor in making Caesar attack his own
country. No, Plutarch says, Antony provided only a pretext for
Caesar's action: "What drove him on against the whole of mankind was the same thing that before him drove Alexander and,
in early times, Cyrus: an inconsolable passion for power and an
insane desire to be the first and the greatest" (*Ant.* 6).

Heroes and Villains

An overview of the biographies of two pairs of conquerors
has made it clear that the *Parallel Lives,* although they present
themselves as portrayals of exemplary individuals, nevertheless leave room for considerable moral ambiguity and sometimes puzzling suspension of judgment. Where we have the
Comparison, it may serve as the equivalent of a study guide,
encouraging the reader to notice certain parallels and to ask
certain questions. This function goes far toward explaining
why the comparisons are so often tedious and uncomfortable
reading. We feel patronized. Suddenly prodded to make deci-
sions, to take stands, we feel betrayed by the author, who has
switched his persona and now returns as a pushy pedant, taking hermeneutic control of his text and dictating our response
to it. Perhaps the loss of the *Comparison* in *Alexander and Caesar*
has a positive side. The *Lives* of these two men, who had more
impact than any other individuals on the history of Plutarch's
world, develop a complexity of judgment that is not analyt-
ically reduced in the end. Contradictions and tensions are left,
and we can, after all, formulate our own questions and conclusions.

Paradoxically, we do have Plutarch's clear, authorial pronouncement on the career of Caesar, but it is elsewhere, in the *Comparison of Dion and Brutus,* where he incidentally offers a comparison between the tyrannies of Dionysius in Syracuse and Caesar in Rome:

> But while the consolidation of Caesar's rule brought considerable troubles to his opponents, once they had been overpowered and accepted it, they found it to be rule in name and in appearance only, and in fact there was nothing savage or tyrannical about it. On the contrary, Caesar seemed to have been bestowed upon them by the divine powers themselves as a very gentle physician when the troubles of the state required a monarchy. That is why the people of Rome immediately regretted his loss and became so harsh and merciless with his murderers. (*Brut.* 55 = *Comp.* 2)

Caesar was the tool of the gods. His least justifiable acts were justified by necessity. Plutarch implies as much in the *Life,* but this was not the closure that *Alexander and Julius Caesar* required, so that is not where Plutarch put it.

These conqueror pairs nevertheless remain eccentric to Plutarch's explicit purpose for just these reasons. The success—the *eudaimonia*—of the individuals described is determined by history—it belongs to the patterns of their lives. What they did overshadows what they were, for all Plutarch's determination to turn them into figures (among other things) exemplary of some virtue or other.

In many pairs of *Lives* the balance is quite different, and there we find Plutarch more consistently doing what the programmatic passages would lead us to expect. If we ask just who Plutarch's heroes were, which figures from the past provided the best models of the qualities he most valued, we will find that they were not the most prominent figures. After all, Er, in

Plato's myth, sees the preeminently wise soul of the mythic tradition, Odysseus, choose "the life of a private individual who minded his own business" (*Rep.* 620c). There are no such individuals among Plutarch's subjects. He did not admire—or teach—withdrawal into private life. But the most striking portrayal of excellence expressed in a life circumscribed by history, a life well lived in spite of circumstances, is that of a man Plutrarch has saved from oblivion, Phocion of Athens. Plutarch's admiring portrait of this contemporary of Demosthenes stands very nearly alone. The Roman biographer Cornelius Nepos had devoted a few pages to him over a century earlier, and these survive, along with four chapters of Diodorus (18.64–67). Both texts throw some light on Plutarch's account and on their common sources. Nepos begins by extolling the integrity (*integritas vitae*) of Phocion (19.1), but his short account gives prominence to Phocion's betrayal of his benefactor Demosthenes and the blatant illegality of the actions that caused his downfall (19.2). Diodorus dwells dramatically on the injustice of Phocion's trial and the thoughts and fears it inspired in sympathizers, "since fortune is unstable and common to all" (18.67). Thus, familiar Plutarchan themes were part of the historiography of Phocion before Plutarch made his contribution, and a submerged negative or at least relatively critical version of the story was known to Nepos.

That Phocion should have been painted in a negative light by Athenian historians is hardly unexpected. The short period that constituted the culmination and catastrophe of his career was one of oligarchy imposed by a foreign power—in this instance, the Macedonian general Antipater. Athenian historiography is permeated by pro-democratic bias. Even the most antidemocratic writers about Athens, including Thucydides and the problematic "Old Oligarch" (Ps.-Xenophon)—provide rich evidence to this effect. Athens's sense of identity, from the

end of the sixth century (and projected back far earlier) was
bound up with its endlessly vaunted, often abused, and period-
ically overthrown democratic institutions. These values even
show through in the explicitly antidemocratic Plutarch (e.g.,
Sulla 43 = *Comp.* 5). It was simply not possible to give a plausibly sympathetic account of the accomplishments of Athens that
was not to some degree informed by the democratic ideology if
the city in its days of greatest achievement. It is this background
that makes Plutarch's *Phocion* stand out as different from the
other Athenian *Lives*, and as something uniquely Plutarchan.

Phocion led the Athenian state through the three and a half
years from Athens's defeat in the Lamian War (322) to the
short-lived restoration of the democracy in 318. The war had
been sparked by a briefly successful alliance and rebellion of
Greek cities against Macedonian rule on the death of Alexander. The Macedonian general Antipater was initially overpowered—he was trapped inside the walls of the Thessalian
city of Lamia, giving the conflict its traditional name—but when
he broke out and turned the tables, he quickly showed his exceptional ability in using a combination of force and diplomacy
to shatter the Greek alliance. Even Athens, preeminent among
the ringleaders, was treated mildly but, negotiating from a
position of helplessness, was forced to accept a radical modi-
fication of its constitution. This introduced a property qualifica-
tion for full citizen rights that reduced the number of the en-
franchised from twenty-one thousand to nine thousand (*Phoc.*
28). The newly disenfranchised poor—clearly in Macedonian
eyes, the ungovernable rabble that had for decades fomented
discontent with Macedonian imperialism—were offered a site
in Thrace to colonize, and many must have gone there, although the net loss of population is a matter of dispute. This
was the trap that history had set for Phocion, now over eighty
years old. The fortunes (*tukhai*) of Greece had blackened the

brilliance of his excellence (*Phoc.* 1). Plutarch takes up the challenge of setting the record straight.

The parallel to Phocion returns us to a more familiar context, one whose relevance is more obvious here than in other comparisons. Cato the Younger (so called to distinguish him from his homonymous great-grandfather, the proverbially severe censor of 189) plays a somewhat larger role in Plutarch's *Julius Caesar* than the summary above would suggest. He emerges repeatedly as the principal senatorial voice against Caesar's abuses. He is ineffectual—Caesar, that combination of divine scourge and "gentle physician" cannot be stopped—but Cato's role in that biography prepares us for Plutarch's presentation of him in his own right. The pair lacks a *Comparison*, but the essentials are laid out in the introduction. This is largely a paean of praise for the politician who has the courage to take the risks of governing a city in crisis. That is when the people, the *demos*, are in danger of destroying the politician who says what they do not want to hear, or of carrying the flatterer along to share in their own ultimate destruction (*Phoc.* 2). Plutarch's metaphor for the politics (and the politician) that can do this successfully is the sun on its oblique path through the universe, neither running directly opposite to the "movement" of the fixed sphere nor traveling with it. In the same way, the government that saves the state mixes severity with generosity: "If the mixture is accomplished, it is the most harmonious and musical of all mixtures of rhythms and scales—the one by which divinity is said to govern the universe, bringing forth that which necessity requires, not by force, but by reason and persuasion" (*Phoc.* 2).

We do not often find appeals to metaphor of this scale in the more ambiguous lives. Plutarch puts us on notice that these two men represent extremes of civic and political excellences of many sorts—they are not just two good politicians you might compare for courage (like Alcibiades and Epaminondas) or intelligence (like Themistocles and Aristides) or other specific excellences. Each of them embodied a complex balance of qualities held in tension: a balance of severity (*austeron*) and fairness or humanity (*philanthropia*), of stability and courage, of care for others and fearlessness for themselves, of caution with regard to what is wrong and the aggressive pursuit of justice (*Phoc.* 3). The mixture and the scale of the metaphors is richly Plutarchan—evocations of celestial mechanics and pre-Socratic physics in the service of a model that is ultimately the juxtaposition of microcosm and macrocosm pervasive in later Platonism. These men embodied and had their place in the harmonious ordering of society in the image of the universe. In the context of the events of his life, each was less fortunate.

Most of the details of Phocion's career, and perhaps all of the sayings that reach us, come by way of Plutarch. We have only his word, for instance, that Phocion listened to Plato "while still a boy" (*meirakion*) and, later, to his successor Xenocrates (*Phoc.* 4). (Diogenes Laertius [6.76] lists Phocion among the students of Diogenes the Cynic, but that would hardly serve Plutarch's purposes.) But Plutarch supplies the information that Phocion was Plato's student (*Phoc.* 4, "Against Colotes" 1126c), and there is no reason to doubt it. Nor should we be surprised that a prominent oligarchic politician emerged from the Academy. Whether Phocion learned from Xenocrates or not—Phocion was about sixty when Xenocrates took over the Academy in 339—the two were co-ambassadors to Antipater on behalf of the Athenians after the defeat of 322.

Beyond the references to his philosophical education, Plutarch has little to say about Phocion's youth, and even these serve principally to counterbalance the claim that he was poor. His behavior as a child and then an ephebe was austere and exemplary. Beyond the restrained, even sullen exterior, he was gentle and humane (*Phoc.* 5), and his wit and conciseness earned even Demosthenes' respect.

Plutarch provides a selection of anecdotes and narratives spanning Phocion's long military and political career, a selection organized around the paradox that even though his policy was regularly one of peace and nonconfrontation, he was nevertheless elected general more often than any other Athenian—forty-five times in the course of about fifty-four years. This is even chalked up to the credit of the *demos*, in that they enjoyed being fawned on by the flattering rhetors but elected the man who told them what they did not want to hear (*Phoc.* 8). Phocion is here credited with Alexander's change of heart toward Athens after the destruction of Thebes (*Phoc.* 17), although in the *Life of Alexander* (13) his change of heart was brought about by sudden and spontaneous remorse, and no role was given to ambassadors.

It will come as no surprise that Phocion's political ideals have a Spartan cast. In the *Life,* this is translated into an anecdote. Phocion's son Phocos competes successfully as an *apobates*—a rider in a complex and difficult sort of dressage event, appropriately the domain of the upper classes, the *hippeis,* or "knights." One of his friends, with Phocion's permission, gives the victory party, whose luxury is offensive. Father says to son, "Phocos, are you going to let your friend go on ruining your victory?" and subsequently sends the boy off to Sparta to complete his education, even though he offends the Athenians by doing so (*Phoc.* 20).

In public matters, Phocion goes on speaking out against war, even when he is a minority of one, and then dutifully goes out as elected general to fight the wars he opposes. The Lamian War was the last. When the assembly shouted him down and insisted on a campaign in Boeotia, he had the heralds proclaim that everyone up to the age of sixty should take five days' rations and follow him immediately. The old geezers (who had a legal right to complain at being taken on a campaign outside Attica) were enraged, and Phocion responded: "That's all right. I'll be going along with you as your general, and I'm eighty" (*Phoc.* 24).

The end of the Lamian War brought what Plutarch presents as history's great test for Phocion. The basic facts have already been outlined. Plutarch adds that the disenfranchised who remained in Athens were like men who had suffered disgrace and loss of citizen rights (*atimia*), while those who went to Thrace were like refugees from a city taken by siege (*Phoc.* 28). The principal political opponents of the Macedonians—Demosthenes and Hypereides—had to be handed over to Antipater. They fled the city. Plutarch credits the demogogue Demades with the motion condemning them to death. They were hunted down by an agent of Antipater known as Archias the Phygadotheras, or "bounty hunter" (*Dem.* 28). In *Phocion*, Demades is developed as a foil to Phocion; he is as self-serving and corrupt as Phocion is austere and incorruptible. Demades ultimately tries, unwisely, to play the Macedonians off against one another. In a version of his end more colorful than that known to Diodorus, Plutarch has Cassander slaughter Demades' son and splash him with the blood before killing the father (*Phoc.* 30). Through all of this, Phocion looks after the city "gently and with respect for the law" (*praos kai nomimos*, 29).

The death of Antipater precipitates the final crisis. Antipater's son Cassander attempts to do an end run around the old general Polyperchon, to whom his father had left his command. Nicanor, on Cassander's orders, takes over the Macedonian garrison in the Piraeus before news of Antipater's death spreads. Polyperchon, to counter Cassander and incidentally to get rid of Phocion, restores the democracy (*Phoc.* 32). At this point and this point alone, Plutarch cannot present Phocion in a wholly positive light. Phocion stood aside and let Nicanor lead his troops out of the garrison and take control of the entire Piraeus. As general, it was Phocion's responsibility to prevent this. The most plausible explanation is that, faced with the restoration of the democracy, Phocion decided that an alliance with Nicanor was his best hope. Other accounts say as much. Plutarch can only soften the judgment by attributing Phocion's lapse not to self-interest but to too-great confidence in Nicanor's trustworthiness (32) and by asserting that when Phocion had realized his error, he wanted to attack Nicanor (33).

It was too late. Phocion was stripped of command. The coda of the *Life* is Plutarch at his most richly theatrical. Two delegations, Phocion's and the Athenians', simultaneously catch up with Polyperchon (who has the idiot Macedonian king Philip Arrhidaeus, his legitimation, in tow). Phocion and his friends are sent back to Athens under guard and taken by cart to the Theater of Dionysus to be judged by an assembly that includes slaves, citizens disqualified by *atimia*, foreigners, and, most outrageous of all, women. The scene has more than a passing resemblance to several in *A Tale of Two Cities*, and the political thrust is identical. The unleashing of radical democracy, putting power in the hands of the brutalized, downtrodden, and abused, results in the unjust and indiscriminate slaughter of those formerly in power, along with their associates. Phocion tries in vain to save the friends fortuitously imprisoned with him. All are condemned without a hearing, in an atmosphere of carnival riot and violence (*Phoc.* 34–35). The city does not even have the hemlock for the executions and Phocion cheerfully contributes twelve drachmas for his own dose: "Well, if not even dying is free in Athens . . ." (36). It is the day of the Festival of Olympian Zeus—a horsey, aristocratic festival recalling the one that had provided the context for Phocion's son's victory. As the mounted elite pass the prison, they remove their festive crowns and weep (37).

That is the final tableau, but there is more: the Athenians

soon repented, gave Phocion a statue, and punished his accusers. The city had committed a crime—and suffered a misfortune—comparable in magnitude to the execution of Socrates (*Phoc.* 38).

Phocion brings us insistently into a problematic area of Plutarch's sociopolitical perspective, and although in context the intensity of his negative portrayal of the restored democracy may not be surprising, it nevertheless needs comment. We have seen that he dreaded tyranny but realized that one must sometimes live with it. He dreaded democracy as well, even though the properly functioning democracy of classical Athens had its admirable side. His nightmare—inherited from Thucydides and passed on to the whole tradition European political thought—is the sudden collapse of social conventions that puts the haves—the aristocracy—at the mercy of the have-nots. To see this as pure self-interest on Plutarch's part would be a mistake. In his analysis, the loss is mutual. The state decapitates itself, and it is not obvious that it will succeed in growing another head.

Phocion was better than his pattern of life, or rather, he in some sense deserved a better one than he got. But if he receives as close to unqualified praise as any of Plutarch's subjects, it is because the qualities he brought to that test stood up to it. Aristotle's teaching failed to equip Alexander for the life that history gave him, but Plato's served Phocion well. He was close to Plutarch's ideal of the philosophically trained man of action, decisive and effective but still more concerned with avoiding the commission of injustice than with suffering from it (*Phoc.* 32, with an interesting twist).

Plutarch's biography of the younger Cato is nearly twice as long as its twin but need not occupy us as long. There is a general tendency for the Roman life to be the longer of the pair, a fact generally traceable to the nature and abundance of the sources Plutarch had available. This disparity is particularly striking in the overlapping late republican *Lives: Cicero, Pompey, Crassus, Sulla, Lucullus,* and *Cato Minor* all dwarf the Greek *Lives* with which they are paired.

Among these major figures of the last decades of the republic, Cato is clearly the one who inspires the most admiration in Plutarch. The reasons are made explicit in the brief comparison at the beginning of *Phocion.* Cato was an idealist, a figure out of the Roman past who genuinely respected republican—and philosophical—values. The mob had no use for him, and unlike his competition, he made few compromises with the mob. Cicero observed that he lost the election for consul by carrying on his campaign "as if he were in Plato's republic, not Romulus's" (*Phoc.* 3, translating Cicero, *To Atticus* 2.1.8, where Cicero is less polite in his description of Rome). And yet, expressing his philosophical principles as politics, Cato did battle with the fortune (*tukhe*) that was bringing the republic down, and because of his efforts, it came close to surviving. That it did not survive is, as we have seen, a something that Plutarch chalks up to destiny, to forces beyond human control. But Cato, more than anyone else, resisted. Plutarch does not celebrate kicking against the pricks as a virtue in itself—in fact, Cicero's moderating advice to compromise and accept the inevitable repeatedly saves Cato from the consequences of his instinctive, rigid adherence to principle.

Cato the Stoic also lived his life on the far side of politics, whereas Cicero was situated squarely in the center of political life. Cato's failure in the consular elections for 51 was for him a signal to withdraw from seeking elected office. His manner, his way of being (*tropos*), clearly offended the plebs, and he chose integrity over elected office. He concluded "that neither to modify one's manner to please others nor to remain consistent and so to suffer another similar defeat was consistent with the behavior of a reasonable person" (*Cato Min.* 50). If there is an element of *Star Trek's* Mr. Spock in Plutarch's Cato, that is because the qualities in question can be traced right to the beginnings of Greek philosophical biography, in the dialogues of Plato. Like Socrates, with whom both Phocion and Cato are explicitly compared (*Phoc.* 38; *Cato Min.* 46), Cato remains calmly—even comically—rational in situations that would evoke an emotional response in an ordinary human being. Cato, we are told, read Plato's *Phaedo* in the hours before his suicide ("they even say he read the whole dialogue through twice," *Cato Min.* 68–70). He spent that time, then, contemplating Plato's portrait of the last hours of Socrates, who calmly and rationally explored possible understandings of the death lying immediately before him, surrounded by disciples who repeatedly broke down and wept. (Plutarch has Cato's admirers reenact the identical scene, in one of his most striking juxtapositions of text and experience [*Cato Min.* 68–69].) Plato's point is that the governing rational principle in Socrates is proof against emotion with its attendant disruption and distortion of experience, even in the most extreme situations. Precisely that juxtaposition of (natural) emotion and (unnatural) rational calm generates humor in the Bergsonian sense: their rationality always in control, neither Socrates, Cato, nor Mr. Spock responds to living in the world with the suppleness of a real person. So Plato's Socrates, Plutarch's Cato, and *Star Trek's* Spock are all reductive portraits—Bergson might say there is something of the machine in them—and they therefore operate on the fringes of the humorous.

    This response is far from irrelevant. Cato's particular mode of *imitatio Socratis* is deliberately pitched at this extreme in Plutarch's account. The single episode of his brother's death and funeral supports the claim that, unseen by most, "sensitivity and affection lay behind the man's unbending rigidity toward pleasure, fear, and shameless demands" (*Cato Min.* 11). Cato's ethical positions were, on the whole, too radical for Plutarch's tastes. As a Platonist, he could hardly sympathize with Cato's suicide (which is portrayed in the most hideous and painful terms, *Cato Min.* 70), though as an expression of Cato's deeply and consistently held Stoic beliefs, even the suicide becomes admirable.

Cato's career is summed up in a string of anecdotes collected by Plutarch from a range of sources, some of which survive while others are lost. From childhood, Cato displays extraordinary courage and a predisposition to asceticism and the study of ethics and politics. He walks around Rome "unshod and unchitoned" (*Cato Min.* 6,44), which is to say, self-consciously affecting the simplicity of dress adopted by Socrates (Xenophon, *Memorabilia* 1.6.2), which many other philosophers had aped. This is initially for Cato a matter of distinguishing what is genuinely shameful from what is "indifferent" and merely "condemned by fashion or convention" (*Cato Min.* 6)—a familiar ethical concern of Stoics and Cynics. Even so, this behavior represents a level of societal disruption in the name of philosophy that is very far removed from the values and practice of the conventional, civilized Plutarch. When Cato adopts this dress in later years when he is praetor, presiding over "capital charges against prominent people" (*Cato Min.* 44), it is one of many aspects of his character and behavior that give offense. Clearly, though, his public character and actions are unimpeachable, and these offenses against the values of the aristocracy do not detract from his growing reputation for justice (*dikaiosyne*), which, Plutarch tells us, automatically generates malicious jealousy (*phthonos*) in rivals, because it endows the bearer with "power and credibility" among the people (44).

Cato's career was a long battle to recover and to maintain the status, power, and credibility of the Senate (and so of the Roman oligarchy) in the face of the efforts of the triumvirs and ultimately of Caesar to destroy that order and replace it with monarchy. As such, this career, when turned into Plutarchan biography, returns us to the story already told in *Julius Caesar* (as also in *Pompey, Cicero, Lucullus,* and elsewhere), but from a new perspective. Cato is a difficult blocking figure in *Julius Caesar.* He had too much credibility, too much authority, for Caesar to throw him in prison when he stood up in lone opposition to some new, self-serving legislation of Caesar's. His integrity, his respectability, were emphasized there as well, but Caesar's biography gives us relatively few glimpses of Cato. The story in that *Life* was the story of Caesar's excellence—the genuine military accomplishments, the seizure of power (somewhat too easily justified by "necessity"), and the benevolent dictatorship cut short by fate.

In contrast, *Cato the Younger* is the story of a loser (by the standards of history) who is turned into the true victor, in the only sense in which victory was possible, over the most ruthless and most successful strongman in Plutarch's collection. We see the familiar confrontations from Cato's perspective: his opposition to public sacrifice in Rome for Caesar's German victories, based as they were on the violation of treaties sworn by Caesar on the good faith of Rome (*Cato Min.* 51). We see Cato in the role of Cassandra—the prophet believed only when it was too late—when it turned out that Caesar was in fact more of a threat to Rome than the million or million and a half Celts and Germans whom his legions had slaughtered in the name of Rome's civilizing mission. Through all of this, Cato served principle while others either served themselves or thought they had done well if they picked, and attached their interests to, a winner. When Pompey's government is the closest thing to legality left, Cato gives advice to Pompey. His gestures are increasingly symbolic, as necessity and Caesar tighten their grip. After Caesar crosses the Rubicon, Cato stops cutting his hair (53). After

Caesar destroys Pompey's forces at Pharsalus, Cato gives up the Greek practice of reclining at meals, henceforth sitting up, and lies down only to sleep (56).

Cato's last stand, in Utica, the capital of the Roman province of Africa, is his finest moment. The scene is worthy of Plutarch's dialogues, for the play of spoken and unspoken and the juxtaposition of the intimate facts of experience with the great sweep of history. Pompey is dead. Cato has unwisely handed his army over to the proconsul Scipio, who ignored Cato's advice and, along with the Numidian king Juba, confronted Caesar at Thapsus. What remains of their armies is in disarray. Cato is in Utica, where the people view him as their savior, but he has already decided that it is time to die (*Cato Min.* 64). His "council" of three hundred Roman citizens resident in Utica vacillates between resistance, submission, and more: detaining those of senatorial rank to hand over to Caesar to save the rest (*Cato Min.* 61). As he plans his own suicide, Cato is still averting injustices and atrocities in Utica. The council proposes to send to Caesar and request pardon, first for Cato, then for themselves, but if the first is refused, to fight to the end.

> In reply, Cato praised their goodwill and said they should send immediately to Caesar for the sake of their own safety, but should not make a request on his behalf, because "requests" were appropriate to those in another's power and "pardon" to the situation of wrongdoers. He, Cato, however, had not only been undefeated all his life but had been victorious over Caesar to the degree he wished, and had defeated him in terms of accomplishments and justice, for Caesar was now the one ensnared and defeated: he now stood indicted and convicted of exactly those crimes that he had long denied he was committing against the state. (*Cato Min.* 64)

The issue, ultimately is freedom—freedom as defined in Stoic ethics (*Cato Min.* 67) and freedom as defined in the political rhetoric of the late republic. Caesar successfully freed himself from all constraints except the need to dominate, to have no constraints. Cato understood both the nature of the victory over him that Caesar craved and the only possible way to subvert that victory. Caesar's response to the news of Cato's death is his apologia: "Cato, I begrudge you your death, since you begrudged me your salvation" (72).

As we can see from this pair of laudatory lives of philosopher-statesmen, the bilateral symmetry that so dominates the rhetorical structuring of the *Parallel Lives* conceals and invites further symmetries and further comparisons. What is missing here, formally, is a *Comparison of Phocion and the Younger Cato* but equally implied is a *Comparison of Caesar and Cato*, the one dragging along his model Alexander and the other, Phocion's parallel excellences.

Plutarch's villains, in contrast, are undeniably more attractive than his rather priggish heroes, and this is immediately clear when we turn from Phocion and Cato to Demetrius and Antony. The preface to *Demetrius and Antony* actually speaks of inserting "one or two pairs" of negative exempla into the model lives, explaining by elaborate illustrations and analogies just why they are needed. The most immediate reasons adduced are pedagogical. Demetrius and Antony will serve in the capacity of the drunken helots displayed to Spartan youth to dissuade them from drink: as examples of "men who acted recklessly and were remarkable, in the power they wielded and in their great undertakings, for vice" (*Demetr.* 1). Among the subjects of the *Parallel Lives,* only Demetrius Poliorcetes ("The Besieger") and Antony (thanks to Shakespeare, more familiar in English as Mark Antony), the last rival of Augustus, are singled out in this way as "bad and legitimately condemned" (1). Other biographies specify failures. Agis, Cleomenes, and the Gracchi, the subjects of the double pair of *Lives*, are identified as leaders led astray by the pursuit of glory (*doxa*), and all suffered reverses—but in their stories there is much more that can be salvaged as admirable than in *Demetrius and Antony*. In complex figures like Nicias, we find a balance of the admirable with the reprehensible: aristocratic philanthropy and (early) military success vitiated in the end but not erased by superstition, hesitation, and misplaced caution. Likewise, in portraying the inherently problematical Alcibiades, Plutarch holds up his subject's charisma and his military skill against his total contempt for the good (*kalon*)—his moral bankruptcy.

If Alcibiades' failure is measured in such terms, it is because he benefited from the tutelage of Socrates. Demetrius and Antony had no such opportunities, and hence no such specific failings, although "moral bankruptcy," in the sense of failure to identify any meaningful or even viable goal, might be seen as a factor in either life (*Demetr.* 52). To the extent that their common failing is defined, Plutarch places it in the broad category of failure of self-restraint (*akrasia, Ant. 91 = Comp.* 4), and so it constitutes a satisfyingly symmetrical mirror of the rational self-restraint that characterizes the admirable Phocion and Cato. On this level of generality, however, Plutarch's judgments sometimes seem quite arbitrary. Was Alexander really so different from these two generals that Plutarch should present him to history as a model of restraint, whereas Demetrius and Antony were the opposite?

The key to the difference—and here we are solidly in the realm of the pedagogical ethics that inform the *Lives*—is pleasure addiction. The prefatory comparison of Demetrius and Antony lays it out:

> They were both given to sex (*erotikoi*), given to drink (*potikoi*), soldierly, generous, prodigal, and domineering (*hybristai*), and fortune shaped their lives similarly in conse-

quence of these qualities: they went through life scoring great successes and suffering great defeats, winning and losing huge prizes, unexpectedly failing, then recovering against all anticipation—and each finally met with catastrophe, the one captured by his enemies and the other barely escaping the same fate. (*Demetr.* 1)

Alexander was (in Plutarch's account) singularly free of the two vices that open the list. He had the strength to resist pleasure and its capacity to take control of a life, and he avoided the oscillations of fortune of these two lesser leaders. That very oscillation, however, gives a sort of vertiginous excitement to these two failed lives; it is bound up with the theme of the radical insecurity of good fortune that informs the *Lives* of Alexander and Caesar.

Alexander is ever present as a model and precedent, or explicitly as a comparison, in Plutarch's treatment of Demetrius, who was perhaps the most colorful of the warlords among Alexander's successors. Demetrius is proclaimed leader (*hegemon*) of Greece at the Isthmus, just as Philip and Alexander had been proclaimed, and at that moment, inflated by power and fortune, Demetrius even thought himself better than his predecessors (*Demetr.* 25). Antigonus and Demetrius were the first outside Alexander's line to be proclaimed "kings" (*Demetr.* 10), and unlike Alexander, Demetrius claimed an exclusive right to the title (25). Alexander's ghostly presence appears twice: Demetrius has an ominous dream of Alexander on the night before the battle that claims Antigonus's life, and the "specter" (*eidolon*) of Alexander's daring is detected by the Macedonians *not* in Demetrius but in his rival Pyrrhus (41). Finally, as Demetrius prepares his ultimate expedition against the kings in Asia, it is a force "such as none since Alexander had previously mounted" (44).

Demetrius is, then, in part a replay of Alexander. This secondariness, this inauthenticity, is also emphasized in an exceptional abundance of theatrical imagery. The *Life* is repeatedly called a play. When Plutarch shifts from stories of Demetrius's womanizing to war, "Fortune is transferring the narrative as if from the comic stage to the tragic" (*Demetr.* 28). Demetrius confronts and intimidates, then pardons, the fickle Athenians—from the stage of the Theater of Dionysus (34). His fancy trappings are "theater" (*tragodia megale*, 41). He slips out "like an actor" when his troops defect to Pyrrhus (44), and in an unusually arch reflexive comment, Plutarch closes his *Life* with: "Now that the Macedonian play has been performed, it is time for the Roman one" (53).

Theatricality is evoked elsewhere in the *Lives*, and, indeed, it is a historiographic commonplace, exploited notably among Plutarch's contemporaries by Tacitus. Plutarch's *Life of Demetrius* nevertheless gives this theme conspicuous prominence. The criticism of mimetic art in Plato's *Republic* is relevant here. One problem with mimetic art—and acting may serve here as an emblem for the other sorts—is that it destroys the integrity of the soul (e.g., *Rep.* 394d–e). The fine-tuned harmony of parts that constitute the individual (and the city) characterized by justice is incompatible with pretense, including mimetic or esthetic pretense. You cannot lead a fully realized life while acting out the lives of others. In a sense, this is exactly the nature of the emptiness of Demetrius's life and the nature of his failure.

In early life, he showed a remarkable capacity to compartmentalize. He had admirable military skills, particularly with reference to preparations, specifically the preparation of glorious equipment—huge ships and siege engines such as had never been seen before. In this he is talented (*euphues*) and studious (*theoretikos, Demetr.* 20). In victory, he expressed his humanity, his fairness (*philanthropia*), and his generosity (*eugnomosyne,* 17).

But all these admirable qualities were expressed in the half of his life that was devoted to duty, most of all to the duty he felt toward his father, Antigonus. When he was not fighting, his life was entirely given over to drunkenness and sex. Antigonus, in his eighties and obese, relied on his son's considerable military skills and chose to ignore the debauchery (19).

Plutarch demonstrates in the end that for all the sublime scale and beauty of the siege engines that Demetrius created—so wonderful that the victims of his sieges asked to keep souvenirs (*Demetr.* 20)—it was never clear that his heart was in it. When, after his father's death, he fell into the hands of his son-in-law and rival, Seleucus, he was kept in Apamea in regal captivity. He responded cooperatively by drinking himself to death—either, Plutarch concludes, because he was depressed by his captivity or because drunkenness and gambling had always been what he really wanted, and his captivity brought home to him that his military career was simply the pursuit of "empty glory," a distraction from the indulgences that were the true focus of his being: "Finally, what other goal is there for bad kings, in their wars and acts of daring? They are worthless and unthinking not only in that they pursue luxury and pleasure rather than excellence and the good but also because they do not even know how to take pleasure in their luxury" (*Demetr.* 52).

In this sense, then, Demetrius lived out his destiny and was complicit in it. This is not his whole story, however, as Plutarch tells it. Viewed in another perspective, the villains of the piece were the Athenians, specifically the fawning demagogues who heaped divine honors on Demetrius, sang outrageous hymns to him, and even treated him as an oracle. The flattery began with crowns and kingship and royal trappings. The Athenians left him literally deranged (although he was "unsound of mind to begin with," *Demetr.* 13). At some level, they were just making fun of him, dressing him up like an actor on the stage, but, like an actor, he lost all sense of himself. He was naturally generous and fair until regal honors hardened him—and so it was that "a single flatterer's voice changed the world," and the evil of tyranny was reinstated in Athens (18). These are the two faces of Plutarch's Demetrius, and both come down to the same failure: a lack of identity, an ability to play roles but not to live a life.

The second act of this two-act drama repeats the pattern of the first, creating a pair with resonant symmetries. Antony's character is much like that of Demetrius: military skill and driving ambition are coupled with the worst sort of pleasure addiction. Unlike Demetrius, Antony does not keep his military career separate from his self-indulgence, and his pleasure has a sadistic edge. He takes real and lingering delight in contemplating the severed head and right hand of his enemy Cicero (*Ant.* 20). Nevertheless, Plutarch reminds us again and again that for those close to him Antony was genuinely likeable. His soldiers liked him, with his simple, crude manner and his jokes, and women liked him. This is what makes *Antony* stand out so prominently among the other *Lives,* and this is why it has had the richest history of retelling and reworking of all of them. It might as well have been entitled the *Life of Antony and Cleopatra.* It is a love story in spite of itself (and in spite of the harsh judgment laid against Antony), and Cleopatra emerges as the single woman the great biographer seriously undertook to portray—although, as we shall see, Octavia in the same *Life* has a powerful supporting role.

Structurally, in terms of the pattern of their lives, Cleopatra is to the self-indulgent Antony what the Athenians were to the self-indulgent Demetrius. Neither of these warlords was really certain whether world conquest or the pleasure of the immediate debauch was the goal closer to his heart. Both were thus predisposed to be manipulated, and both found their manipulators. The Athenians clouded Demetrius's sense of self and his simple humanity by telling him he was a king and a god, and the demagogues who proposed these outrageous honors had absolutely no illusions about what they were doing. Cleopatra, as Plutarch presents her, was a similar mistress of illusion, and her calculated assault on Antony was, like the Athenian demagogues' flattery, built on ridicule, contempt, and the will to dominate (*Ant.* 26). This explains just how Antony's story becomes Cleopatra's story and why Plutarch's *Life of Antony* goes on for ten chapters after Antony's death. Cleopatra usurped Antony's life and his *Life*, so his story can end only with hers. He in fact becomes less interesting as the story progresses—reduced and immobilized, after Actium, in a three-day funk, crumpled alone on the bow of Cleopatra's ship, then withdrawn into self-conscious Timonian dudgeon on the island of Pharos, at Alexandria. But he is just sulking—he will come back to the party.

The story of Antony before Cleopatra (a little more than a quarter of the *Life*) is another colorful chapter in the wars of the alpha males who tore down the Roman republic. Young Antony was seduced early by extravagance, by drinking parties, and by sex. He modeled himself on his "ancestor" Heracles, although as the *Life* evolves his attendant deity comes to be Dionysus. He was "brilliant" (*lamprotatos, Ant.* 3) in his early military exploits, and after Pharsalus, he ruled Italy as Caesar's protégé while Caesar was in Spain. He was a terrible administrator, indifferent to injustices that he could ignore and ready to abuse his power in various ways, notably in affairs with other men's wives. If Caesar's benevolent dictatorship looked like a tyranny, the blame lies with Antony (6). Still, he delivered the goods militarily, through a combination of bravado and good luck, and Caesar (remember Antigonus) looked the other way. Meanwhile, Antony installed himself in the house of the late, austere Pompey in Rome and turned it into a brothel (9, 10, 21). This violation of revered space by debauchery echoes Demetrius's treatment of the Parthenon in Athens.

Caesar as patron is ultimately more vigilant than Antigonus as father, however, and he marries Antony off to Fulvia, widow of the "demagogue" Clodius, a woman whose goal was "to rule a ruler and give orders to a general"; Cleopatra, Plutarch observes, should have paid Fulvia tuition for training Antony to be ruled by a woman (*Ant.* 10). Antony's motives in 44 B.C.E. are kept deliberately vague. As Caesar's protégé, he was not a participant in the conspiracy, but he knew about it and did not expose it. With Caesar dead and Brutus and Cassius stopping short of a general massacre of Caesarians, Antony emerges as the great conciliator, the great statesman—but slow as he is (*Ant.* 24), he realizes that with Brutus out of the way, he himself could be "first" (14). The funeral oration that Shakespeare was to make famous drives the conspirators from Rome and leaves Antony the leader of the avengers. He initially underestimates the nineteen-year-old Octavian and is defeated by his armies at Mutina in 43, but adversity always brings out the best in Antony, just as its opposite destroys him (17). He sets the standard for endurance, seeing his starving, defeated army across the Alps, where he assembles seventeen legions and ten thousand horsemen for the next confrontation with Octavian (18). The Second Triumvirate is put in place. Octavian, Antony, and Lepidus divide the world among themselves, and Antony is lord of everything east of the Adriatic. The triumvirs do not make the mistake of Brutus and Cassius. They kill everyone they have the slightest reason to suspect or fear. Friends and relatives are traded: Octavian consents to let Antony kill Cicero in exchange for the proscription of Antony's uncle (as it turns out, his mother dramatically saves her brother). Lepidus's brother is also among the three hundred on the list. In a context of murderous brutality on a scale that numbs the imagination, Plutarch nevertheless marks this as an extreme: "I do not believe that anything happened more savage and brutal than this exchange." They killed without hatred. They killed relatives and friends (*philoi*, 19).

The subsequent rule of the triumvirs is harsh and oppressive. Antony returns to his debauchery in Pompey's house, and then, after eliminating Brutus and Cassius in Macedonia, he visits Greece and Asia, the land for which he has a special affinity, both as an orator (*Ant.* 2) and as the "new Dionysus" (24, 26, 60). In his capacity of governor of the East, he summons the twenty-eight-year-old reigning queen of Egypt, Cleopatra the Seventh, to Tarsus to answer charges of supporting Cassius in the Civil War. That, in a sense, is the end of Antony's story. The passion that she provokes in him is the "last blow" (*teleutaion kakon*) to his poorly defined character, wiping out anything "upright and salutary" (*khreston, soterion*, 25) that may still have been present in it. An ambassador has briefed her on how best to deal with Antony. She arrives at the mouth of the Kydnos River, just south of Tarsus, with gifts and treasure, "but putting her greatest hopes in the charms and spells that surrounded her person" (25). The passage describing her entry is deservedly famous:

> She had received repeated letters summoning her, both from him and from those close to him, but she treated him with such dismissiveness and mockery that she sailed up the Kydnos River on a barge with a golden platform and purple sails set, while rowers timed the strokes of their silver oars to the music of a flute accompanied by pipes and lyres. She was reclining under a gold-embroidered canopy, adorned like Aphrodite in a painting, while boys gotten up like painted Erotes stood on either side and fan-

ned her. The most beautiful of her maids, dressed up as
Nereids and Graces, stood by the steering oar and the ca-
bles. Fabulous odors spread over the banks from many
incense burners. Some of the people accompanied her
from the mouth of the river, on both banks, and others
came down from the city to see the spectacle. As the crowd
poured out of the civic center, Antony was finally left all
alone sitting on the speaker's platform. They were all saying that Aphrodite was coming to revel with Dionysus for
the benefit of Asia. (*Ant.* 26)

Antony was outclassed. His response was an invitation to
dine, but she countered with her own invitation, and he accepted. She was in control and in her medium. Plutarch's description of Cleopatra is extraordinarily subtle. She is beautiful,
but not incomparably so. Rather, her power lies in her charm
and in the imaginative range of her deployment of that charm.
The barge is analogous to Antony's—or Demetrius's—huge
warships and siege machines. The note of mockery (*kategelase,*
26) sounded at the outset does little more than mark the rather
forced parallel to the Athenians' treatment of Demetrius. It is
never repeated. Cleopatra's act is flawless, fitted perfectly to
the desires of her targeted audience, Antony, and increasingly
indistinguishable from the true identity of the actress. Plutarch's Julius Caesar invented the role of king—of benevolent
dictator to the Romans—and became what he invented. Plutarch's Cleopatra does much the same. She becomes the "new
Isis" as consort to the "new Dionysus"—the mistress, in all the
ambiguity of the term, of the lord of the richer half of the inhabited world.

The dynamics of the representation of gender roles is complex here. It is largely assumed that Plutarch wrote the *Parallel
Lives* primarily, if not exclusively, for a male readership—I

would envision a male readership aged roughly fifteen to
twenty. In the exemplary tale of Antony, Cleopatra is his downfall. The results of his infatuation are disastrous. Only when he
pries himself away from her and campaigns in Central Asia
does he recover something of his true excellence, and even that
is vitiated by the urgency of his desire to return to her. By
allowing her to come to Actium and even to dictate the decision
to risk it all on a naval battle, he changed the course of history.
Antony, not Octavian / Augustus, could have been the successor of Julius Caesar, and the center of the Roman world would
have shifted eastward, to Alexandria. In the middle of the Battle of Actium, which could still have been won, Cleopatra took
her sixty ships and fled. Antony abandoned the troops fighting
and dying for him to follow her. The battle lost, the troops
defected to the victor. Augustus succeeded his adoptive father,
the deified Julius, as sole ruler of the Roman empire.

For Plutarch's projected readership, this is unambiguously
a cautionary tale about the power of women to unman men and
about the vulnerability of a self-indulgent, erotically susceptible soldier to that power. The message to those readers is pon-
derously and repeatedly emphasized: Antony's is a failed life
on a heroic, a cosmic scale. What sets this *Life* apart from all the
others, however, is the women. Octavia, married to Antony by
her brother to secure the *fides* of the triumvirate, is one of a
small number of exemplary women who play minor roles in the
Lives. She is uncomplicated and wholly admirable, refusing to
be used as an excuse for more internecine bloodshed and remaining faithful to Antony and his interests while he lives an
outrageous life with Cleopatra, acknowledges his children by
Cleopatra, and hands much of the world over to them to rule
(*Ant.* 31–35). Octavia is also the survivor, and she raises those
children when they are no longer the monarchs Alexander He-
lios and Cleopatra Selene but ten-year-old orphans (*Ant.* 87).

Her integrity and consistent devotion to duty are particularly striking against the backdrop of the actions of her warlord relatives, all notable for their betrayals and for allegiances violated for the sake of power.

If Octavia puts the principal actors of the *Life of Antony* to shame, however, it is certainly the portrait of Cleopatra that captures the imagination. Excluded from the dreary mechanisms of evaluation by comparison, the women of the *Lives* are liberated by that very exclusion. The Cleopatra of the *Comparison* is only Omphale, taking away Heracles' club and lionskin (*Ant.* 90 = *Comp.* 3). But like so much in the comparisons, this fails to do justice to the vividly imagined figure of the *Life* itself. With her breathtaking flamboyance, Plutarch's Cleopatra is the worthy counterpart of Demetrius and Antony—and even, as I suggested above, of Caesar, in that her actions achieve the desired result. The ultimate failure is inherent in the enterprise, but she cannot be—and is not—held responsible for that. By taking possession of Antony erotically, she attached herself and her kingdom to the interests of the most powerful man in the world. If by the same stroke she rendered him incapable of removing the last obstacle to that power and brought about his downfall, the reason lies in the soul of Antony, not in anything she can be held accountable for. Plutarch is unambiguous on that score.

Cleopatra's last days are worthy of Cato and infinitely more colorful. Those final chapters when Antony is dead and she is treacherously forced from the monumental stronghold that is also her tomb—one of the richest of Plutarch's many dreamlike imagined spaces—are the sort of writing that has guaranteed Plutarch appreciative readers for millennia. Octavian will say and do anything to keep her alive and in his power: she is to be the finest display in the triumph he is planning in Rome for his recent victories. Threats and promises regarding the fate of her children are his principal tools for manipulating her into accepting food and medical care (*Ant.* 82). Octavian comes to visit her and he is no more a match for her than Antony was. She acts like someone who wants to live, "and he went away thinking he had put something over on her, but he was rather the one fooled" (83). Told she will soon be sent away with the children, she has herself carried to Antony's urn, apostrophizes it, then takes a bath and is served a sumptuous meal. Octavian's guards examine a basket of figs brought from the country and find nothing remarkable beyond the figs themselves. She has the timing under perfect control. She sends a message to Octavian and in the time he needs to respond is bitten by the asp hidden in the figs, and then laid out in state. Octavian's envoys find the guards still at the door. When it is opened, one of the dying maids is still arranging Cleopatra's diadem and is still able to speak.

> "That's a fine thing!" said one of [Octavian's envoys] in a rage. And the maid responded, "A very fine thing, and fitting for the descendant of so many kings." She said nothing more, but dropped there, alongside the bier. (*Ant.* 85)

Nothing could provide a better illustration of the fundamental tensions in the *Lives* between the pedagogical moralizing, the wonderfully theatrical manipulation of anecdote, and the anarchic, unstated second level of judgment beyond the two. Cleopatra lives out to the full the two stages of their life together that she and Antony called "The Company of Inimitable Living" and "The Company of Those Awaiting Death Together." That life and that death are her victory over Octavian. Surely, not even stuffy, ambitious teenage students of rhetoric could have found the emperor more admirable.

The Project in Retrospect

Plutarch's *Parallel Lives*, with their idiosyncratic symmetries, their pedantic comparisons, and their overdetermined symmetry of the past, resemble an enormous textbook. But what is the subject of the course? It is not history in the usual sense—Plutarch makes that much clear. One might argue for ethics, because each life is so insistently presented as exemplary of specific qualities of character, even when what is known of the individual in question makes such claims difficult to maintain. But if ethics were the main thrust, why include all those early lives at all, the ones on the fringes of the map and so remote that we have little hope of reconstituting a living, complex person from the shreds of unreliable anecdote and myth? And why do some of the *Lives*—including the most attractive among them—seem to break the rigid but fragile mold into which they are poured and to revel in the beauty and the wonder of what it was to be Demetrius the Sacker of Cities, or to be Cleopatra, or Alexander the Great? The anecdotes, the speeches, and turns of phrase that make these figures from the past emerge suddenly and vividly as people whom we can imagine as present, imagine as individuals we can know as we know living people—all of this seems so often at odds with the apparent goals of the textbook. What excites wonder here is not always what Plutarch invites us to admire but too often its opposite.

If there is a solution to this dilemma, this disparity between form and content, medium and message, I suspect it is to be sought in the context of rhetoric and rhetorical training. In Lucian's *Dream*—the little speech mentioned in Chapter 1 that depicts Education (specifically, rhetorical education) and Sculpture competing over the teenage Lucian—Education says to him:

If you do what I say, first of all I will show you the accomplishments of the men of the past and tell you their wondrous deeds and what they said, and I will give you experience . . . well, of everything! And your soul—the really
important thing—I will shape that with many fine qualities: self-mastery, justice, piety, gentleness, fairness, understanding, courage, passion for the good, and an impulse toward the sublime. These are the soul's true and
pure ornaments. You will know everything in the past and
in the present—with me, you will even look into the future.
I will teach you absolutely everything, human and divine—and it won't take long! (Lucian, *Dream* 10)

That, I think, is the course for which Plutarch wrote the textbook, or at least the volume about the past. The schematic,
antithetical organization has its analogy in the exercises of the
rhetorical schools, so often visible in Plutarch. The focus on
memorable anecdote, and particularly on "what they said"—
the dicta, the witticisms—these are the tools of rhetoric, the
building blocks for assembling that most precious of all com-
modities (and the one that Lucian and, no doubt, Plutarch
would claim transcends commodification): the effective speech,
the persuasive speech, the speech that encapsulates and em-
bodies everything you are and everything you know, that
reaches the ears of listeners and takes possession of their imagination—and, when need be, their judgment.

In Plutarch's school—whether he had teenage boys come
to him in Chaeronea for rhetorical training or not—as in Lucian's, rhetoric promised a great deal. It was, as for Lucian, a
propaedeutic to philosophy, a first crucial stage in the molding
and shaping of the person. As in Lucian's *Dream*, rhetoric advertised itself not as a dreary analysis of language or the memo-
rization of tropes but as the acquisition of empowering know-

ledge—most of all, knowledge of the wondrous deeds and sayings of the great men of the past. These could be snipped out and reused in new contexts. Plutarch himself shows us how, and the collections of "Sayings" that reproduce so many of the anecdotes scattered through the *Lives* and the essays constitute handbooks of that material.

The *Parallel Lives* may well be best understood as a huge, hybrid textbook to complement rhetorical training, where the student can simultaneously absorb principles about the structure of argument and a wide range of sayings and anecdotes. Some principles and judgments are fixed. The excellences in Lucian's list do not differ substantially from those extolled by Plutarch—but the very reason for the existence of the anecdotes and sayings is their vividness. They can be used and reused in new arguments and contexts. They become part of the student, ornaments of the soul that can be deployed in the service of new agendas. If this education is truly successful, then self-restraint, gentleness, and the rest of those endlessly praised excellences will govern the student's use of those tools—but there are no guarantees.

III BETWEEN PAST AND PRESENT: THE DIALOGUES

The Dialogue as a Genre

THE *LIVES* GAINED A RAPID AND LONG-LIVED POPULARITY that has tended to eclipse the rest of the Plutarchan corpus. The most unfortunate victims of this neglect in modern times have been the dialogues, representatives of a literary genre that thrived in antiquity, lived on into the Middle Ages, was revived in the Renaissance and survived into the eighteenth century, but since then has had relatively few practitioners. Plutarch, to judge by the surviving evidence, considered the dialogue central to his literary activity. Despite all the work he put into the *Lives*, one might even argue that his creations in the genre that was preeminently Plato's were the ones that mattered most. Certainly they provided him with a vehicle whose obliqueness he savored and whose capacity to juxtapose the complementary and the contradictory, argument for argument's sake, and multiple tentative solutions he found congenial.

Although we hear of a few earlier, lost dialogues, the talk of one brilliant talker—Socrates—seems to have given birth to the dialogue as a genre in the Greek world. Antecedents can be found in Herodotus and in Thucydides, dialogues embedded in historical narrative that sometimes seem to be re-creations of actual debates, with the issues marshaled plausibly on either side (e.g., the Melian Dialogue [Thucydides 5.84–114]) and that in other instances are purely literary creations, with ideas and arguments dramatized in contexts that can hardly be historical (e.g., Herodotus 3.80–83). The independent dialogue, however, the freestanding work consisting entirely of the display of a discussion presented as historical, was for all practical purposes the invention of the Socratics, with their teacher as protagonist. Plato may not have been the first among them to do create one. We know, in any case, of at least half a dozen others who wrote Socratic dialogues, although only Plato's and Xenophon's survive, along with fragments of the competition. The Socratic dialogue was never an exercise in transcription. Rather, it was a literary genre, and one with subgenres, including *Socrates' Defense Speech (Apologia)*.

Right from the start, then, the dialogue was an elusive combination of memoir and fiction. Plato's own dialogues are by no means uniform. The ancient historian of philosophy Diogenes Laertius (3.49–51) divided and subdivided them, using as his major categories "instructional" and "inquisitive," and he acknowledged that others used categories such as "narrative" and "dramatic," but he thought these more appropriate to plays than to Plato. But the analogy to drama was lost on no one. In Aristotle's lost dialogue *On Poets*, the Socratic dialogue was juxtaposed with Sophron's prose mimes (frs. 72, 73 Rose), and the later Platonists had a story that the young Plato was on his way to a career as a dramatist until he was redirected by Socrates toward writing a prose drama of intellectual inquiry instead of plays for the stage.

Plato's dialogues defy reductive summary. There is no satisfactory answer to the question of why he chose to make the Socratic dialogue the unique vehicle for the publication of his ideas. There is a general agreement that the simpler, aporetic dialogues, such as the *Ion* and *Euthyphro*, where Socrates is seen testing and refuting others' claims to wisdom, are concerned in large part with the representation of the activity and the thought of the historical Socrates, whereas the "middle" dialogues, such as the *Republic*, and "late" dialogues, such as the *Parmenides* and the *Sophist*, use Socrates and his interlocutors as personae to develop notions and concerns that were Plato's own and not his teacher's. There is also a general agreement that at some level Plato's motive must have been protreptic and that the dialogues present intellectual inquiry for the interested spectator while they invite that spectator to come closer and embrace the philosophical life.

Of the many puzzling and elusive conventions of the Platonic dialogues, two are of particular importance in approaching the dialogues of Plutarch: the frame and the myth. By frame, I mean the explanation, provided within the dialogue, of the conditions and occasion of the original conversation to be re-created for the reader, including the chain of transmission of the account. Some are direct and uncomplicated, either lacking a separable frame (e.g., the *Crito*) or narrated by Socrates in an autobiographical mode (as is the *Republic*). Others, however, are oddly insistent on the distance that separates the original conversation from the retelling.

Plato's *Symposium*, for instance, opens as a dialogue between Apollodoros (devoted Socratic and weepiest of the attendants of Socrates on his last day) and a nameless friend. The friend has asked for an account of a dinner party "a long time ago" at the home of Agathon, the tragic poet, a dinner party attended by Socrates and Alcibiades. Apollodoros begins by telling the friend that he has it all clearly in mind because he happened to be asked "just the other day" by Glaucon to recall the same evening. Glaucon had already heard it from a man named Phoenix, who heard it from Aristodemos, who was actually present at the party. Phoenix's account was unsatisfactory, however, so Glaucon came to Apollodoros, whose source for the whole matter is the same Aristodemos who had told Phoenix about it in the first place.

The *Symposium* presents itself, then, as a re-creation by Apollodoros for his anonymous interlocutor of an account he gave a few days ago to Glaucon, based on a report by Aristodemos, who was there, of a conversation many years in the past. Apollodoros mentions that he subsequently checked "a few things" with Socrates, who confirmed Aristodemos's account. Why all this confusing narrative paraphernalia? The most satisfying answer is that it problematizes from the start the issue of knowledge—knowledge, in this case, of the past, of what was said on a specific occasion. How do we know such things? By repetitions of reports of reports of (perhaps) eyewitnesses. Our knowledge, in other words, is mediated. We have no direct and verifiable perception of a truth as ordinary and everyday as a dinner-party conversation some years ago. Given the frailty of the chain that links us to this truth, what must we think of the larger epistemological dilemmas that confront us?

This explanation of Plato's odd, distancing frame stories combines the philosophical with the esthetic. Other explanations have been offered: there is no way to prove, for instance, that this cumbersome frame is not simply Plato's way of legitimating the account he is about to deliver and rendering it more credible. Our explanation, however, has the tacit approval of at least one ancient student of Plato's dialogues: Plutarch. As we shall see, Plutarch manipulates the frames of his dialogues in precisely this spirit, savoring the paradox of our endlessly frustrated attempts to know the truth.

The myths of Plato's dialogues are even more problematic than the frames. The bulk of most of the dialogues consists of attempts to solve problems, attempts that we may broadly categorize as analytic. The specific techniques illustrated range from the Socratic elenchus, or refutation, to the "division" tested in the *Sophist*. Plato's arguments are not always logically sound, and in a number of instances we cannot say whether their failures of logic were clear to Plato or not. It is nevertheless fair to characterize all of this material as rational analysis, as attempts—successful or failed, seriously portrayed or ironically parodied—to use the resources of mind, reason, and discourse to reach certainty on some issue or other. These arguments sometimes include illustrations, analogous to mind experiments, that serve to clarify or focus some matter under discussion. Thus in *Republic* 7 (514a–520a), Socrates uses the illustration of the cave to sum up what has already been said about education and to introduce the notion that the state will have to compel the philosopher to rule. The story of the people trapped in the cave, vivid as it is, is circumscribed. Its function within the argument is adequate to explain its presence and to exhaust its significance.

In roughly ten instances, however, Plato introduced stories—myths, nonanalytic, nonverifiable narratives, characterized by fabulous and folkloric elements—into contexts that do not wholly exhaust them. Some, including the wonderful comic creation myth fabricated by Aristophanes in the *Symposium*, may be explained as illustrations, like the cave story. One way or another, though, each takes over the exposition, as if it constituted an alternative to the analytic discourse, another way of talking about the world, unfettered by the demands of proof or logical demonstration. In two instances—the creation story of the *Timaeus* and the story of Atlantis in the *Crito*—this sort of discourse dominates to the point that the dialogue is reduced to storytelling, and any possible philosophical value is obscured, if such value can be equated with rational inquiry.

One of the most outrageous of Plato's myths is the "Myth of Er," which brings the *Republic* to a close. It has greatly offended some of Plato's most devoted and careful readers. Julia Annas denounces it as a blatantly "consequentialist" reversal and subversion of what has gone before. Socrates, she points out, spends many hours (the content of 286 Stephanus pages) attempting to demonstrate to his interlocutors that justice, or simply doing right, is an end in itself in the context of the successful life—and then in the final seven pages he tells a colorful fairy tale about reward and punishment in the afterlife (*Introduction to Plato's Republic*, 349–53). Various solutions to this dilemma have been explored, but for our purposes it suffices to note the problem itself. Plato in his dialogues repeatedly shifts gears, often at or near the end of a dialogue, abandoning rational inquiry in favor of colorful and implausible storytelling, sometimes seemingly at odds with whatever gains have been attained up to that point by the use of rationally structured language.

These two problematic aspects of Plutarch's primary model, the Platonic dialogue, are central to his own creative reworking of the genre. Much has been lost between Plato and Plutarch. Aristotle wrote perhaps fifteen dialogues that circulated to a general public. Cicero and Plutarch both read them. Remarks of Cicero's suggest that Aristotle's dialogues opened with proems and that Aristotle was at least sometimes the principal speaker, but neither claim is certain, given the nature of the surviving fragments.

More likely to have influenced Plutarch's practice are the dialogues of two fourth-century thinkers whose works have almost totally vanished, Dicaearchus and Heraclides of Pontus. Of the first, we can say only that he wrote dialogues and that Plutarch read him. He wrote a book whose title is reported as "The Descent to the Oracle of Trophonios" (cited by Athenaeus 594e–f), which might lurk in the background of the myth of *Socrates' Sign*. Heraclides wrote nearly fifty dialogues, if we can believe Diogenes Laertius (5.86–94), who lists all his titles under that rubric. Although Heraclides frequented philosophers in Athens, he is generally treated as an intellectual lightweight, a judgment shared by ancients and moderns. Plutarch, though, refers to him at least ten times and recommends him especially warmly for children:

> It is clear that in the area of philosophical discourse the very young take more pleasure in books that do not seem philosophical or even serious, and they enjoy listening to them and pay attention. They enjoy not just *Aesop's Fables* and stories from the poets but the *Abaris* of Heraclides and the *Lycon* of Ariston as well, with ideas about souls mixed up with mythology, and they are excited by them. ("Poetry" 14e)

Abaris was a Hyperborean shaman of whom all sorts of fabulous tales were told. The two random snippets of Heraclides' dialogue that survive (as illustrations of points of syntax) support Plutarch's description (Heraclides frr. 74, 75 Wehrli):

> Snakes crawled out of their lairs nearby and rushed at the corpse, but they were held off by the dogs that snarled and barked at them.

> And [Abaris?] said the *daimon*, now transformed into a young man, turned to him a second time and told him to believe that the gods exist and that they concern themselves with human affairs.

Heraclides' dialogue *On the Soul* contained a firsthand account of the fate of souls reported by one Empedotimos of Syracuse. This was very widely read and commented on by later Platonists and was compared to what clearly was its literary model, the Myth of Er in Plato's *Republic*. Heraclides seems to have embellished his version of the near-death tale with precisely the sort of poetic metaphysics that we find in Plutarch, centuries later. The Neoplatonist Iamblichus gives us the most elaborate reconstruction:

> Again, another group of Platonists [postulates that] the soul is always in a body, but that it spends time in a lighter body and then returns to live in a flesh-and-blood body. They say that souls go off into some portion of the perceptible universe and that they descend into a solid body at various times and from various places—Heraclides of Pontus defines this place as the Milky Way, but others distribute souls through all the heavenly spheres and maintain that they descend from there to return here (Heraclides fr. 97 Wehrli)

What we see in the Milky Way in the night sky, then, was claimed by a character in a dialogue of Heraclides to be souls, wrapped in the fiery vehicle that sustains them between incarnations. We know from Plutarch's testimony (*Cam.* 22) that he himself had read the dialogue in question. Clearly, then, Heraclides was not exclusively for children. Plutarch also noted ("Live Unknown" 1130b) that "some philosophers consider the soul to be light, as far as its substance is concerned," and he may well have been thinking of Heraclides' myth. As we shall see, it was certainly to his taste.

After Heraclides, it is difficult to identify specific practitioners of the dialogue who are likely to have influenced Plutarch's practice. The best candidate among preserved authors might well be Cicero, whose *De Republica* is modeled on Plato's *Republic*. This dialogue is only partially preserved, but we have the end, a dream reported by the principal speaker, the younger Scipio Africanus. The discussion that immediately preceded the account of the dream is lost, but it seems to have included reference to Plato's Myth of Er (whose place the dream occupies in Cicero's *Republic*), perhaps dismissing it as a fiction. Scipio's dream is a visitation from his homonymous older relative by adoption, the great general of the Second Punic War. It consists of a string of prophecies, followed by a tour of the universe not unlike Er's. Cicero and Plutarch made their respective contributions to the genre of the dialogue by looking back on much the same models, some evident and some lost to us. Those contributions seem, however, to be largely independent of one another. Cicero's dialogues do not contain the poetically elaborated myths that are the beauty of Plutarch's, and Plutarch in turn shows little knowledge of Cicero's dialogues.

Of the seventy-some preserved pieces in the *Moralia* generally accepted as authentic, sixteen make some use of dialogue form, but four of these quickly turn into speeches or monologues. Of the remaining twelve, the ninety-one short dialogues of the *Table Talk* constitute a separate subgenre, although participants in those symposia often appear in the more elaborate dialogues as well. All of the rest (and much of the *Table Talk*) might be broadly characterized as philosophical, though varying considerably in presentation and imaginative elaboration.

The most fanciful consists of a discussion between Odysseus and a pig named Oinker (*Gryllus*)—formerly one of his men, now transformed by Circe—about the rationality of animals. *The Symposium of the Seven Sages* presents itself as a first-person account of the table talk of the pre-philosophical wise men of archaic Greece. Seven of the remaining eight dialogues present discussions among individuals close to Plutarch; he himself is present and named in only one. Plutarch is presumably the "I" of *The E at Delphi* as well and may be lurking behind other personae. Several of these dialogues include elaborately and self-consciously developed myths, but the dialogue *Love* attractively substitutes a love story—or a story of passion and abduction—for the myth. This unfolds simultaneously with the discussion and ultimately provides closure in a wedding scene. *Socrates' Sign* is the most ambitious of the dialogues, and the only one where Plutarch presumes to join Plato and Xenophon in expanding the Socratic corpus. Set twenty years after Socrates' death and appropriating two of the speakers Plato used in the *Phaedo,* this major dialogue with its fabulous and colorful myth marks Plutarch's most successful venture into combining philosophy, (exemplary) history, and rhetoric into a single, coherent whole.

The Delphic Dialogues

It seems appropriate for most of what concerns the god to be concealed in riddles.

—*The E at Delphi* 385c

Plutarch is the only insider to provide us with evidence regarding the oracular shrine at Delphi, but it will come as no surprise that this evidence is in large part infuriatingly indirect and notoriously difficult to use. The bulk of it is concentrated in three dialogues, all set at the site and all implying, but never explicitly claiming, the presence of Plutarch himself. Of the three, *The E at Delphi* is in this sense the most straightforward. The nameless first person addresses the dialogue to Sarapion (a poet, mentioned in the *Table Talk* and a participant in another Delphic dialogue), claiming that a recent discussion of the E had reminded him of a discussion of this odd dedication that occurred "long ago" ("E" 385b), when Nero was in Delphi (67 c.e.). In the recalled conversation that follows, the speaker—let us call him Plutarch to avoid periphrasis—discusses the E with Lamprias (Plutarch's brother) and others. His teacher Ammonios had the last word ("E" 391e–394c), and although Ammonios's explanation does not replace the others, it carries an authority the others lack. Here, the distancing static introduced by the frame is minimal, but the recent discussion of the E to which the speaker refers, which was attended by his grown sons, is imposed as a sort of silenced echo across generations. *The Disappearance of Oracles* is also presented by a nameless first person, who addresses it to Terentius Priscus (identifiable, but not mentioned elsewhere in the Plutarchan corpus), precisely (and uselessly) specifying the date of the conversation as just before the Pythian Games presided over by the undatable Callistratos ("Disappearance" 410a). What is ingenious and playful about the obfuscating frame here, though, is that the "I" is belatedly identified as Plutarch's brother Lamprias ("Disappearance" 413d), whereas everything up to that point would suggest that we are hearing Plutarch's own voice—an assumption that *The E at Delphi* allows us to sustain. Plutarch thus remains absent (or disguised) in this discussion. The other Delphic dialogue never mentions Plutarch, although several of the interlocutors are denizens of the *Table Talk*, and there are plausible reasons for taking the character named Theon to be a mask, or a mouthpiece, for the author.

This, then, is the way Plutarch the Delphic priest turns his insider's information into literature. He uses the distancing convention of the frame, developed by Plato, to erase himself from the picture—or, rather, to obscure his own identity in the manner of a protected witness whose image is optically blurred to prevent recognition. In this case, however, we know all along—or think we know—whose voice we are hearing. The blurring is for purely esthetic reasons, even though these impinge on the issue of knowledge and ignorance and consequently on much else besides. Nothing is less authentic, less transparent, than Plutarch's voice speaking from within the Delphic shrine. These characters in dialogue, exploring, arguing, and counterarguing, are doing exactly what the Delphic priesthood rigorously refused to do: they are explaining, interpreting, unfolding, Delphic mysteries. The dialogue itself is not forbidden, but its closure decidedly is. The priest cannot possibly speak in his own voice, and ultimately no conclusion can be reached that is not subject to further interrogation and revision.

Plutarch comes as close as he ever does to making this explicit in Ammonios's imposing speech closing *The E at Delphi*. The dialogue as a whole consists of attempts to explain the dedication at Delphi of a series of objects in the form of the letter *epsilon*, E ("E" 385f–386a). The dedications apparently have a symbolic value—they are signs with some obscure referrent—but the frame of reference is undefined and potentially cosmic in scope. The E could designate the number 5 (represented in Greek by the fifth letter of the alphabet, *epsilon*), and this in turn could be referred to historical or numerological levels of meaning. Alternatively, as the second vowel in the alphabet, *epsilon* could have to do with secondness—perhaps the sun (Apollo) as the second planet. Finally, *epsilon*, whose name is written "epsilon-iota" (εἶ, in the sense that the letter *D* may be designated by the name "dee" in English), could have any of the meanings of that combination of letters in Greek. In fact, several words consist of these two letters and are more or less distinguished one from another by accents and other diacritics. As εἰ, *epsilon* could mean "if"—an appropriate dedication here, either as an opener for oracular inquiries (people ask "if" they should do this or that) or as symbolic of the power of the syllogism ("if" *x*, then *y*). It could also point to the inquirer's desire: " 'If' only . . ." But accented differently, εἶ is the second-person singular of the verb "to be," meaning "you are" or "you exist."

This last is the interpretation that Ammonios privileges, so it stands at the top of the hermeneutic hierarchy of the dialogue, though without entirely displacing the others. It is half of an exchange, Ammonios claims, the other half of which is the famous Delphic maxim "Know yourself" (*gnothi sauton* 392a). In effect, the god says to the inquirer approaching the temple,

"Know yourself" (in your ephemeral, mortal being, radically divorced from the unity and eternity of the divine and of truth), to which the inquirer replies with an acknowledgment: "You exist" (i.e., you have being in Plato's sense, eternal and unchanging, whereas we are only becoming, only fragmented creatures with a beginning and an end). What Plutarch's Ammonios does not go on to point out—perhaps because it is self-evident—is that this exchange is strikingly relevant both to the ontology and to the hermeneutics of oracular inquiry and response. The priests never interpret. They accept the inquiries (which may well be the wrong questions or questions asked in the wrong way, for lack of essential knowledge on the part of the seekers), they submit them to the transcendent intelligence accessible through the prophetess, and they deliver the response, Zeus's response, mediated by Apollo and articulated by the prophetess. What comes back is a text, and as the story of human folly so dear to Herodotus reiterates, the inquirer is very likely to get it wrong, to do the wrong thing on the basis of the hard-won text—to fail, in other words, as an interpreter. The ritual exchange into which Ammonios inserts the E is the limit of the god's hermeneutic assistance to the inquirer. Apollo is saying: You had better know who *you* are (and the relationship to my being of your becoming) or else you will never manage to fit my answer to your question.

The *E at Delphi* begins, then, as a hermeneutic dilemma, with the dialogue form providing the perfect vehicle for the juxtaposition of competing interpretations, and develops into a pretext for Ammonios to deliver a short lecture on being and becoming. The remaining Delphic dialogues address more general issues regarding the Delphic shrine and prophecy in general, but each likewise ends up with a colorful meditation on an aspect or aspects of Platonic metaphysics.

The order of the dialogues in the modern editions is uniform but rather arbitrary. Robert Flacelière argued influentially a generation ago that *The Delphic Oracles Not Now Given in Verse* must be the last. It makes mention both of the "recent" eruption of Vesuvius in 79 C.E. ("Oracles" 398e) and of a recent benefactor of the Delphic shrine (409b–c), whose name has disappeared into a lacuna in the text. Flacelière argued that this must be the same Hadrian whose statue Plutarch erected near the end of his own life. He may have been correct, but the evidence is not compelling. Flacelière's argument for placing this essay at the very end of Plutarch's career rests further on the observation that *The Disappearance of Oracles* remains aporetic on the nature of oracular communication, whereas the other essay seems more conclusive—Plutarch's last thoughts on the matter, perhaps. My own inclination is to believe that Plutarch was as evasive, tentative, and respectful of the limits of knowledge at the end of his life as he had been throughout it. Some matters do allow conclusions to be reached: the Delphic responses, couched in human language and specifically in Greek, are in a medium that belongs to the priestess, not to the god. *The Disappearance of Oracles* addresses much larger issues, where certainty is more elusive.

Not the least of the problems that surround the essay *The Delphic Oracles Not Now Given in Verse* is that the title—and hence the central issue of the dialogue—is misleading. It is certainly possible that at the dramatic date of the dialogue (whenever, between 79 and 120, we may imagine that to be) the oracular shrine offered only prose responses, but responses of the traditional sort, in hexameter verse, are nevertheless well documented for Plutarch's time and later, and not simply in literature, where we must suspect tampering or manipulation, but in inscriptions, which are far more likely to accurately represent the responses as they were returned to their cities by the delegates sent to Delphi. In fact, the Pythia's most ambitious recorded effort, as believable as any other literary oracle, was a fifty-one-verse hymn on the fate of the soul of the Neoplatonist Plotinus, who died a century and a half after Plutarch. (This oracle is certainly a fabrication, but one that based on the assumption that, in 270 C.E., an oracle of Apollo ought to speak in hexameters.) These facts call seriously into question the nature and thrust of Plutarch's dialogue.

The dialogue has a minimal frame: an otherwise unmentioned and presumably fictional Basilocles asks Philinos, a well-attested friend of Plutarch's, to repeat to him a conversation that has just ended. Philocles agrees and re-creates a guided visit to the shrine just carried out for the benefit of a visiting philosopher, Diogenianus of Pergamon. Aside from Philinos himself and some professional guides, the party included Sarapion, the poet to whom *The E at Delphi* is addressed, as well as a mocking Epicurean named Boethos (who thinks prophecy is bunk and any apparent accuracy a matter of pure chance) and a character named Theon, who emerges as the principal interpreter of Delphic matters and the principal defender of the oracular shrine against the general skepticism of Boethos, as well as the specific doubts that trouble Diogenianus regarding responses delivered either in bad verse or in prose. This Theon both is and is not Plutarch. He is as much of Plutarch as the author will let us glimpse in this context. Characters with this name occur in the *Table Talk,* dining and conversing with Plutarch (626e, 728f), and in *The Face in the Moon* (where Plutarch is absent), *The E at Delphi,* and *Epicurus Actually Makes a Pleasant Life Impossible,* where Theon is one of those who have listened to and now discuss Plutarch's lecture "Against Colotes." There are several other references to this or other Theons as well. All of this, combined with Plutarch's own observation (*Roman Questions* 30, 271e) that "Dion and Theon" are names of convenience used in philosophical formulations (i.e., "Tom and Dick") leaves us here face to face with Plutarch's thickest and least penetrable disguise, a figure deliberately situated on the margins of identity: a dissolving mask.

Philinos's account of a distinguished visitor's experience of the Delphic shrine around 100 C.E. begins with the professional guides (*periegetai*) who would present the site to an ordinary visitor. It is not clear just why Diogenianus, who has more expert and specialized guidance at his disposal, is initially in their hands. Philinos, Sarapion, and even Theon apparently have to wait until the guides are through, however impatient they may be with their reading the inscriptions through aloud and delivering their speeches. The inscriptions, however, are a nice touch. This passage is unique in making explicit the fact that inscriptions on sites such as the Delphic shrine were performance pieces for guides, and we must imagine much of their ancient readership experiencing them in this way.

After a sotto voce digression within the little group on the qualities of Delphic air, Diogenianus observes (apropos of a guide's reading of a verse response from an inscription) that he has often been amazed at the terrible, second-rate poetry that is the vehicle of the oracles: "We can see that most of the oracles are full of defects in meter and diction and poetically incompetent" ("Oracles" 396d). This, then, is the initial formulation of the problem, and Theon cuts through distracting comments by Sarapion and Boethos to formulate a solution: the voice of the response, including sound, diction, and meter, is no more the god's than the handwriting would be if the Pythia wrote the responses rather than speaking them. The god places mental images (*phantasiai*) in her head, a "light directed toward the future," but from there on, the medium is human, not divine (397c). Diogenianus's rejoinder (taking his cue from Theon) shifts the question in the direction that the title anticipates: "There isn't one of us who is not looking for an explanation of how it is that the oracular shrine has stopped using epic verse and meter" (397d).

Diogenianus has to wait quite a while for an answer, in deference again to the guides. As the party climbs along the sacred way, past monument after monument, Boethos mocks prophecy and invokes chance while Sarapion and Theon defend providential prophecy. Amid general and sarcastic disapproval of the infamous golden statue of the prostitute Phryne, displayed "among generals and kings," Theon does indeed sound like the subversive and semi-submerged moralist of the *Lives:*

> You seem to me to want to drive from the shrine a wretched woman who made disgraceful use of her body, while you see the god and his temple surrounded by the firstfruits and tithes of murders and wars and plunder. . . . Praxiteles [should be praised] for putting a golden prostitute up next to those golden kings and throwing in the face of the rich the fact that what they have is nothing wonderful or deserving of reverence. ("Oracles" 401c–d)

That is, it is the *big* crooks, who laundered the spoils of their rapacious brutalities by putting up dedicatory monuments at Delphi, who bring shame to the shrine, not the sculptor who added a portrait of his girlfriend.

But Diogenianus is not troubled by any of this so much as by the question that he keeps insisting on, which is for him "the major obstacle to faith in the oracle" ("Oracles" 402b): the abandonment of poetic form seems to show either that the prophetess no longer gets close to the god or that the spirit has died, the power departed.

Theon's resolution of Diogenianus's misgivings about the replacement of poetry by prose in the oracular responses is delivered in a lecture filling the final third of the dialogue. He begins with a corrective, more nuanced account of the relation of prose to verse in the history of the oracle. There were always prose oracles, he says—even the confirmation that Lycurgus sought of the validity of his constitution was delivered in prose ("Oracles" 403e)—and there are still oracles delivered in verse, however rarely. The issue has already been resolved in any case, and the lecture consists of elaborations and new metaphors developing Theon's earlier description of the nature of inspiration and its relation to the medium of the prophetess's language ("Oracles" 397c). What is envisioned is a series of analogous relationships, constructed from the bottom up: the body uses tools, the soul uses the body, and the god uses the soul (404b). Each medium aspires to transparency. The tools do the best they can to translate the craftsman's design into an object. The body does the best it can to express the intention of the soul, which in turn transmits the intention of the god, but each medium fails in a necessary way, and at each new level the medium generates an artifact whose relation to its antecedent is both intimate and remote.

At this point ("Oracles" 404d–e), Theon puts on the table a sentence he attributes to Heraclitus (fr. 93 DK) and assumes to be generally familiar: "The lord whose oracle is in Delphi neither speaks nor conceals, but gives signs (*semainei*)." It is no exaggeration to say that semiotics, in the tradition of European thought, starts here, with this notorious, sententious claim, and were it not for this passage of Plutarch's, this Heraclitus fragment would be unknown. Indeed, without the passage we would have little or no evidence for articulated, analytic concern with signs, signification, and meaning among the pre-Socratics. These are matters that come into their own in Greek thought with the Stoa and then again in later Platonism, a development to which Plutarch provides the essential background. What Plutarch delivers seems to be in Heraclitus's own words, but it is nevertheless predigested. What Heraclitus was getting at remains obscure, but what Plutarch is using his words to say is quite clear. Heraclitus, according to Plutarch, used the verb *semaino*, "indicate by signs," to designate the action of Apollo through the prophetess (or perhaps more properly, through her utterances). The ontological hierarchy that Plutarch projects onto this sentence can hardly have anything to do with Heraclitus, and is steeped in Platonism, but to Plutarch's mind, if Heraclitus pointed to a tertium quid for the pair "speak—conceal," he must have meant the projection of meaning down the hierarchy, with the attendant necessary distortion introduced by the medium. Apollo "signs," and the prophetess "speaks." She is his tool, but he is not implicated (although his meaning may be expressed) by her utterance.

Much of what remains is a meditation on history, and one that strikes an uncharacteristically positive note. The past—along with the priestesses of the past—was more poetic than the present. Similarly, love was more poetically expressed in the past, but we do not say that love has changed ("Oracles" 406a), and as was pointed out earlier, philosophy over time has also made the transition from the poetic medium of the early pre-Socratics to prose. These changes all favor clarity (*to saphes, sapheneia* 496e–f). We have seen that the sententious obfuscation of archaic philosophers—and Pythagoreans in particular—was not to Plutarch's taste. If he approves of it (e.g., in *Numa*), it is justified as a legitimating pose, a means of impressing and imposing on the public. The change in oracular style is an escape from this deliberate obscurantism. The allegories (*hyponoiai*) and ambiguities (*amphilogiai*, 407e) that the priestesses used to indulge in were necessary in part because the consultations were about important matters, and the responses had to be encoded so only the inquirer would understand them (407d –e). This resulted in misinterpretations (408a).

The conclusion of the dialogue is the paean of praise for the Pax Romana evoked above (Chapter 1). These days, people generally come to ask modest, personal questions, but at least they receive clear answers ("Oracles" 408f), and the shrine, along with the rest of the world, has entered a period of renewed prosperity. The responses given now are not imposing, and so they provoke skepticism in people like Diogenianus, but the very prosperity of the shrine is testimony to their accuracy. Prose for a prosaic world, but one that has peace, unlike in the past, and so can be said to have been transformed "for the better" (*pros to beltion*, 406b).

The Disappearance of Oracles, like the dialogue just discussed, is about prophecy and history—or, better, history and prophecy—but the resemblance does not go much further than that. In overall orientation, the two are in fact so fundamentally at odds that they might be compared to Plutarch's paired rhetorical exercises that support opposite theses. Where *The Delphic Oracles Not Now Given in Verse* reaches an optimistic conclusion, celebrating the present and the Delphic shrine's new prosperity with its new mode of prophecy, *The Disappearance of Oracles* explores the decline and disappearance of oracles in a shrinking world.

Plutarch's moment in history was viewed retrospectively by the Christian West as one of transition and decay. With Christian self-satisfaction removed, the view is nicely summed up in a phrase from a letter of Flaubert's (cited in Marguerite Yourcenar's notebooks for *Hadrian's Memoirs*): "When the gods were no more and Christ did not yet exist, between Cicero and Marcus Aurelius, [there was] a unique moment when man alone existed."

One would not have any trouble finding abundant support for this picture of dying gods (or demons) in Christian writers from the late second century to Augustine's time and beyond.

What is amazing, though, is to find Plutarch, a traditional polytheist, offering primary evidence generations earlier. Platonists
like Plutarch genuinely understood the world to be a living,
ensouled entity inhabited or visited by complex hierarchies of
other ensouled beings, ranging from plants to gods. The gods—
manifest as the hypercosmic bodies and phenomena—are the
only immortals. All the rest will have an end. *The Disappearance
of Oracles* is haunted by the sublime sense of loss inherent in the
spectacle of the aging and the anticipated death of that complex
living being.

The dialogue is also fascinating for its mix of information
and of methodologies, ranging (in our terms) from the scientific
to the religious. Plutarch both does and does not respect that
distinction, a fact that is even more evident in *The Face in the
Moon*. He emerges, once again, as a pluralist in ways that make
it difficult for us to take him seriously. Driven by the sheer
pleasure of intellectual work and discourse, he embraces every
mode of explanation and rejects none. The positive gains are
few, but some modest conclusions can be reached. Much more,
however, is left suspended in uncertainty, and the long, rather
rambling conversation concludes with the acknowledgment of
that fact.

The frame—which consists simply of the narrator Lamprias's explanatory note to the addressee—quickly establishes the
cosmic scale of the discussion. The occasion of the conversation
is the intersection at Delphi of the trajectories of two travelers,
Demetrius, coming from Britain, and Cleombrotos, coming
from Siwa, in the Libyan desert—like the Delphic eagles coming from the ill-defined ends of the earth to its ambiguous center. The first thing we learn is that Cleombrotos has brought
from the priests of Ammon at Siwa the observation that their
permanent sacred lamp uses less oil every year. They interpret
this to mean that the years are becoming progressively shorter.

Taking off from this (supposed) fact and its interpretation, the discussion turns to disparity of scale in explanation—tiny indicators of events of cosmic scale. Ammonios extrapolates (he is apparently older than in *The E at Delphi* and no longer as dominant in the conversation). If the priests were right, then the consequences not just for the sun but for celestial mechanics would be devastating. To save the phenomena (here, the progressively smaller annual oil measures, which Cleombrotos has actually seen), an answer can and must be sought in the conditions of combustion or in the quality of the oil. This initial exercise in explanation is very much in the tradition of Plato. It will be echoed at the end of the dialogue in the unresolved attempts to mediate between Ammonios's explanation of the disappearance of oracles as an expression of divine will and Lamprias's explanation in terms of the fluctuations of terrestrial exhalations that stimulate a capacity for prophecy that is innate in the soul.

On the whole, Cleombrotos seems to have accepted the Egyptian priests' conclusion that time is shrinking, but he cannot sustain this position against Ammonios's objections. This complicates the problem of interpreting his deliberate silence when asked by Lamprias whether the Oracle of Siwa is "wasting away" ("Disappearance" 411e). His silence is filled, in any case, by Demetrius, who supplies a long list of local—mainly Boeotian—oracles that have been silenced since the classical period (411e–412d). This list in turn leads into the discussion—continued in the Lesche (or clubhouse) of the Cnidians at the upper end of the Delphic sanctuary—of the meaning of the failure of oracular shrines.

At this point, some others have joined the group, and the first attempt to explain the phenomenon takes the form of a harangue from a Cynic named Didymus, who chalks it all up to human wickedness, which has caused the providence of the gods to withdraw from mankind. In its violence and simplistic moralizing, Didymus's speech is a re-creation of a type of Cynic discourse familiar in Plutarch's world and often parodied (e.g., Lucian *Peregrinus* 4–6). Not unlike the violent Thrasymachus in the first book of Plato's *Republic,* Didymus seems to represent an irreconcilable position that can be neither incorporated into the analysis of the problem nor entirely ignored. Like Thrasymachus again, he hits a nerve when he proposes changing the question to "why this oracle as well has not refused to function" ("Disappearance" 413a), a matter clearly not on the table for debate. Lamprias's rather gentle rebuttal—the badness of mankind is constant, and if anything, there was more of it in the larger populations of the past; therefore badness cannot explain the decline of prophecy (413c–d)—is sufficient to make the Cynic stalk out in high dudgeon.

Lamprias's rebuttal contains the first mention in the dialogue of a decline in population—yet another aspect of this shrinking, dying cosmos. The passage where Ammonios takes up that theme and turns it into a sufficient explanation for the decline of oracles is often cited as social history. He claims that "now" the whole of Greece could produce only three thousand footsoldiers, the number that Megara alone sent to Plataea in 479 B.C.E. ("Disappearance" 414a). Avoidance of excess is essential to Ammonios's notion of the divine (413f): a diminished population needs fewer oracles, and therefore the god provides fewer. Delphi once had two alternating prophetesses as well as one in reserve, but now one is quite sufficient (414b–c). Lamprias, however, refuses to take seriously the notion of a divine efficiency expert downsizing the oracle delivery system. The divine by its nature creates and gives. Nature (i.e., the necessary condition of being in the world) causes decay and destruction. The god, however, never wills the cessation of an oracle (414d). There is an implicit competition here between Lamprias and Ammonios, and it is Lamprias, with his optimism about the gods combined with pessimism about nature and natural decay, who sounds more like a Platonist in the style of Plutarch.

The issue seems to be settled, then, that the decline in population is related to the decline in number of functional oracular shrines. The difference remaining has to do with the role of divine will and/or nature in the actual failure of the oracles. Cleombrotos steps into the breach with the most Platonic of solutions: oracles are controlled not by gods (at least directly), nor by exhalations or other functions of the natural world (*physis*), but by mediating *daimones*, the bridge between mortality and immortality, between human ignorance and divine knowledge ("Disappearance" 415a).

This entire section of the dialogue, dominated by Cleombrotos (414f–421e), is built on evidence that is poetic or mythic. In other words, we are in the same realm of discourse as in Plato's *Timaeus*, where the subject is the creation of the universe, a realm where the goal is the "most plausible" or "likely" account and where certainty will not be reached. Cleombrotos is explicit about this: we must try to "proceed in our opinions to the most probable" ("Disappearance" 418f). A further, less Platonic limit is set to this theological speculation. Cleombrotos opens his lecture with the ancient evidence, which shows "that there exist entities occupying, so to speak, the border area between gods and men, susceptible to mortal emotions and to the changes brought about by necessity, entities it is correct for us to revere according to ancestral custom and to designate and call *daimones*" ("Disappearance" 416c).

The deliberately vague phrase "changes brought about by necessity" designates in the broadest terms what everything in the world of nature (*physis*) experiences, culminating in decay and death. This is precisely the point that will not go down with one of the listeners. Heracleon accepts as plausible and theologically acceptable the notion that it is these intermediaries who speak through prophets and prophetesses in the oracular shrines: "But to take by the handful out of the verses of Empedocles crimes and violent acts and divinely imposed wanderings and attribute these to the *daimones*, and to postulate that they meet their end in death as humans do—this seems to me too bold (*thrasuteron*) and too barbarous (*barbarikoteron*)" ("Disappearance" 418e).

Theological correctness, then, is a matter of tradition, specifically, of Hellenism. There is a body of texts complemented by a history of interpretation that can be distilled into correct theology. Plutarch at this point seems considerably more optimistic than Plato had been.

Cleombrotos does not have much trouble disposing of Heracleon's objection. He has already invoked a beautiful (and otherwise unknown) passage from Hesiod to the effect that the Naiad nymphs, though extremely long-lived, eventually die ("Disappearance" 415c). Now, in his support and in response to Heracleon, another speaker calls to witness the father of a respected rhetor, the teacher of some of those present. This mediated first-person account (by one Epitherses) is among the most characteristically Plutarchan of myths:

> [Epitherses] told the story that once he got on board a ship for Italy, packed with cargo and passengers. In the evening, among the Echinades Islands, the wind dropped, and the ship drifted toward the island of Paxi. Most of the passengers were still awake, and some were still drinking after-dinner wine. Suddenly a voice was heard coming from Paxi, someone shouting for Thamous, and everyone was both amazed and confused. This Thamous was the Egyptian pilot of the ship, and not many of the passengers knew him by name. He did not respond to the first two

calls, but the third time he answered, and the other shouted still louder and said: "When you reach Palodes, report that the great Pan is dead." When they heard this, as Epitherses reported, they were all astounded and discussed whether it was better to carry out the order or not to get involved and just let it be. Thamous decided that if there was a breeze when they passed the island of Palodes, he would just sail by and keep quiet, but if they were becalmed on a flat sea, he would repeat what the voice had said to him. When they arrived and there was no wind or wave, Thamous climbed up on the elevated stern of the boat and spoke the words he had heard, in the direction of the shore: "Great Pan is dead." Before he could finish, a great sighing groan was heard, composed of many voices and full of wonder. There were many witnesses to this, and the story spread quickly in Rome. Tiberius Caesar sent for Thamous and was so convinced by his story that he had an inquiry undertaken concerning Pan. The numerous literary scholars he employed reached the conclusion that this must be Pan the son of Hermes and Penelope. [This odd genealogy is confirmed by Herodotus.] ("Disappearance" 419b–d)

The story is known to some of the others present, presumably by way of their teacher, Epitherses' son. Demetrius has a further story, gathered during his recent travels in Britain, of the deaths of *daimones*. The locals there attribute atmospheric disturbances to "the death of one of the greater ones" ("Disappearance" 419e–f). Plutarch has a better use in store for the best part of this story, however: the prophetic, sleeping Kronos attended by *daimones* on an island at the end of the world will return in *The Face in the Moon* (941a–f).

There is no need for us to follow this long and digressive

dialogue through in detail to its aporetic end. Cleombrotos reports his conversations with an Arabian prophetic sage, who confirmed and elaborated a great deal of demonic lore ("Disappearance" 421a–e). The lore made some odd claims about the plurality of worlds, a subject that takes hold of the conversation (421f–431a). When the speakers return to the metaphysical hierarchy of souls, *daimones*, and gods, Lamprias has the opportunity to expand on his exhalation theory, locating the agency of prophecy in exhalations from the Earth (Gaia, Apollo's predecessor at Delphi, according to the myth), which act on a natural capacity in souls—now equated with embodied *daimones*—analogous to memory but directed toward the future. We are back to Lamprias's original differences with Ammonios and to a problem of causality that will not admit of resolution.

The Disappearance of Oracles, like the other dialogues, is best understood as a protreptic piece, seducing the reader or listener into a predisposition to delve deeper into philosophy, particularly speculation about metaphysics and psychology. With its vertiginous scale and unforgettable myth, it responds to the demands we have seen Plutarch make on literature that will serve the young as a propaedeutic to philosophy, incorporating "ideas about souls mixed up with mythology."

A brief look at two more dialogues, still more ambitious, will indicate how he further implemented this program.

The Face in the Moon

If the dialogue particularly suited Plutarch because it clothes philosophy in the imaginatively engaging trappings of drama, the genre also offered him the opportunity to juxtapose incompatible modes of explanation without sacrificing one to the other. Nowhere is this aspect of his cultivation of the dialogue more apparent than in *The Face in the Moon*. The subject before the speakers is stated in the title, and although they proceed with characteristically Plutarchan circumambulation, they do in fact address it repeatedly and insistently. Starting from the question of why we see what looks like a face on the lunar disk—our "Old Man in the Moon," although the Greeks apparently saw a girl's face—they go on to the larger question of which this forms a part: What *is* the moon? What is it made of, and what keeps it up there in the sky? The striking thing about the answers offered is that they are so nearly equally divided between what we might call science ("Face" 920–938) and exotic, metaphysical mythmaking ("Face" 938–943).

The opening of the dialogue seems to be mutilated. There is no indication of where the discussion is taking place, and we are given even less of an account of the interlocutors than we might expect from Plutarch. Particularly elusive is the "I" of the dialogue, who will turn out much later ("Face" 937d) to be not Plutarch himself but his brother Lamprias. The loss of the opening sentences—perhaps more—leaves us unable to say whether this is another instance of authorial hide-and-seek like the one played out in *The Disappearance of Oracles*. The opening as we have it immediately directs our attention forward to Sulla the Carthaginian's "story" (*mythos*), the most elaborate and ambitious of Plutarch's myths, which will clearly be the explicit payoff of the conversation. In other words, the "scientific" portion of the dialogue is bracketed between Sulla's promise of more imaginatively and esthetically rewarding fare and its delivery much later. (Also missing here is some account of the "stranger," who, we find out belatedly at 942b, was Sulla's source for the fabulous tale.)

The narrative cultivates the tension between rational or scientific explanation on the one hand and sublime storytelling on the other, and out of that tension emerges the richest presentation we have of Plutarch's teleological Platonist cosmology. The myth will take over and prevail, but once again, nothing is lost. There are many ways of apprehending the world and giving an account of it.

The "scientific" portion is a recapitulation, orchestrated by Lamprias, of an earlier conversation, itself apparently dominated by a figure designated only as "our friend" (*hetairos*). Many readers of the dialogue have claimed to see Plutarch himself lurking behind the anonymity of this distanced, mediated persona. The slippage between ill-defined past and featureless present is constant and serves to throw into relief the arguments themselves (or reports of arguments). The positions of various schools are crystallized around speakers who act as their spokesmen—including an Aristotelian curiously labeled simply "Aristotle" and a Stoic with the exotic Persian (or Pontic) name Pharnaces.

The initial accounts rejected out of hand include a subjectivist one (the "face" is an artifact of glare and our weak vision) as well as a simplistic hypothesis contradicted by the phenomena (the moon is a mirror, the image the reflection of the terrestrial continent with its internal sea and surrounding ocean). This discussion provides a bridge from the issue of the face to the broader one of the nature and substance of the moon. The arguments raised and refuted or endorsed by Lamprias are complex in their claims, sometimes easily shown to lack logical coherence but more often simply inaccessible to any available mode of testing or refutation. As we saw in Chapter 1, Lamprias's principal target is the formulation attributed to the Stoa ("Face" 921f) that the moon is a mixture of congealed mist and soft fire, maintained in its position by ineluctable laws that draw heavier, solid bodies down to an earth that attracts them by virtue of its centrality in the universe.

Lamprias dismantles this supposed web of necessity piece

by piece ("Face" 924–925), exposing absurd consequences even of some cosmological principles that he apparently embraces (e.g., the sphericity of the earth, 924a–c). His rhetoric becomes vertiginous as he dismisses the notion that an infinite universe has, in any meaningful sense, a center (925e–926b), claiming that such a center would in any case be "an immaterial point," which by the Stoics' own account could not act or exert force on material things. The orderly Stoic system, intolerant of anomaly, is shown to crumble when confronted by the task of explaining the phenomena. The Stoics have got it backwards. They assert the existence of divine providence (*pronoia*, 927a), but their claims that everything is as and where it is "according to nature" (*kata physin*) leave no room for that providence to be active. They should realize that the rational and beneficial order imposed by divine mind (*to kata logon*) is prior to the merely "natural." Lamprias deconstructs the notion of nature, along with "natural order, position, or motion" (927d), quickly filling the void with teleology: "Rather, it is when each component makes its contribution usefully and appropriately to that whole for whose sake it has come into existence and in terms of which it develops or is shaped, and when each by its action, reaction, and disposition contributes to the preservation, beauty, or capacities of that whole—that is precisely when it seems to have its "natural" place, motion, and disposition" ("Face" 927e).

What follows is an exemplary elaboration of the microcosm / macrocosm analogy so dear to Plutarch and other Platonists. Look at man: the fire in his eyes is not up there "naturally," nor that in his guts situated below "unnaturally." "Rather, each is located where it is appropriate and useful" (927f; cf. the discussion in Chapter 1). The same is true of the living organism that is the *kosmos*, where benevolent reason (*to kata logon*) determines that everything is where it is "because that is the better way" (928b). That is why the solid moon is suspended in the ether between the solid earth and the sun: there is no better place for it to be.

At this point, Lucius takes over to relate how "our friend" explained the relation of the sun's light to the moon, conceding that the issue of the nature and motion of the other celestial bodies is a separate one, from which the problem of the moon can fruitfully be isolated. Throughout this "scientific" discussion the moon again and again turns out to be a tertium quid, belonging neither to this world nor to the more durable and remote realm of the stars. It will be no surprise to see this role transformed in the myth into one of mediation between the unchanging superlunary realm and this sublunary sphere of coming-to-be and passing away. For the present, though, it is enough to show that the moon's phases and eclipses mark it as a solid, earthy thing ("Face" 930–933). The Stoics are still not ready to give in, and they try to turn this discussion to their advantage (933f) and reassert the fiery nature of the moon, but Lamprias gets the final word, coming full circle back to the relation of the moon's light to the visual ray emitted by the eye. The moon *does* reflect the sun's light to us, but that light has become featureless, like a reflection in milk rather than water— whether because of the nature of the reflective surface or the nature of the visual ray is a question left unresolved.

Lamprias now demands Sulla's *mythos* ("Face" 937c), but the telling of it is again deferred when Theon interjects the question of the habitability of the moon. Lamprias's reply focuses on Theon's false corollary that an uninhabitable moon would be a useless thing, infertile and incapable of supporting human life, and in no sense an "earth" (937d–e). Even such a moon, Lamprias asserts, could mediate between the fiery sun and stars on the one hand and the earth on the other. In any case, we must remain agnostic concerning the habitability of the moon. We have sufficiently established that it is earthy, not

fiery—and to deny that it could support life, based on our imperfect knowledge, would be to fail to acknowledge the amazing diversity of life forms and habitable environments right
here on earth (940b–c). When Lamprias invokes the sublime
perspectives of Homeric cosmology to reinforce the notion that
the earth might well appear a Hades or a Tartaros from a lunar
perspective, Sulla the Carthaginian intervenes to lay claim to
this mode of explanation of lunar phenomena (940f). The transition is carefully orchestrated. The "scientific" discussion has
in any case been larded with poetic citations and arguments
invoking the poets. This last one carries the dialogue into a new
realm, as mediated analytical discourse yields to mediated poetic fiction.

The heart of this fiction, as we shall see, is a discourse on
the nature of the moon that Sulla reports as the teaching of a
"stranger / foreigner" (*ksenos*), a devotee of Kronos whom he
met in Carthage. The tale that grounds and validates the
stranger's claim to privileged knowledge is unforgettable. It is
a story set in a fabulous geography of the limits of the world
and an account of oracular mediation as beautiful as any in the
corpus of Plutarch.

The stranger told Sulla of a population of Greeks, wor-
shipers of Heracles and of Kronos, who live at the limits of the
world, somewhere in the vicinity of Britain. The text is lacunose, and much is unclear, perhaps by design. Is the stranger
one of those Greeks, or was he a stranger among them as well—
as later among the Carthaginians? He joined them, in any case,
in an astrologically regulated thirty-year expedition to an oracular shrine in a faraway archipelago associated with Ortygia
(Calypso's island in the *Odyssey*), five thousand stades (more
than five hundred miles) from the mainland, across a "congealed" sea. The goal of the delegation is an island where
Kronos sleeps deep in a golden cave—this is how Zeus keeps

his superseded but immortal father out of mischief—attended
by various unidentified *daimones*. The members of the delegation, themselves "servants of Kronos," converse with these oracular *daimones* and study philosophy for the duration of their
thirty-year vocation, most (unlike the stranger) choosing to remain on the island when the time is up. The crowning motif in
this sublime conceit is the source of the deepest insights of the
oracular *daimones:* they tap and report the dreams of the sleeping Kronos, which in turn are visions of the content of the mind
of Zeus ("Face" 942a).

   This is why, Sulla tells Lamprias and the others, they should
take seriously the story he is about to retell: its source is those
remote servants of Kronos who report the content of his dreams.
What remains of the dialogue (942c–945d) is the stranger's account of the moon. The gist of it has already been summarized in
Chapter 1: the moon mediates between life and death, between
the sublunary realm of birth and decay and the eternal heavens
with their "visible gods." This mediation is obscurely communi-
cated in the story of Demeter and Persephone, the former presiding over the "first death," when bodies are left behind to
decay into the earth, while Persephone receives the souls, still
united to mind, into the lunar realm, where the stories about the
fate of souls in Hades in fact have their origin. Some souls are
excluded, others punished. Some return to earth intact as *daimones* to preside over oracular and other shrines. The ultimate
fate of all the purified dead is nevertheless the same: they leave
behind their souls to decay into moon-stuff and ascend as pure
mind to union with the sun, into which they are absorbed. There
are variants on this scenario. When souls from the lunar realm,
already devoid of mind and reason, occasionally escape back to
earth and take control of bodies, they become monsters like the
Tityus and Typhoeus of myth (945b). The moon can ultimately
absorb even these violent spirits, however, and becomes in turn

the source of souls for new earthly bodies when the sun provides a spark of mind.

Viewed in this perspective, the three Fates represent the
three phases of birth, initiated in the sun by Atropos. Klotho in
the lunar realm adds soul to the mind sent by Atropos, and on
earth, Lachesis seals the union of spirit and (previously inanimate) matter.

> The inanimate is feeble and acted upon from outside,
> whereas mind is free of outside influence and self-deter-
> mining—but soul is a mixed, intermediate thing, like the
> moon, which the god brought into being as a mixture and
> compound of things from above and things from below,
> and moon is to sun as earth is to moon. ("Face" 945c–d)

Socrates' Sign

The Face in the Moon is an extreme instance of Plutarch's
determined program to have his cake and eat it, too. As the
metaphor implies, he spends a great deal of time savoring his
subject, slicing it up in different ways and nibbling at it. The
frosting is the myth, reveling in the pure pleasure of discourse,
where the imagination asserts its rights alongside (and, finally,
at the expense of) rational, analytical discourse.

We have seen how Plutarch weaves his seductive discourse around matters of theology and physics. In perhaps his
most ambitious single work, the dialogue *Socrates' Sign*, he
presents the reader with a yet more complex and eclectic inter-
weaving of philosophy with myth and with history.

Plutarch's other dialogues (*The Symposium of the Seven
Sages* and *Gryllus* aside) are set in his own era and represent his
own intellectual and social world (albeit idealized), his relatives
and friends, and sometimes himself. In *Socrates' Sign*, Plutarch

turns back in time to the source of his genre, the dialogues of
Plato, and writes as a belated Socratic. The dramatic date of the
dialogue, 379 B.C.E., falls twenty years after the death of Socrates—a characteristically ingenious Plutarchan variation on Plato's own distancing of his dialogues. Twenty years after their
teacher's death, Socrates' students are seen still trying to figure
out what he meant when he spoke of a spirit or sign—a *daimonion*—that warned him when he was in danger of doing
something he should not (Plato, *Apology* 40a). There is no question now of asking Socrates—although he, unlike the poets
whose inspired but uncomprehended utterances are evoked in
the *Ion* and *Republic*, could presumably have supplied a reasoned, rational answer to such a request. Leaving no mode of
apprehension (and its failure) untapped, however, Plutarch
does incorporate direct interrogation into his fiction: Simmias,
the Theban Pythagorean whom Plutarch borrows from Plato's
Phaedo, did in fact put the question to Socrates, over twenty
years ago, only to be met with silence (*Socrates' Sign* 588c). So
now, older and convalescent, Simmias and others who knew or
knew of Socrates can only try to reconstruct what his answer to
that question might have been, had he chosen to give one. That
the dramatic date of the dialogue is nearly a half millennium in
the past, from Plutarch's perspective, is also significant. Plutarch's dialogue takes on qualities of a historical novel that
marks its distance from its models.

The question of the nature of Socrates' *daimonion* was one
whose time had arrived. In an age when demonology was of
intellectual and literary interest, we have treatments of the
same subject from two more philosopher-rhetors of Plutarch's
stamp —Maximus of Tyre and Apuleius—within a generation
or so of Plutarch's death. Plutarch's version, however, mixing
praise of famous Thebans with the dramatized inquiry (itself a
pretext for unlawful and conspiratorial assembly) is unique. He

narrated the same historical moment—the liberation of Thebes from an occupying Spartan garrison in December 379—rather differently in *Pelopidas*, and no doubt in the lost *Epaminondas* as well, but here, dramatized and elaborated with a myth in the manner of Heraclides, these events provide the vivid and heroic context for the inquiry. The result is, admittedly, something of a two-ring circus, with history and the present repeatedly impinging on philosophy and the interrogation of the past.

Socrates' *Sign* is a dialogue framed within a dialogue, much like its principal model, Plato's *Phaedo*. The framing narrative is set in Athens, presumably in the house of the pre-Boeotian Archedamos (*Socrates' Sign* 575d), where a group of prominent Athenians provide the audience for a narrative of recent events in Thebes, delivered by a Theban ambassador named Caphisias, said to be a brother of Epaminondas but otherwise unknown. What this audience wants to hear about is, presumably, the events themselves, although Archedamos insists that they will relish "the specifics" (*ta kath'hekasta*, 575c), and Caphisias warns them from the start that an account of both the deeds and the discussions (*prakseis kai logoi*, 575e) will not be short.

Why, indeed, juxtapose these disparate sorts of information at all? We have seen Plutarch the educator, philosopher, and scholar repeatedly singing the praises of the active life, and we have noticed the tension between that commitment and the life he in fact led. In this unique dialogue, Plutarch comes as close as he ever does to confronting that paradox. History invades and interrupts philosophy as deliberately and discordantly as farce invades opera seria in Strauss's *Ariadne auf Naxos*—the esthetic gain lies in the outrageousness of the juxtaposition, in the sheer daring of forcing the two genres into the same space. But there is something more. The assembled Athenian aristocrats who listen, with patient fascination with detail, to this mix of history and ideas mirror the Theban aristocrats, assembled in Simmias's house a few weeks or months earlier, on the evening of the coup. Collectively, these groups—simultaneously men of action and intellectuals—represent a genuine Plutarchan ideal. The world in which they are the ones in control, who steer their cities on paths mapped out by philosophy, is one that by Plutarch's standards is a well-ordered world. That it finds its richest expression in a relentlessly literary and self-referential dialogue retrojected half a millennium into the past is a strong indication of Plutarch's relation to his own historical present and to that ideal.

Even if the events leading up to that evening in December 379 were familiar to Caphisias's audience, they are unlikely to be known to Plutarch's modern readers. The ancient sources, aside from Plutarch himself, are Xenophon (a contemporary) and Cornelius Nepos and Diodorus Siculus centuries later. Archedamos does provide Caphisias (and so the reader) with a general outline of what the Athenians know of recent events in Thebes (*Socrates' Sign* 575f–576b), and Caphisias's account contains a few references to the background of the situation on the night he re-creates for his listeners. Briefly, in the aftermath of the Peloponnesian War, the Thebans joined Argos and Corinth, all disillusioned Spartan allies, and along with the Athenians went to war against Sparta. This is known as the Corinthian War (395–386 B.C.E.), and in its aftermath the victorious Spartans burdened their fractious onetime ally with an occupying Spartan garrison and a pro-Spartan oligarchy (in 382). Many prominent Thebans went into exile, some of them to Athens. In December 379, on the day Caphisias describes, a conspiracy of some thirty Thebans (*Socrates' Sign* 586c), along with the returning exiles, killed the oligarchs and some of their associates. Then Epaminondas, who had refused to participate in the killing of the oligarchs because they were fellow citizens, led a victorious army to drive the garrison from the citadel. It was eight years later that the same Epaminondas defeated a Spartan army at Leuctra (371) and effectively put an end to Spartan military dominance in Greece.

Within the dialogue, Epaminondas is the figure who comes closest to uniting the threads of philosophy and military-political action. His refusal to kill countrymen without trial—even quislings—is three times at issue, first when Caphisias defends his brother's position (*Socrates' Sign* 576d–577a), later, implicitly, when Epaminondas himself holds forth in Socratic fashion on the subject of profiting from injustice (585b–d), and finally when the crisis is at hand (594b–c). But for the most part, the philosopher-conspirators talk of matters remote from the present situation while events draw them into the thick of history.

As if the plot were not sufficiently cluttered, much of Caphisias's narrative concerns a Pythagorean from Italy named Theanor, who has chosen this particular day to arrive in Thebes to collect the bones of a Pythagorean teacher named Lysis and to offer Epaminondas money to compensate for the costs of Lysis's support during his old age. It is the report of this stranger's arrival and incubation at Lysis's grave in search of a divine sign that ushers in the issue of Socrates' *daimonion*. Galaxidoros, an admirer of Socrates, reacts to the news of the incubation with a tirade against superstition (*deisidaimonia*) and pompous obscurantism (*typhos*, 579f). When accused of lending credence to the charges of impiety that the Athenians brought against Socrates, he responds with a eulogy that says a great deal about Socrates' position in the history of philosophy:

> [Socrates did not dismiss] the truly divine, but philosophy as it came to him from Pythagoras and his followers was full of phantoms and fables and superstitions, and Empedocles in particular had left it babbling ecstatically. Socrates taught philosophy wisdom in the face of the facts and

taught it to go after the truth with sober reason. (*Socrates'*
Sign 580c)

Galaxidoros's portrait of Socrates the rationalist is vulnerable on one point, the *daimonion*. Theocritos—described as a
"seer" (*mantis*) both here (595f) and in *Pelopidas* 22 and portrayed below as a dubious, if correct, dream interpreter—jumps
on this, calling on first-person reminiscences. Theocritos was
present one day when the sign stopped Socrates in his tracks,
and those present who foolishly went on ahead were met by a
herd of pigs that left them covered with mud and excrement
(*borboros*, 580f). This starts the debate, and Galaxidoros coun-
ters that the "sign" had no supernatural power, but, like an
ominous sneeze, allowed Socrates to arbitrarily resolve equally
balanced dilemmas. Polymnis, the father of Epaminondas and
Caphisias, intervenes with the claim (supported by second-
hand anecdote) that Socrates' *daimonion* was, in fact, a sneeze—
that it was sneezes that Socrates took as warnings and guides—
but Polymnis himself is reluctant to give credence to the story,
because Socrates is said often to have proved prescient. Further,
why would the unpretentious, straightforward Socrates indulge in the pompous theatricality of calling a sneeze a *daimonion*? Simmias, whose firsthand knowledge of Socrates should
throw light on the issue, is about to speak when Epaminondas
and the Italian Pythagorean enter, and the topic is dropped
(582c–d).

Meanwhile, tension is growing in the tangled plot of the
conspiracy. There is fear of exposure. Alarmed by an ominous
dream, one Hippostheneidas has taken it upon himself to send
a messenger to the exiles nearby on Mt. Cithaeron to warn them
to delay their return (586c). This report of a rash action that
threatened the success of the coup will turn out to have been a
false alarm—the messenger never set out because his wife had

lent out an essential part of his harness (587f). It is at this point that Theocritos jumps in to counter Hippostheneidas's interpretation of his own dream and turn it into a divine promise of victory. Predictive dreams, it seems, are at best ambiguous, like sneezes.

Caphisias and Theocritos are at last able to join in the discussion of the sign, although they arrive too late to hear Simmias's response to Galaxidoros (*Socrates' Sign* 588b). It is at this point that we learn of Socrates' refusal to answer Simmias on the matter, along with Simmias's testimony that Socrates considered claims to have *seen* divine beings false and outrageous, but took reports of divine *voices* seriously (588c). Simmias goes on to elaborate a theory of telepathic communication—transmission of thought freed not only from the organs of speech but from grammar itself—from divinities to exceptionally receptive humans (588d–589f)—and presents this as the Socratics' own understanding of Socrates' *daimonion* when Socrates was still alive.

This is as close as we will get to a privileged solution to the principal question that gives the dialogue its title, but Simmias doubles that solution with a "story" (*mythos*, 589f, 592f), explicitly its complement: "first the reasoned account, then the story" (592f). He coyly allows Theocritos to coax him into telling it: "Even if it is not the most exact way, still myth has its way of getting at the truth" (589f).

Timarchos, Simmias explains, was a young Socratic who predeceased Socrates. This fictional young man from Chaeronea (*Socrates' Sign* 589f), whose name is modeled on and echoes that of Plutarch himself, is one of this author's oddest disguises. Mimicking Chaerophon's trip to Delphi to ask about Socrates' wisdom (*Apology* 21a), young Timarchos went to the oracle of Trophonios at Lebadeia to ask about his *daimonion*.

On this bizarre Boeotian oracle—Timarchos (or Ploutar-

chos) would have had to travel less than an hour from home to
reach it—we have little beyond this wonderful account, supplemented by that of Pausanias, perhaps fifty years later. Pausanias, whose narrative is hardly less fabulous than Plutarch's
myth, insists that he writes from personal experience, having
himself consulted the oracle (Pausanias 9.39.14). Despite some
naive or rash claims in the literature, the shrine itself continues
to elude archaeologists. Plutarch's "story" of Timarchos's visit
to the oracle has already been cited and paraphrased at length
in Chapter 1. It is the most disorienting and vertiginous of Plutarch's soul-myths and perhaps the best example of a rhetorical
mode we might call the Plutarchan sublime.

Timarchos, once he has entered the subterranean shrine
and embarked on his hallucinatory journey of discovery, un-
derstandably seems to forget the question he came to ask and,
in response to the disembodied voice that greets him, can only
say that he wants to find out about "everything" (591a). He gets
his answer anyway, spontaneous and unsummoned. The *daimones* are the little flames of mind-stuff of his vision, the rational or higher soul that is part of—or attached to—each of us.
We either drag them down into the abyss of matter—the Styx—
or they raise us up to the moon and beyond, out of the cycle of
generation. The significant difference among humans is one of
sensitivity—degree of docility in the hands of our little bit of
mind-stuff. Although Socrates is not mentioned, we are left to
conclude that he was one of the exceptionally receptive, the
exceptionally docile.

The answer to the dialogue's question has been distanced
from any possible human apprehension in multiple ways: by
deliberate silence, by death, and by history. This does not prevent its being formulated in a variety of rhetorics, from the
ironic (Galaxidoros and the sneeze) to psychological (Socrates
used his intellect) to the theological (the intellect itself is di-

vine). It is Theanor the Pythagorean who speaks up when Simmias has finished his story. Theanor calls attention to the silence
of Epaminondas, as if to defer to him (as a student of Lysis and
fellow Pythagorean), but that silence remains unbroken. Un-
daunted, Theanor picks up the theological rhetoric of the myth
and delivers a stream of inflated, groundless, soteriological
bombast that exemplifies everything Galaxidoros said earlier
about the damage that Pythagoras had done to philosophy.
This is met by a wonderfully bathetic silence and a return to the
world of action. Epaminondas says nothing in response to Theanor, but turns to his brother, the narrator, and says, "It's about
time for you to go and join your friends in the gymnasium"
(*Socrates' Sign* 594a).

Socrates, *daimones,* and souls receive no further mention.
Caphisias narrates the comings and goings of the conspirators—who begin in the palaestra by exchanging information
and plans as they wrestle, one after the other, with different
partners. The gymnasium joins the philosophical *thiasos* in the
list of aristocratic institutions that lend themselves to conspiracy and political action. The plot is executed, the oligarchs
killed, the garrison removed.

Once again, with a different emphasis and in a different
genre, Plutarch's concern has proven to be the interaction of
character, intellect, chance, and history. Intellectually, the dialogue concerns itself with foreknowledge and with the nature
of judgment. History, as it impinges on the discussion, is rid-
dled with signs, true and false, and their interpreters, as well as
plans that go awry and plans that succeed. The difference is
something as liminal as a sneeze, or as imponderable as divine
providence.

IV PLUTARCH'S READERS

PLUTARCH'S SEDUCTIVE RHETORIC WON HIM A SUCCESS THAT
was immediate and enduring. From his own time to the present, he has had a decisive impact on the European tradition's
perception of its Greek and Roman antecedents. This popularity is responsible in large part for the remarkable state of
preservation of the corpus of his writings—and that in turn
makes his work the major window we have into the changing
intellectual world of the Roman empire. Themes that surface
for the first time as literary subjects in Plutarch come to have an
unexpected afterlife—as with Socrates' *daimonion,* just discussed in Chapter 3. Several other subjects that are prominent in
Plutarch but difficult to find in earlier authors likewise anticipate the later empire's obsession with souls and their fate,
along with *daimones* and other disembodied spirits. Philosophical vegetarianism and animal rights ("Land or Sea Animals")
are examples. Other emerging themes, including the hermeneutics of not only myth and cult but also literary texts—along
with larger issues of pedagogy—make Plutarch a critically important figure in documenting the emergence of the characteristic concerns that mark the literature of the later empire.

Few of the late-antique authors whom Plutarch influenced,
explicitly or implicitly, are widely read today, but they included
both polytheists and, in increasing numbers, Christians. It will
come as no surprise that an important channel for the influence
of Plutarch was the schools of rhetoric. He provided a rich mine

of exempla, and the works transmitted in the corpus that consist of unconnected collections of anecdotes and sayings (*Sayings of Spartans, Bravery of Women,* and so forth) may well have
had their origin in the schools that exploited that mine. Canon-
ization in the schools was the principal factor in the survival of
ancient authors, and there is a peculiar symmetry in the ancient
and modern reception of Plutarch from this point of view. The
Lives have always been the principal Plutarchan textbooks, and
this is reflected no less in their richer manuscript tradition than
in their availability today in inexpensive paperbacks, chopped
up into anthologies covering specific periods in the history of
Greece and Rome. Those paperbacks are destined for and sustained by the lucrative textbook market. The "Dryden" translation, comfortably in the public domain, is parceled out as fare
for ancient history courses. The reasons are not unlike the ones
that created for the same texts a niche in the ancient schools of
rhetoric: the narratives are vivid (if often historically uncritical),
the characters bigger than life. They sustain interest where Diodorus Siculus—or even Livy, for all his own rhetorical color—
does not. The units are short and do not require an exceptional
attention span.

The history of Plutarch's readers from the ancient schools
of rhetoric to the modern classroom is a forbiddingly large subject. It has not been surveyed as a whole since the First World
War, but in the decades since Rudolf Hirzel's *Plutarch* (Leipzig,
1912)—a general description of Plutarch that devotes three-
fifths of its bulk to the reception of the corpus—Plutarch's influence has been the subject of numerous narrower studies, each
exploring and detailing the specific impact of Plutarch's writing
in a given period in a given literature. There are few periods
where his influence cannot be found, although the absence of
Latin translations before the Renaissance rendered the corpus
largely inaccessible to the Latin West during the millennium

that followed the decline of Greek in Italy in the fifth century. When Plutarch did return to western Europe, however, he returned in style. Only Aristotle and Plato, among writers of Greek prose, were better represented in the collections of manuscripts in the Italian libraries of the fifteenth century. By 1450, there were at least fifty separate Latin translations of individual biographies, and a complete Latin *Parallel Lives* existed twenty years later. The essays were slower to appear in Latin, but among the earliest was *The Education of Children*, translated in 1411. Clearly it was Plutarch the educator who first attracted interest, after the biographer. The *Lives* could be read in Italian a scant decade after the first complete Latin translation appeared, but it was Jacques Amyot's translation of the entire corpus into French (*Lives* 1559, *Moralia* 1572) that brought Plutarch to a wide European vernacular audience, and Amyot lies in the background of the first English translation of the *Lives*, Thomas North's, which followed his own by twenty years (1579).

More important even than the translation history of the Plutarchan corpus is the prominent role of the text itself in the humanistic education of the Renaissance. From the first hellenizing schools in the fifteenth century to the widespread Jesuit schools of the sixteenth, Plutarch was among the first Greek prose authors studied, along with Isocrates, Plato, and Demosthenes. The lowest common denominator here, once again, is rhetoric, and Plutarch is present for the same reason he was dear to the schools of rhetoric of the later empire.

There is abundant praise of Plutarch in Renaissance authors, but eulogy in general is not a fruitful source of information about what was valued in an author by the eulogist. We may well wonder whether the Plutarch read in the humanist schools was appreciated for any of the values that this book has brought into relief. For the properly rhetorical qualities, there is no doubt, and he was certainly appreciated for the exempla that

could be recycled into new texts—it is striking that some of the
collections of sayings were among the items from the *Moralia*
that received early vernacular translations. But what about the
rambling, self-contradicting Plutarch? The Plutarch who is all
too likely to inspire in the frustrated reader the conviction that
this is the most fatuous of authors? At least one reader recorded
his admiration for these very qualities, and it will not come as a
surprise that this was Montaigne, the single Renaissance vernacular author who most warmly embraced Plutarch's mode of
writing and, to a considerable extent, his view of the world.

The passage is not in every edition of Montaigne, but it is in
some of the earliest, from his own lifetime, and how it was
eventually dropped from Montaigne's text is unclear. It is a
precious document, not only for Montaigne's own appreciation
of Plutarch but for its surprising evidence that qualities so infu-
riating to many modern readers were both intellectually and
esthetically rewarding for sixteenth-century readers. Montaigne's "Apologie de Raimond Sebond" (*Essais* II, ch. 12) is the
touchstone text for the skeptical Montaigne, the Montaigne
whose motto was "Que sais-je?" Its explicit message is the one
we have seen dramatized again and again in Plutarch, the
frailty of human knowledge, the abyss that separates us from
the truth. A natural corollary of this profound sense of alienation from certainty is a mistrust of dogmatism, and Montaigne's
essay is largely directed against the arrogance of intellect that
proclaims its success in bridging the abyss. The passage in
question is in praise of the inquiring, as opposed to the dogmatic, style:

> In whom can this be seen more clearly than in our Plu-
> tarch? How variously does he discourse on the same topic?
> How many times does he present us with two or three
> contradictory explanations of the same subject, along with

a variety of causes, without making a choice and telling us which we must embrace? (*Essais*, ed. P. Villey and V. L. Saulnier [Paris: PUF, 1965], p. 509 n. 15)

Shakespeare, Montaigne's younger contemporary, read Plutarch (in North's translation), and many echoes have been detected in the plays—and especially in *Antony and Cleopatra* and *Julius Caesar*. Shakespeare, one suspects, would have had little patience for the qualities of Plutarch's style praised by Montaigne. What he taps is the sharp image, the telling detail. Plutarch is pervasively rhetorical, and to be rhetorical is to be theatrical. Shakespeare's rhetoric owed much to Plutarch's (or at least to North's, through which Amyot's expansive French can often be seen). Still, it is no surprise that what Shakespeare does with Plutarch emerges utterly transformed. Plutarch (*Antony* 4) gives us an Antony who deliberately associated himself with his "ancestor" Heracles, and Shakespeare repeatedly exploits the motif of the "Herculean Roman" (*Antony and Cleopatra* 1, 3, 82). Plutarch tells us that Antony was endowed with "a not ignoble beard" (*pogon tis ouk agennes*). North elaborates: "He had a goodly thick beard." And Shakespeare has Enobarbus observe,

> By Jupiter,
> Were I the wearer of Antonius' beard,
> I would not shave't today. (2, 2, 4–6)

The eighteenth century saw the beginnings of a reaction against the anecdotal and uncritical Plutarch, especially among historians. Voltaire had little use for his dithering. But in others he still inspired respect. The most inclusive edition ever of the relatively neglected *Moralia* was completed, with voluminous annotation, by Daniel Wyttenbach in the first years of the nineteenth century. In France, a scholar-translator named E. Clavier,

hot on Wyttenbach's trail, contributed to a revised and ex-
panded reprint of Amyot (1801–1805), incorporating the ad-
vances of Wyttenbach's text and translating for the first time
some pseudepigrapha first published there in association with
the corpus. In one of Clavier's prefaces (vol. 23 [1804]) he la-
ments the intervention of history, which has slowed down his
scholarly work. Had he not been so busy serving as a judge in a
revolutionary tribunal, his Plutarch might have appeared more
quickly. Plutarch might not have approved of his translator's
politics, but he would have applauded his simultaneous engagement with scholarship and with the great events of his
time.

Nineteenth-century historians largely discredited Plutarch
as a historical source. This loss of prestige was reflected in the
scholarly industry that was grounded in the postulate that
plodding Plutarch must, in each biography, have been making
use of some single preexisting account of his subject—a principal source he simply excerpted and reshaped as the skeleton of
his narrative. Scholarly success was equated with identifying
that source (and convincing others that you had done so). Like
numerous other scholarly industries, this one was crushed under its own weight and its inability to build a persuasive account of the matter at hand.

It would be a mistake, however, to represent the nineteenth century as uniformly hostile to Plutarch. He had a significant place in the classical canon of the New England Transcen-
dentalists, thanks in large part to the admiration of Emerson.
There was an extraordinary level of interest in Platonism in
mid-nineteenth century America. Emerson, again, was the
principal leader of this movement, but for all his praise of Plato,
he may well have known the text of Plutarch more intimately,
and his Platonism was of Plutarch's stamp. Here was a reader
who was not content with savoring the rhetoric of the *Lives*,

even if he was unable to read them "without a tingling in the blood" ("Uses of Great Men," in Emerson, *Collected Works*, ed. R. E. Spiller [1971], vol. 4, p. 9). He found Plutarch's inquiring intellect, his passion for hermeneutics, for deciphering the message beyond the phenomena, entirely congenial. Emerson had none of the scruples of the professional historians, none of the condescension of the scholars. In fact, his very egocentrism links him to the author he so appreciated:

> The whole value of history, of biography, is to increase my self-trust, by demonstrating what man can be and do. This is the moral of [Plutarch]. ("Literary Ethics," in *Collected Works*, vol. 4, p. 102)

What about our own time? Well, the scholarly industries are thriving, though now on a basis of greater respect for Plutarch the writer and a more sympathetic, less reductive reading of his text. Editions (often bilingual) and commentaries on individual lives appear annually in all the scholarly languages, although lately the Italians seem to be generating them faster than anyone else. Many of the essays in the *Moralia* have received similar treatment since the mid-twentieth century. But who *reads* Plutarch? The scholars, of course, but frankly we don't count for much. We can pick away at well-known problems and perhaps even open up some new ones, savor the qualities of Plutarch's style, and read papers to each other: audiences of the converted. Plutarch has a remarkable number of readers of this sort, and although the cost may be disproportionate to the gain, we do manage, little by little, to advance the world's sum of knowledge and understanding of this enormously influential and oddly attractive author. But his real readership, the one that counts, is right where it was in antiquity and in the Renaissance. The core readership is in university classrooms, where students read Plutarch's *Nicias* and *Alci-*

biades and his *Themistocles* and his *Pericles* as a supplement to—
for many, doubtless, a substitute for—Herodotus and Thucydides. The professors in those classrooms know what they are
doing when they assign Plutarch: they know the difference between Plutarch and history and do their best to communicate
that difference to their students. For all Plutarch's idiosyncra-
sies, though, he remains the most palatable—no, the most en-
joyable—of all the ancient writers on the history of Greece and
Rome and the principal actors in that history. He focused the
fascination of the literati of the Renaissance on Cleopatra, and
he continues to exert a similar power today. His rhetoric, for all
its artificiality, paradoxically breathes into those ancient lives a
new energy, illuminates them with a bright and engaging light.

APPENDIX 1: THE WORKS OF PLUTARCH

I HAVE LISTED HERE ALL THE SURVIVING WORKS OF PLUTARCH (AND A few of the lost works, where relevant), as well as entrenched pseudepigrapha. The list should serve as a guide to the corpus and, more specifically, to the Loeb Classical Library bilingual edition of the *Lives* (11 vols.), and particularly the *Moralia* (15 vols. in 16). The list of the *Parallel Lives* provides a convenient tabular overview of the project in all its idiosyncracy.

I. The Parallel Lives

Plutarch provides some characteristically tantalizing scraps of information about the order in which some of the twenty-three pairs of *Parallel Lives* were written, but we have no basis on which to reconstruct the arrangement that he would have given to the completed set. The order of modern editions has generally been based on the historical sequence of the Greek subjects, and the Loeb edition, followed here, applies that principle as systematically as possible. Included with the *Parallel Lives* are the unpaired *Aratus* and *Artaxerxes,* as well as *Galba* and *Otho* from the otherwise lost sequence of biographies of Roman emperors. Pairs marked with an asterisk (*) lack a *Comparison.* The one known lost pair is bracketed, as are the lost emperors' *Lives.* Numbers in parentheses indicate the position of the pair in the sequence of composition, where known. Longer names are abbreviated as indicated for purposes of references in this book.

Theseus (Thes.)	and	Romulus (Rom.)
Lycurgus (Lyc.)	and	Numa
Solon	and	Publicola (Pub.)
*Themistocles (Them.)	and	*Camillus (Cam.)

Aristides (Arist.)	and	Cato the Elder (Cato Maj.)	
Cimon	and	Lucullus (Luc.)	
Pericles (Per.)	and	Fabius Maximus (Fab.)	(10th)
Nicias (Nic.)	and	Crassus (Cras.)	
Alcibiades (Alc.)	and	Coriolanus (Cor.)	
Lysander (Lys.)	and	Sulla	
Agesilaus (Ages.)	and	Pompey (Pom.)	
[Epaminondas	and	Scipio	(1st)]
Pelopidas (Pel.)	and	Marcellus (Mar.)	
Dion	and	Brutus (Brut.)	(12th)
Timoleon (Tim.)	and	Aemilius Paulus (Aem.)	
Demosthenes (Dem.)	and	Cicero (Cic.)	(5th)
*Alexander (Alex.)	and	*Julius Caesar (Caes.)	
Sertorius (Sert.)	and	Eumenes (Eum.)	
*Phocion (Phoc.)	and	*Cato the Younger (Cato Min.)	
Demetrius (Demetr.)	and	Antony (Ant.)	
*Pyrrhus (Pyr.)	and	*Gaius Marius (Mar.)	
Agis and Cleomenes (Ag. & Cl.)	and	*Tiberius Gracchus and Gaius Gracchus (Grac.)	
Philopoemen (Phil.)	and	Flamininus (Flam.)	

[Augustus, Tiberius, Claudius, Nero, Gaius, Vitellius]
Aratus (Arat.)
Artaxerxes (Arta.)
Galba
Otho

II. The Moralia

The *Moralia* are listed in the order of the first comprehensive edition (Wyttenbach, 1800–1830). Wyttenbach's order follows the nearly complete Frankfurt edition of 1599, the pagination of which provides the basis for the system of reference in general use, here indicated after the full English title. That edition in turn followed the order established by Stephanus in his edition of 1572. The Loeb *Moralia* follows Wyttenbach's closely, but the Budé (in progress) divides the essays differently and so diverges in numeration. This list gives first the number in Wyttenbach's sequence, then the number in Planudes' fourteenth-century collection, preceded by P, and that in the Lamprias catalogue, preceded by L (with either, "om." = "omits"), then any short title used in this book, followed by the full English title used here, then by the Greek and finally by the Latin titles by which they are commonly cited. The Greek titles are fairly consistent in manuscripts and printed editions (although there is no reason to assume they are Plutarch's), the Latin less so. The Latin titles used here are in general those adopted for the Loeb edition; in some instances I have substituted shorter (and I think more widely used) traditional titles. I have added a brief indication of the nature of each of the items. Bracketed items are widely believed not to be by Plutarch.

LOEB VOLUME 1

[1 (P2, L om.) ("Education") *The Education of Children* 1A–14C (Περὶ παίδων ἀγωγῆς, *De liberis educandis*)]
  Wide-ranging essay on education, praised by Montaigne and Rousseau, but probably not to be attributed to Plutarch.

2 (P6, L103) ("Poetry") *How the Young Should Listen to Poetry* 14D–37B (Πῶς δεῖ τὸν νέον ποιημάτων ἀκούειν, *De audiendis poetis*)
  Essay on the usefulness and role of poetry in education, where Plutarch draws significantly on Stoic precedents (the same title is attributed to Chrysippus) to justify the study of poetry and elaborate a pedagogic hermeneutics.

3 (P15, L102) ("Listening") *Listening to Lectures* 37C–48D (Περὶ τοῦ ἀκούειν, *De audiendo*)
  Lecture (*schole*) presented in written form to a young man who had just taken up the *toga virilis* (i.e., who was fifteen to eighteen years old), concerning his future education.

4 (P7, L99) ("Flatterers") *How to Tell a Flatterer from a Friend* 48E–74E (Πῶς ἄν τις διακρίνειε τὸν κόλακα τοῦ φίλου, *De adulatore et amico*)
  Essay on flatterers and on frank criticism (*parrhesia*) and the relationship between the philosopher and the rich and powerful people whom it is his role to advise.

5 (P3, L87) ("Progress") *How Progress in Virtue Might be Perceived* 75A–

86A (Πῶς ἄν τις αἴσθοιτο ἑαυτοῦ προκόπτοντος ἐπ᾽ ἀρετῇ, *De profec-tibus in virtute*)
Essay directed against the Stoic position that virtue or excellence (*arete*) is the exclusive possession of the wise man (*sophos*) and that it is attained, if at all, by a sudden transition, not by gradual progress.

LOEB VOLUME 2

6 (P5, L130) ("Enemies") *How to Profit by Your Enemies* 86B–92F (Πῶς ἄν τις ὑπ᾽ ἐχθρῶν ὠφελοῖτο, *De capienda ex inimicis utilitate*)
Essay on the profit to be gleaned both from deriding your enemies and from being derided by them.
7 (P16, L om.) *Too Many Friends* 93A–97B (Περὶ πολυφιλίας, *De amicorum multitudine*)
Essay on avoiding having an excessive number of friends at the expense of true friendship.
8 (P18, L om.) *Chance* 97C–100A (Περὶ τύχης, *De fortuna*)
Brief, fragmentary essay, rhetorical in character, on chance or fortune.
9 (P1, L om.) *Virtue and Vice* 100B–101E (Περὶ ἀρετῆς καὶ κακίας, *De virtute et vitio*)
Brief essay in praise of excellence or virtue (*arete*) as the foundation of the successful life (*eudaimonia*).
10 (P22, L om.) *Consolation to Apollonius* 101F–122A (Παραμυθητικὸς πρὸς Ἀπολλώνιον, *Consolatio ad Apollonium*)
Letter of consolation on the death of a son. Authenticity doubtful.
11 (P29, L94) *Advice About Health* 122B–137E (Ὑγιεινὰ παραγγέλματα, *De tuenda sanitate praecepta*)
Dialogue on preserving health through diet and exercise, demonstrating Plutarch's considerable interest in medicine.
12 (P34, L115) *Advice on Marriage* 138A–146A (Γαμικὰ παραγγέλματα, *Praecepta coniugalia*)
Essay in the form of a letter to a newlywed couple. The genre is well represented in the early Christian literature, but this piece provides a unique polytheist background.
13 (P31, L110) *Symposium of the Seven Sages* 146B–164D (Τῶν ἑπτὰ σοφῶν συμπόσιον, *Septem sapientium convivium*)
Historical dialogue, rich in anachronisms, assembling the "Seven

Sages," the forerunners of philosophy, along with other characters, at a banquet arranged at Lechaion, one of the ports of Corinth, by Periander. Authenticity has been doubted.

14 (P21, L155) *Superstition* 164E–171F (Περὶ δεισιδαιμονίας, *De superstitione*)

Essay, rather rhetorical, describing the terrible effects of "god fearing" (*deisidaimonia*), which is compared to atheism and found to be more destructive.

LOEB VOLUME 3

15 (P59, L108) *Sayings of Kings and Commanders* 172A–208A (᾽Αποφθέγματα βασιλέων καὶ στρατηγῶν, *Regum et imperatorum apophthegmata*)

Compare 16, 18. Collection of anecdotes containing *dicta* (apophthegms) of rulers and generals, many of which also occur scattered through the *Lives*. Addressed to Trajan, although the dedication may well be a forgery. The latter part (194E–208A) is isolated under the title "Sayings of Romans." As with the other collections, this may or may not have been assembled by Plutarch.

16 (P60[a], L169) *Sayings of Spartans* 208A–236E (᾽Αποφθέγματα Λακωνικά, *Apophthegmata Laconica*)

Compare 15, 18. Collection of anecdotes centered on *dicta* of Spartans.

17 (P60[b], L om.) *Spartan Customs* 236F–240B (Τὰ παλαιὰ τῶν Λακεδαιμονίων ἐπιτηδεύματα, *Instituta Laconica*)

Compilation of Spartan customs, many of which are also mentioned in the *Life of Lycurgus*. Authenticity questioned.

18 (P60[c], L om.) *Sayings of Spartan Women* 240C–242D (Λακαινῶν ἀποφθέγματα, *Lacaenarum apophthegmata*)

Compare 15, 16. Many of these occur elsewhere in the corpus as well.

19 (P33, L126) *Bravery of Women* 242E–263C (Γυναικῶν ἀρεταί, *Mulierum virtutes*)

Collection of stories about admirable women, presented to Clea, the addressee of *Isis and Osiris* (27).

LOEB VOLUME 4

20 (P62[a], L138) *Roman Questions* 263D–291C (Αἴτια 'Ρωμαϊκά, *Quaestiones Romanae*)
Compare 21. Collection of 113 questions regarding Roman customs, with discussion. Often the material occurs in the Roman biographies as well.

21 (P62[b], L166) *Greek Questions* 291D–304F (Αἴτια 'Ελληνικά, *Quaestiones graecae*)
Compare 20. Collection of 69 questions regarding Greek customs, with discussion.

[22 (P61, L128) *Greek and Roman Parallel Stories* 305A–316B (Συναγωγή ἱστοριῶν παραλλήλων 'Ελληνικῶν καὶ 'Ρωμαϊκῶν, *Parallela Graeca et Romana*)]
Juxtaposed stories from ancient history. On stylistic grounds, clearly not the work of Plutarch.

23 (P56, L175) *The Fortune of the Romans* 316C–326C (Περὶ τῆς 'Ρωμαίων τύχης, *De fortuna Romanorum*)
Rhetorical essay on the role of *tuche / fortuna* in the success of Rome.

24 (P57a, L176) *The Fortune of Alexander, 1* 326D–333C (Περὶ τῆς 'Αλεξάνδρου τύχης ἢ ἀρετῆς, λόγος α΄, *De Alexandri fortuna aut virtute i*)
Compare 25. Rhetorical essay on the role of *tuche / fortuna* in the accomplishments of Alexander. This speech has little to say about his "virtue."

25 (P57b, L186) *The Fortune of Alexander, 2* 333D–345B (Περὶ τῆς 'Αλεξάνδρου τύχης ἢ ἀρετῆς, λόγος β΄, *De Alexandri fortuna aut virtute ii*)
Compare 24. This speech seems to make the case for his "virtue," with less attributed to good luck.

26 (P27, L197) *The Fame of the Athenians* 345C–351B (Πότερον 'Αθηναῖοι κατὰ πόλεμον ἢ κατὰ σοφίαν ἐνδοξότεροι, *De gloria Atheniensium*)
Rhetorical piece supporting the thesis that the fame of the Athenians rested more on their military than on their intellectual accomplishments.

LOEB VOLUME 5

27 (P32, L118) *Isis and Osiris* 351C–384C (Περὶ Ἴσιδος καὶ Ὀσίριδος, *De Iside et Osiride*)
Essay addressed to Clea (see 19). Analysis of the Egyptian myth and related lore. Along with Herodotus, book 2, and Manetho, among the most important Greek sources for Egyptology.

28 (P68, L117) ("E") *The E at Delphi* 384D–394C (Περὶ τοῦ ΕΙ τοῦ ἐν Δελφοῖς, *De E Delphico*)
Dialogue placing the young Plutarch and his teacher Ammonios at Delphi, where they and others discuss the meaning of the *E* (*epsilon*) that was a prominent dedication to Pythian Apollo.

29 (P72, L116) ("Oracles") *The Delphic Oracles Not Now Given in Verse* 394D–409D (Περὶ τοῦ μὴ χρᾶν ἔμμετρα νῦν τὴν Πυθίαν, *De Pythiae oraculis*)
Dialogue on the Delphic oracle, taking as its point of departure the (supposed) fact that in Plutarch's time the oracles were delivered exclusively in prose and not, as earlier, in verse.

30 (P69, L88) ("Disappearance") *The Disappearance of Oracles* 409E–438D (Περὶ τῶν ἐκλελοιπότων χρηστηρίων, *De defectu oraculorum*)
Dialogue on the reasons why oracular shrines cease to function.

LOEB VOLUME 6

31 (P55, L180) *Can Virtue Be Taught?* 439A–440C (Εἰ διδακτὸν ἡ ἀρετή, *An virtus doceri possit*)
Fragmentary, rhetorical essay, maintaining that the realized life (*eudaimonia*) is attainable through education.

32 (P52, L72) *Moral Virtue* 440D–452D (Περὶ τῆς ἠθικῆς ἀρετῆς, *De virtute morali*)
Essay on psychology and ethics, supporting Platonic and Aristotelian positions against the Stoa.

33 (P9, L om., cf. 90) *The Control of Anger* 452D–464D (Περὶ ἀοργησίας, *De cohibenda ira*)
Dialogue between Plutarch's friends Fundanus and Sulla. The former advises the latter to overcome anger and tells him how.

34 (P11, L95) *Tranquillity of Mind* 464E–477F (Περὶ εὐθυμίας, *De tranquillitate animi*)

Essay in the form of a letter on peace of mind and how it can be achieved.

35 (P13, L98) *Brotherly Love* 478A–492D (Περὶ φιλαδελφίας, *De fraterno amore*)

Essay on the correct relations between brothers.

36 (P46, L om.) *Love of Offspring* 493A–497E (Περὶ τῆς εἰς τὰ ἔκγονα φιλοστοργίας, *De amore prolis*)

Fragmentary, rhetorical essay on love of offspring in animals and humans.

37 (P45, L om.) *Whether Vice Is Sufficient to Cause Failure* 498A–500A (Εἰ αὐτάρκης ἡ κακία πρὸς κακοδαιμονίαν, *An vitiositas ad infelicitatem sufficiat*)

Fragmentary, rhetorical essay. The familiar "luck or virtue" theme of the rhetorical exercises (cf. 23–26), viewed from the opposite perspective.

38 (P19, L208) *Whether the Misfortunes of Soul or Body Are Worse* 500B–502A (Πότερον τὰ τῆς ψυχῆς ἢ τὰ τοῦ σώματος πάθη χείρονα, *Animine an corporis affectiones sint peiores*)

The beginning of a speech, perhaps delivered in Asia (501F), elaborately demonstrating that afflictions of the soul are worse than those of the body.

39 (P14, L92) *Talkativeness* 502B–515A (Περὶ ἀδολεσχίας, *De garrulitate*)

Essay on the vice of garrulousness (which is dangerous, contemptible, and comic all at once [504E–F]) and how to avoid it.

40 (P10, L97) *Curiosity* 515B–523B (Περὶ πολυπραγμοσύνης, *De curiositate*)

Essay on the vice of *polypragmosyne*—more a matter of restless prying and being a busybody than curiosity in general—and its cure.

LOEB VOLUME 7

41 (P17, L211) *Love of Wealth* 523C–528B (Περὶ φιλοπλουτίας, *De cupiditate divitiarum*)

Essay on the vices of misers and prodigals and on the empty show that is the only *eudaimonia* of the rich, that form of a "successful life" finally being compared to the real thing, which comes from philosophy.

42 (P12, L96) *Shame* 528C–536D (Περὶ δυσωπίας, *De vitioso pudore*)

Essay on the vice or rather the passion that allows us to be shamed into granting a request that we would rationally reject, along with advice for avoiding this.

43 (P47, L om.) *Envy and Hate* 536E–538E (Περὶ φθόνου καὶ μίσους, *De invidia et odio*)

Essay juxtaposing envy and hate, of which the former passion is the principal subject.

44 (P8, L85) *Inoffensive Self-Praise* 539A–547F (Περὶ τοῦ ἑαυτὸν ἐπαινεῖν ἀνεπιφθόνως, *De laude ipsius*)

Essay on self-praise, which is inherently offensive but sometimes necessary in public life. How to neutralize the offensiveness.

45 (P4, L91) ("Slowness") *The Slowness of Divine Justice* 548A–568A (Περὶ τῶν ὑπὸ τοῦ θείου βραδέως τιμωρουμένων, *De sera numinis vindicta*)

Dialogue, set at Delphi, in which Plutarch and others discuss the Epicurean objection to the notion of divine providence that points to the slowness of divine retribution. The justice of punishing descendants of the offender is also discussed.

[46 (P37, L om. cf. 58) *Fate* 568B–574F (Περὶ εἱμαρμένης, *De fato*)]

Essay, not by Plutarch and probably by a second-century Platonist, seeking to accommodate notions of fate and providence.

47 (P75, L69) *Socrates' Sign* 575A–598F (Περὶ τοῦ Σωκράτους δαιμονίου, *De genio Socratis*)

Historical dialogue relating events in Thebes in 379 B.C.E., in which discussion of souls, taking Socrates' *daimonion* as point of departure, is carried on while returning exiles under Epaminondas liberate the city from its Spartan garrison.

48 (P24, L101) *Exile* 599A–607F (Περὶ φυγῆς, *De exilio*)

Consolatory essay in the form of a letter to an exile from Sardis.

49 (P23, L112) *Consolation to His Wife* 608A–612B (Παραμυθητικὸς εἰς τὴν γυναῖκα τὴν αὐτοῦ, *Consolatio ad uxorem*)

Consolatory letter on the death of a daughter.

LOEB VOLUMES 8 AND 9

50–58 (P78, L om., cf. 125) *Table Talk* (in 9 books) 612C–748D (Συμποσιακῶν προβλημάτων βιβλία θ΄ , *Quaestionum convivialium libri ix*)

Dinner-table conversations of Plutarch, his family, and friends on a host of subjects.

LOEB VOLUME 9

59 (P70, L107) *Love* 748E–771E ('Ερωτικός, *Amatorius*)
Dialogue recounting an episode at Thespiai and the Valley of the
Muses at Mt. Helicon. A problematic marriage is the occasion for a
discussion of the pros and cons of pederasty and marriage.

LOEB VOLUME 10

60 (P49, L222) *Love Stories* 771E–775E ('Ερωτικαὶ διηγήσεις, *Narrationes
amatoriae*)
Five short stories, perhaps by Plutarch.

61 (P28, L om.) *That Philosophers Ought Especially to Talk to Rulers* 776B–
779C (Περὶ τοῦ ὅτι μάλιστα τοῖς ἡγεμόσι δεῖ τὸν φιλόσοφον διαλέ-
γεσθαι, *Maxime cum principibus philosopho esse disserendum*)
Essay on the importance, for philosophers, of leading an active life
advising the powerful.

62 (P35, L om.) *To an Uneducated Ruler* 779D–782F (Πρὸς ἡγεμόνα ἀπ-
αίδευτον, *Ad principem ineruditum*)
Short essay or speech—the title is misleading—on various matters
relating to political authority.

63 (P30, L75) *Whether an Old Man Should Engage in Public Life* 783B–
797F (Εἰ πρεσβυτέρῳ πολιτευτέον, *An seni sit gerenda res publica*)
Essay in the form of a letter, encouraging Euphanes (otherwise
unknown) to remain active in public life. A few shared anecdotes
and illustrations suggest either dependence on Cicero's *On Old
Age* or a common source.

64 (P58, L104) ("Precepts") *Precepts on Statecraft* 798A–825F (Πολιτικὰ
παραγγέλματα, *Praecepta gerendae reipublicae*)
Essay advising a young man on matters of politics and government.

65 (P48, L om.) *Monarchy, Democracy, and Oligarchy* 826A–827C (Περὶ
μοναρχίας καὶ δημοκρατίας καὶ ὀλιγαρχίας, *De unius in republica
dominatione*)
Fragmentary essay comparing the three "constitutions"—a commonplace subject from the fifth century B.C.E.

66 (P65, L215) *Avoid Borrowing* 827D–832A (Περὶ τοῦ μὴ δεῖν δανεί-
ζεσθαι, *De vitando aere alieno*)
Essay encouraging avoidance of debt.

[67 (P63, L41) *Lives of the Ten Orators* 832B–852E (Βίοι τῶν δέκα ῥητό-ρων, *Decem oratorum vitae*)]
Brief biographies of the ten canonical Attic orators of the fifth and fourth centuries B.C.E. Written in the first or second century, but not by Plutarch.

68 (P41, L121) *Comparison of Aristophanes and Menander* (Summary) 853A–854D (Συγκρίσεως Ἀριστοφάνους καὶ Μενάνδρου Ἐπιτομή, *Comparationis Aristophanis et Menandri Compendium*)
Not the original essay but a fragment of a summary of Plutarch's essay on the subject.

LOEB VOLUME 11

69 (P76, L122) *The Malice of Herodotus* 854E–874C (Περὶ τῆς Ἡροδότου κακοηθείας, *De Herodoti malignitate*)
Essay (or, rather, tirade) directed against Herodotus, who is accused, among other things, of misrepresentation, prejudice (especially against the Boeotians and Corinthians), flattery, and being *philobarbaros*.

[70 (P51, L61, cf. 196, 183) *Opinions of the Philosophers* (in 5 books) 874D–911B (Περὶ τῶν ἀρεσκόντων φιλοσόφοις φυσικῶν δογμάτων βιβλία ε΄, *De placitis philosophorum libri v*)]
Very substantial doxographic work, sometimes attributed to one Aëtius, roughly contemporary with Plutarch (H. Diels, *Doxographi Graeci*). Not by Plutarch, but an important collection for late antiquity and the Arabs. Omitted from the Loeb *Moralia*. See Guy Lachenaud, ed., *Opinions des philosophes* = Plutarque, *Oeuvres morales*, vol. xii, pt. 2 (Paris: Les Belles Lettres [Budé], 1993).

71 (P50, L218) *Natural History Questions* 911C–919D (Αἴτια φυσικά, *Quaestiones naturales*)
Collection of forty-one questions regarding natural phenomena, with discussion.

LOEB VOLUME 12

72 (P71, L73) ("Face") *The Face in the Moon* 920B–945D (Περὶ τοῦ ἐμφαινομένου προσώπου τῷ κύκλῳ τῆς σελήνης, *De facie in orbe lunae*)
Dialogue on the nature of the moon, incorporating cosmology, physics, and ultimately psychology.

73 (P53, L90) *The Principle of Cold* 945F–955C (Περὶ τοῦ πρώτως ψυχροῦ, *De primo frigido*)
Essay on the question of which element is to cold as fire is to heat. Plutarch's solution is that what is "primarily cold" is earth.

[74 (P20, L206) *Is Fire or Water More Useful?* 955D–958E (Περὶ τοῦ πότε-ρον ὕδωρ ἢ πῦρ χρησιμώτερον, *Aqua an ignis utilior sit*)]
Rhetorical exercise, but not by Plutarch (on the basis of prose rhythms, style, and choice of vocabulary).

75 (P67, L147) ("Land or Sea Animals") *Whether Land or Sea Animals Are Cleverer* 959B–985C (Πότερα τῶν ζῴων φρονιμώτερα τὰ χερσαῖα ἢ τὰ ἔνυδρα, *De sollertia animalium*)
Dialogue frame for a formal debate between a boy defending land animals (and hunting) and another defending sea creatures (and fishing).

76 (P64, L om.? cf. L127, L135) *Gryllus; or, The Rationality of Animals* 985D–992E (Περὶ τοῦ τὰ ἄλογα λόγῳ χρῆσθαι, *Bruta ratione uti*)
Dialogue between Odysseus, Circe, and a pig named Gryllus ("Oinker"), who refuses to be re-transformed into a man and expounds at great length on the superiority of other animals to human beings.

77 (P36a, L om.) *Eating Meat, 1* 993A–996C (Περὶ σαρκοφαγίας α', *De esu carnium i*)
Fragmentary essay (lecture) urging vegetarianism as "natural" for man.

78 (P36b, L om.) *Eating Meat, 2* 996D–999B (Περὶ σαρκοφαγίας β', *De esu carnium ii*)
Another fragmentary lecture, paired with 77, where the element of anti-Stoic polemic on this issue is more explicit.

LOEB VOLUME 13, PART 1

79 (P38, L136) *Platonic Questions* 999C–1011F (Πλατωνικὰ ζητήματα, *Quaestiones platonicae*)
Ten problems in Platonic philosophy presented in question-and-answer format.

80 (P77, L65) ("Generation of the Soul") *The Generation of the Soul in the Timaeus* 1012B–1030C (Περὶ τῆς ἐν Τιμαίῳ ψυχογονίας, *De animae procreatione in Timaeo*)
Essay addressed to two of Plutarch's sons on Plato's ideas about

the soul, taking as its point of departure the interpretation of *Timaeus* 35A–B.

81 (P42, L om.) *Summary of "The Generation of the Soul in the Timaeus"* 1030D–1032F (Ἐπιτομὴ τοῦ Περὶ τῆς ἐν Τιμαίῳ ψυχογονίας, *Compendium libri De animae procreatione in Timaeo*)
Paraphrase, largely a copy of four chapters of number 80 (1023B–1025B).

LOEB VOLUME 13, PART 2

82 (P66, L76) *Stoic Self-Contradictions* 1033A–1057C (Περὶ Στωικῶν ἐναντιωμάτων, *De Stoicorum repugnantiis*)
Polemical essay paraphrasing various claims and arguments of the early Stoics and then showing them to be contradictory.

83 (P40, cf. L79) *Summary of "The Stoics Talk More Paradoxically Than the Poets"* 1057D–1058E (Σύνοψις τοῦ "Ότι παραδοξότερα οἱ Στωικοὶ τῶν ποιητῶν λέγουσιν, *Compendium argumenti Stoicos absurdiora poetis dicere*)
Extract from an essay composed of a series of juxtapositions of paradoxical poetic passages and idiosyncratic Stoic notions (which the Stoics themselves called *paradoxa*).

84 (P74, L77) *Common Conceptions* 1058F–1086B (Περὶ τῶν κοινῶν ἐννοιῶν πρὸς τοὺς Στωικούς, *De communibus notitiis adversus Stoicos*)
Dialogue attacking the Stoics' "common conceptions" (which served them as criteria for making truth-judgments) on the grounds that these involve them in contradictions and claims contrary to widely held (and true) beliefs.

LOEB VOLUME 14

85 (P43, L82) ("No Pleasant Life") *Epicurus Actually Makes a Pleasant Life Impossible* 1086C–1107C ("Ότι οὐδὲ ζῆν ἔστιν ἡδέως κατ᾽ Ἐπίκουρον, *Non posse suaviter vivi secundum Epicurum*)
Dialogue criticizing Epicurean notions. The scene is a gymnasium, where Plutarch and some of his audience have gone after his lecture against Epicureanism (essay 86).

86 (P73, L81) ("Against Colotes") *Reply to Colotes in Defense of the Other Philosophers* 1107D–1127D (Πρὸς Κωλώτην ὑπὲρ τῶν ἄλλων φιλοσόφων, *Adversus Colotem*)

Essay (originally a lecture—see number 85) responding to a book by Colotes, a student of Epicurus, entitled *Conformity with the Other Philosophers Actually Makes It Impossible to Live.*

87 (P44, L178) ("Live Unknown") *Is "Live Unknown" a Wise Precept?* 1128A–1130E (Εἰ καλῶς εἴρηται τὸ Λάθε βιώσας, *An recte dictum sit latenter esse vivendum*)
Essay devoted to refuting this Epicurean maxim.

[88 (P39, L om.) *Music* 1131B–1147A (Περὶ μουσικῆς, *De musica*)]
Dialogue, set at a feast during the Saturnalia, on the nature and history of music. Not by Plutarch.

LOEB VOLUME 15: FRAGMENTS
(including the Lamprias Catalogue)

Wyttenbach included five additional works, all of which he declared inauthentic, and all have been explicitly excluded from the Loeb *Moralia* as pseudepigrapha (*see* Sandbach in *Moralia* 15, appendix A, 403–6). Only number 90 was in the Frankfurt edition of 1599 and so has pagination uniform with the essays above.

[89 (P om., L203) *Nobility* (Περὶ εὐγενείας, *De nobilitate*)]
A forged essay, patched together from excerpts in Stobaeus. See Frags. 139–41.

[90 (P om., L om.) *Names of Rivers and Mountains* 1149A–1166C (Περὶ ποταμῶν καὶ ὀρῶν ἐπονυμίας, *De fluviorum et montium nominibus*)]
Wonderful collection of exotic lore about distant rivers and mountains and the gems and fabulous animals found there.

[91 (P 54, L om., but cf. L42, with Frags. 122–27) *The Life and Poetry of Homer* (Περὶ τοῦ βίου καὶ τῆς ποιήσεως Ὁμήρου, *De vita et poesi Homeri* or *De Homero*)]
The most complete surviving ancient introduction to Homer for the first-time reader, influential among Renaissance and early modern readers. See [Plutarch,] *The Essay on the Life and Poetry of Homer,* ed. and trans. J. J. Keaney and R. Lamberton (Atlanta: Scholars Press, 1996).

[92 (P om., L142) *Alexandrian Proverbs* (Παροιμίαι αἷς Ἀλεξανδρεῖς ἐχρῶντο, *Proverbia quibus Alexandrini usi sunt*)]
Collection of proverbs, perhaps deliberately misattributed to Plutarch.

[93 (P om., L om.) *Meters* (Περὶ μέτρων, *De metris*)]
An elementary manual on Greek metrics.

APPENDIX 2:
TRANSLATIONS AND
SELECT BIBLIOGRAPHY

PLUTARCH'S OVERALL MANNER AND HIS ANECDOTES ARE EMINENTLY translatable, but the rhetorical texture of his prose—unquestionably the focus of much of his concern—is not. Recent translations are pedestrian, almost without exception. The earliest English translations, from the sixteenth and seventeenth centuries, belong to an age when formal English prose was shaped by classical (and especially Latin) models, much as classical Latin style was shaped by Greek. This lends to such early efforts as Wyatt's "Quyete of Mynde" an interest that is more than antiquarian. Wyatt's style (or North's, whose 1579 translation of the *Lives*, based on Amyot's French, was Shakespeare's window into Plutarch) is simply more like Plutarch's than any twentieth-century translation could aspire to be, and the fact that much of Wyatt's vocabulary is quaint and even obscure to our ears adds to the effect. Much of Plutarch's own vocabulary must have had such a ring for his own contemporaries, not to mention his readers over time. The most accessible edition of the *Lives* in their entirety represents a compromise between old and new. It is the Modern Library edition of the seventeenth-century translation "by several hands" that generally goes under the name of Dryden, as "freely revised" by Arthur Henry Clough in the 1860s and 1870s: *Plutarch's Lives*, trans. John Dryden (Modern Library, Random House, 1932).

Penguin has for decades kept in print three volumes of translations of *Lives* by Ian Scott-Kilvert under the titles *The Rise and Fall of Athens, The Age of Alexander,* and *The Makers of Rome,* joined more recently by a fourth volume translated by Rex Warner, *The Fall of the Roman Republic.* The plan of these volumes shows clearly that Plutarch's grand scheme is of little interest to modern publishers, as is the very nature of his enterprise. Geographical and chronological selections of biographies are patched together into potted history, or substitutes for history—precisely what Plutarch emphatically tells us he did not set out to write. Of writers in the Western tradition, perhaps only Dante has been so consistently and ruthlessly butchered. Both created sublimely and architectonically idiosyncratic works of literature, built of complementary elements in balance and symmetry, and both are consistently read only in truncated excerpts, the equivalent of the left arm of Polykleitos's Doryphoros (the statue that represents his "canon" of the human form) or a slice of the left wing of Bernini's courtyard at the Vatican. But the Penguin volumes of selections still offer the least expensive access to more than half of the individual lives, and they are widely used on history courses (*pace* Plutarch).

There have been at least two excellent volumes of selections from the *Moralia* in recent years, whereas a decade ago there were no inexpensive editions in print:

> Plutarch, *Selected Essays and Dialogues,* trans. Donald Russell. Oxford World Classics. Oxford University Press, 1993.
> Plutarch, *Essays,* ed. Ian Kidd, trans. Robin Waterfield. Penguin, 1992.

Both contain *Socrates' Sign, Consolation to His Wife,* and *Gryllus,* and each offers as well a generous selection of other material.

For the corpus in its entirety in English, the reader must turn to the Loeb Classical Library, where all the undisputed works and an inevitably arbitrary selection of the doubtful and the clearly inauthentic can be found together, with facing Greek text, in twenty-seven volumes. The *Lives* were published between 1914 and 1926 by Bernadotte Perrin (very likely the only translator of the entire series into English in the twentieth century). The translations remain readable and are certainly careful representations of the facing Greek, but in practical terms they are unlikely to be used except as aids in reading that Greek or as a reading text for those with enough Greek to make at least occasional use of it. The notes are confined to clarification of obscurities that might trouble an informed reader, as well as a few dates and cross-references.

The Loeb *Moralia* is another story (see Appendix 1). The first five volumes were completed by Frank Lloyd Babbitt between 1927 and his death in 1935. These, along with volumes 6 and 10, likewise published in the 1930s, are, as bilingual editions, closely comparable to Perrin's *Lives.* Introductions are brief and unobtrusive, and notes are kept to a minimum. It was twenty years before the series came to life again, in the late 1950s, with contributions by such scholars as Harold Cherniss, Phillip De Lacy, and F. H. Sandbach, who generally offered far richer and more generous introductions and annotation. Cherniss's volumes (volume 12, with William Humbold, and volume 13, in two parts) represent a level of scholarship and commentary unique in the Loeb series. The last four volumes, including Sandbach's *Fragments* (volume 15) are not the humble bilinguals for those with a little Greek that the Loeb series originally set out to provide; rather, along with meticulous translations, they offer essential commentaries and introductions that form the basis for contemporary scholarship on these texts.

The scholarly literature on Plutarch is vast, and much of it the work of German, French, and Italian scholars. Two outstanding general studies, to which I am constantly indebted in this volume, are C. P. Jones, *Plutarch and Rome* (Oxford University Press, 1971), and D. A. Russell, *Plutarch* (Duckworth, 1972). Tim Duff's *Plutarch's Lives. Exploring Virtue and Vice* (Oxford University Press, 1999), which appeared as this book was in the final stages of correction, addresses in a fresh and helpful way the problem of reading Plutarch's *Parallel Lives*. With its rich bibliography, it is an excellent starting place for further exploration of the *Lives*. Finally, volume II.33.6 (1992) of *Aufstieg und Niedergang der Römischen Welt* (ANRW), a brobdignagian encyclopedia of classical scholarship that blossomed and grew out of a *Festschrift*, is entirely devoted to Plutarch. It is polyglot, with contributions in all four major scholarly languages, but in this volume the majority of the contributions are in English. ANRW is available in most general research libraries in the humanities, and this volume gives access to much of the important recent work on Plutarch while providing a valuable source of further bibliography.

INDEX

Abaris, 152
Aeschylus, 19, 103
Alcibiades, 120, 131, 148
Alexander Romance, 99
Alexander the Great, 14–15, 97–107, 109, 114, 121, 124, 130–33, 143; successors of, 14–15, 118–24, 132
Alexandria, 10
Allegory, 48–50
Ammonios, 3–4, 10, 155–58, 167–69
Amphictyonic League, 52–53
Amyot, Jacques, 190, 192–93, 211
Anaxagoras, 8
Annas, Julia, 150–51
Antigonus (Gonatas), 132, 134, 136
Antony, 8, 72–73, 130–32, 135–42, 192
Apollonius of Tyana, 3
Apuleius, 54, 180
Aristippos, 43
Aristotle, 7, 16–17, 24–25, 42, 46, 72, 85–87, 104, 106, 124, 147, 151, 174, 190
Arrian, 99, 101
Atheism, 57–59
Athens, 2, 6, 10, 67, 75–76, 79–80, 94, 134–35
Augustus (Octavian), 1, 89, 137, 140–42
Autoboulos (Plutarch's father), 7–10, 46, 56
Autoboulos (Plutarch's son), 8

Babbitt, Frank Lloyd, 212

Caesar. *See* Julius Caesar
Callisthenes, 99, 104

Camillus, 83
Cato the Younger, 119, 124–31, 141
Chaeronea, 1–2, 6, 10–13, 46
Cherniss, Harold, 213
Christianity / Christians, 33–36, 40–41, 58, 165–66, 188
Chrysippus, 18, 50
Cicero, 12, 18, 21, 41, 50, 106, 108, 115, 125, 135, 137, 151, 153–54
Claudius, 1
Clavier, E., 192–93
Cleanthes, 18
Cleopatra (the Seventh), 8, 135–43, 195
Crantor, 37
Curtius Rufus, Quintus, 99
Cynics, 42, 127, 167–68

Dante, 35–36, 212
Deification, 76–77, 81–82
De Lacy, Phillip, 213
Delphi, 6, 11–12, 52–59, 94, 155–72; guides at, 11, 59, 161–62; oracle of, 2, 156–72
Demetrius Poliorcetes, 72, 130–35, 139, 141, 143
Democritus, 42–43
Demosthenes, 20, 117, 121–22, 190
Dicaearchus, 151
Diocles of Peparethos, 79
Diodorus Siculus, 15, 99, 117, 182
Diogenes Laertius, 120, 147, 151
Diogenes the Cynic, 85, 120
Dionysius of Halicarnassos, 15, 79
Domitian, 11

Emerson, Ralph Waldo, 193–94
Empedocles, 170, 183
Epaminondas, 67, 120, 181–87
Ephippos, 102
Epicurus / Epicureans, 17–18, 33, 43,
    56–59
Eudaimonia, 41–42, 91–94
Eunapios, 3, 68
Euripides, 56

Fabius Pictor, Quintus, 79, 83
Flacelière, Robert, 159
Flaubert, Gustave, 165

Galen, 18
Gellius, Aulus, 68
Gibbon, Edward, xiii, 1
Gnostics, 33

Hadrian, 1, 12, 24, 52–54, 59, 63–64,
    69, 159
Heracles, 23, 77, 79, 136, 141, 177, 192
Heraclides of Pontus, 151–53, 181
Heraclitus, 163–64
Herodotus, 14–15, 55, 62, 69–72, 83,
    146–47, 195
Hesiod, 8, 19, 23, 37, 50, 77–78, 170
Hieronymos of Cardia, 14–16
Historiography, ancient, 70–71
Homer, 5, 16, 19, 24, 37, 48–50, 62–63,
    177

Iamblichus, 152–53
Islam / Moslems, 35
Isocrates, 190

Jones, C. P., 12, 213
Judaism / Jews, 7, 35, 57–58
Julian, 57
Julius Caesar, 21, 97, 100, 106–16, 119,
    128–30, 136–37, 139

Kronos, 171, 177–78

Lamprias (Plutarch's brother), 5, 38–
    40, 155–56, 166–69, 172–78
Lamprias (Plutarch's grandfather), 8

Lamprias Catalogue, 22–23, 58
Livy, 79, 81, 83, 98, 106, 189
Lucian, 44, 143–45
Lycurgus, 51, 84–90, 110
Lysander, 94–97
Lysias, 18

Macedonians, 62–63
Mann, Thomas, 75
Maximus of Tyre, 180
Montaigne, Michel de, 3, 26, 191–
    92

Nepos, Cornelius, 117, 182
Nero, 23–24, 155
Nicarchos (Plutarch's great-
    grandfather), 8
North, Thomas, 190, 211
Numa, 51, 84, 87–90

Octavia, 135, 140–41
Octavian. *See* Augustus

Pan, death of, 170–71
Panhellenic Council, 63–64
Pausanias, 54, 59, 80, 186
Peripatetics, 42, 85
Perithous, 78
Perrin, Bernadotte, 212
Philip of Macedon, 62, 100–101
Philochoros, 78
Philodemus, 58
Philopappus, 6
Philotas of Amphissa, 8
Phocion, 117–25, 130–31
Pindar, 19
Pisistratids, 62
Pittheus, 77
Planudes, 22
Plato, xiii–xiv, 16–18, 25–26, 33–38,
    85–89, 92–93, 116–17, 120, 124, 126,
    133, 146–52, 154–55, 169–70, 180–
    81, 190
Platonic philosophy, xvi, 10, 16, 24,
    27–44, 51–52, 58–59, 73, 120, 163–
    64, 167–69, 173–74
Plotinus, 32–33, 160

Plutarch: dialogues of, 5, 25–26; hermeneutics of, xv, 47–51; Latin reading of, 19–21; reputation of, 14, 68, 188–95 passim; rhetoric and, xv, 45–48, 65, 66, 97–98, 143–45, 188–90, 192–93, 211–12; self-presentation of, 1–59 passim, esp. 2–12; sources used by, 13–18; style of, 18.

WORKS: *Lives of Attic Orators*, 23; *Lives of Emperors*, 23; *Moralia*, 23–26, 40–41, 198–210, 212–13 (*see specific titles below*); *Parallel Lives*, 22–23, 60–145 passim, 189–90, 197–98 (*see specific titles below*); *Parallel Lives*, comparisons (*synkriseis*) in, 65, 115, 141

—*Moralia: Bravery of Women*, 189, 201; *Common Conceptions*, 5, 209; *Consolation to His Wife*, 55, 205; *Curiosity*, 11, 204; *Delphic Oracles Not Now Given in Verse*, 2, 5, 158–65, 203; *Disappearance of Oracles*, 5, 55, 57, 159, 165–72, 203; *E at Delphi*, 5, 46–47, 154–60, 203; *Education of Children*, 45–46, 190, 199; *Epicurus Actually Makes a Pleasant Life Impossible*, 5, 45, 160, 209; *Face in the Moon*, 29, 38–40, 160, 171–79, 207; *Fame of the Athenians*, 44, 66–67, 202; *Fortune of Alexander*, 44, 97, 202; *Fortune of the Romans*, 44, 83, 97, 202; *Generation of the Soul in the Timaeus*, 34–38, 44, 208; *Greek and Roman Questions*, 5, 25, 160, 202; *Gryllus*, 154, 179, 208; *How Progress in Virtue Might Be Perceived*, 51, 200; *How the Young Should Listen to Poetry*, 46–51, 199; *How to Profit by Your Enemies*, 40, 200; *How to Tell a Flatterer from a Friend*, 24, 104, 199; *Isis and Osiris*, 47, 55–56, 203; *Is "Live Unknown" a Wise Precept?* 12, 43, 153, 210; *Listening to Lectures*, 46, 51, 199; *Love*, 5, 9, 19, 56, 154, 206; *Malice of Herodotus*, 69–72, 207; *Natural History Questions*, 25, 207;

Platonic Questions, 16–17, 25, 208; *Precepts on Statecraft*, 8, 206; *Principle of Cold*, 44, 208; *Reply to Colotes in Defense of the Other Philosophers*, 5, 24, 45, 120, 209; *Sayings of Spartans*, 189, 201; *Slowness of Divine Justice*, xv, 5, 58–59, 205; *Socrates' Sign*, 28–31, 154–55, 179–87, 205; *Stoic Self-Contradictions*, 24, 209; *Superstition*, 57–59, 201; *Symposium of the Seven Sages*, 154, 179, 200–201; *Table Talk*, xvi, 5–11, 25, 53, 54–55, 74, 101, 154, 155–56, 160, 205; *That Philosophers Ought Especially to Talk with Rulers*, 104, 206; *Tranquillity of Mind*, 13, 24, 31–33, 43, 44, 203–4; *Virtue and Vice*, 40, 200; *Whether an Old Man Should Engage in Public Life*, 53, 206; *Whether Land or Sea Animals Are Cleverer*, 9, 46, 188, 208

—*Parallel Lives: Aemilius Paulus*, 74; *Agesilaus*, 67; *Agis and Cleomenes*, 67, 130–31; *Alcibiades*, 131; *Alexander*, 71–72, 97–107, 113–16, 121, 132; *Antony*, 8, 95, 115, 130–32, 136–42; *Aristides*, 70; *Brutus*, 116; *Camillus*, 153; *Cato the Elder*, 70, 92; *Cato the Younger*, 46, 101, 110, 124–30; *Cicero*, 12; *Cimon*, 72; *Demetrius*, 15, 72–73, 92, 97, 130–35; *Demosthenes*, 10, 13, 20, 67; *Epaminondas*, 67, 181; *Eumenes*, 15; *Galba*, 23; *Gracchi*, 130–31; *Julius Caesar*, 22, 97, 107–16, 119, 128, 132; *Lycurgus*, 67, 75, 81–88, 95; *Lysander*, 67, 94–97; *Marius*, 11, 73; *Nicias*, 131; *Numa*, 51, 75, 83–84, 87–90, 95, 164; *Otho*, 11, 23; *Pelopidas*, 67, 181, 184; *Phocion*, 67, 117–26, 130; *Publicola*, 4; *Pyrrhus*, 15, 67, 73; *Romulus*, 68, 75, 79–83; *Sulla*, 94–97, 108, 118; *Themistocles*, 70; *Theseus*, 22, 68, 75–79
Pollio, Gaius Asinius, 106
Polybius, 64–65, 69, 98
Pompey, 71, 107–9, 111–14, 128–29, 137–38

Pouqueville, François C. H. L., 52
Proclus, 37
Providence (*pronoia*), 40, 175–76, 187
Pythagoras / Pythagoreans, 9, 84, 88–
  89, 164, 180, 183–87
Pythian Games, 53

Rome, 6, 10–12, 79–80, 97–98
Roman imperialism, 1–2, 63–64, 89–
  91, 94–97, 108–11, 128
Romulus, 75–76, 79–83
Rusticus, 11

Sandbach, F. H., 213
Seneca, 90
Shakespeare, William, 108, 130, 137,
  192, 211
Simonides, 6
Soclaros, 9, 46
Socrates, 25, 51, 86, 92, 124, 126–27,
  131, 146–51, 155, 179–80, 183–87,
  188
Sosius Senecio, Quintus, 74, 75
Sparta, 67, 81–88, 96, 121
Stoics, 17–18, 28, 33–42, 50–51, 56,
  125–27, 130, 163, 174–75
Sulla, 94–97
Superstition, 57–58, 105, 131, 183

Tacitus, 90, 133
Thebes, 67, 69, 94, 101–2, 121, 181–
  87
Themistocles, 70, 83
Theon, 5, 160–63, 176
Theseus, 75–79
Thucydides, 14–15, 83, 117, 124, 146–
  47, 195
Trophonios, oracle of, 29–31, 151,
  185–86

Vegetarianism, 9
Virgil, 61, 66
Voltaire, François-Marie Arouet de,
  32, 192

Wilamowitz-Moellendorff, Ulrich
  von, 7
Wyatt, Thomas, 31, 211
Wyttenbach, Daniel, 45–46, 192–93

Xenocrates, 37, 120
Xenophon, 25, 147, 154–55, 182;
  Pseudo-Xenophon, 117

Yourcenar, Marguerite, 165

Zeno, 85